D0855677

Jewish Life in the United States:
Perspectives from the Social Sciences

Jewish Life
in
the United States:

Perspectives from the Social Sciences

edited by
Joseph B. Gittler

New York · New York University Press · *1981*

Library of Congress Cataloging in Publication Data
Main entry under title:

Jewish life in the United States.

Contents: Towards a definition of a Jew and
implications of general systems theory for the
study of Jewish life / Joseph B. Gittler—Jews
in the United States / Sidney Goldstein—Jewish
life in the United States, perspectives from
psychology / Morris N. Eagle—[etc.]
Includes index.
1. Jews—United States—Social conditions—
Addresses, essays, lectures. 2. United States—
Social conditions—Addresses, essays, lectures.
3. United States—Ethnic relations—Addresses, essays, lectures. I. Gittler, Joseph Bertram,
1912–
E184.J5J575 973'.04924 81-9661
ISBN 0-8147-2982-7 AACR2

Manufactured in United States of America

PREFACE

Several decades ago, Professor Morris Raphael Cohen, one of America's major philosophers, recognized the need for the scientific study of Jewish life in the United States. Since then, abundant and important researches, and their publications have developed. However, one would obtain notable difficulty in finding even an occasional and exiguous concerted multi-social discipline approach to the study of Jewish life. This volume seeks to fill this gap.

In May, 1978, the Max Weinreich Center for Advanced Jewish Studies of the YIVO Institute for Jewish Research, sponsored a two-day colloquium on "Jewish Life in the United States: Perspectives from the Social Sciences." The authors in this volume presented papers from the perspectives of their respective disciplines. The chapters in this volume are an outgrowth of these papers. Seven of the eight papers were significantly revised and up-dated for this volume.

Appreciation and thanks are due several persons who made the colloquium possible. I wish to express my gratitude to the following people: Morris Laub, executive chairman of the YIVO Institute for Jewish Research at the time of the colloquium; Hannah Fryshdorf, associate director of the YIVO Institute; and Yadja Zeltman, without whose assistance neither the colloquium nor this publication would have been realized. I wish to express special appreciation to the several sectional chairpersons and discussants of the papers during the colloquium.

My thanks is also emphatically extended to Sandra Berger, Mary S. LaClaire, Joseph A. Scimecca, May L. Thompson, and Thomas R. Williams of George Mason University and to Robert Bull and Despina Papazoglou of New York University Press. They facilitated the preparation of the manuscript for the printers and publishers in a variety of resourceful ways.

To Susan W. Gittler I remain indebted for her steady encouragement and assistance in pursuing the publication of the papers while we were thousands of miles removed from the United States for twelve months.

Fairfax, Virginia
August 1980

Joseph B. Gittler

v

CONTENTS

Preface   v

Notes on Contributors   ix

Chapter I: Towards a Definition of a   1
                  Jew and Implications of
                  General Systems Theory
                  for the Study of Jewish
                  Life
                  Joseph B. Gittler

Chapter II: Jews in the United States: 31
                  Perspectives from Demography
                  Sidney Goldstein

Chapter III: Jewish Life in the United   103
                  States: Perspectives from
                  Psychology
                  Morris N. Eagle

Chapter IV: Jewish Life in the United   123
                  States: Social and Political
                  Values
                  Everett Carll Ladd, Jr.

Chapter V: Four Sociologies of American   173
                  Jewry: Methodological Notes
                  Samuel Z. Klausner

Chapter VI: Jewish Life in the United   237
                  States: Perspectives from
                  Economics
                  Arcadius Kahan

Chapter VII: Jewish Life in the United   271
                  States: Perspectives from
                  History
                  Henry L. Feingold

Chapter VIII: Jewish Life in the United   297
                  States: Perspectives from
                  Anthropology
                  Sol Tax

Index   315

NOTES ON CONTRIBUTORS

Morris N. Eagle, Ph.D., is professor of psychology at York University and the Clarke Institute of Psychiatry, Toronto, Canada. During 1967-75, he was professor of psychology at the Ferkauf Graduate School of Humanities and Social Sciences of Yeshiva University. He has held many research and clinical positions at various institutions including the Institute of Human Learning, University of California at Berkeley; Psychological Laboratory, University of Cambridge, England; Research Center for Mental Health, New York University; Department of Psychiatry, Mt. Zion Hospital, San Francisco. Dr. Eagle is the author of numerous articles and chapters in books, including: "Some Conceptual Issues in Psychotherapy," "The Concept of Self in Psychoanalytic Theory," "Puerto Ricans in New York City," "The Nature of Psychodynamic Interpretation."

Henry L. Feingold, Ph.D., is professor of history at Baruch College and the Graduate Center of the City University of New York. He is editor and Chairman of the editorial board of American Jewish History and is also a member of the editorial boards of Shoah (a journal on the holocaust), Reconstructionist, YIVO Annual. His many publications include Politics of Rescue: The Roosevelt Administration and the Holocaust 1938-1945; Zion in America: The Jewish Experience from Colonial Times to the Present. Dr. Feingold is currently at work on The Limits of Ethnic Power: The Jewish Question in American Foreign Relations.

Joseph B. Gittler, Ph.D., is Distinguished Visiting Professor of Sociology at George Mason University. From 1966 to 1978 he was dean of the Ferkauf Graduate School of Humanities and Social Sciences and University Professor of Sociology (1966-1979) at Yeshiva University. During 1979 and 1980 he was a Fulbright professor at Hiroshima University, Japan. His book publications include Social Thought Among the Early Greeks; Social Dynamics; Understanding Minority Groups (author and editor); Ethnic Minorities in the United States: Perspectives from the Social Sciences (author and editor, International Journal of Group Tensions, volume 7, numbers 3 and 4, 1977); Virginia's People, Review of Sociology: Analysis

ix

<u>of a Decade</u> (author and editor). He is now
completing a study of <u>The Jewish Family in the</u>
<u>United States</u>. His numerous articles include
"Jews As An Ethnic Minority in the United States,"
"Cultural Pluralism in the United States," and
"Towards the Definition of an Ethnic Minority."
Dr. Gittler was also director of research and
author (with Lami Gittler) of <u>Your Neighbor Near</u>
<u>and Far</u>, a published report of a study of inter-
ethnic prejudice in a rural county of Iowa.

   Sidney Goldstein, Ph.D., holds the George
Hazard Crooker University Professorship at Brown
University and is Professor of Sociology and
Director of the Population Studies and Training
Center. An internationally recognized expert on
urbanization and migration, he has published
widely in these fields. His particular focus is
on the experience of the less developed countries. Dr. Goldstein has also done extensive
research on the demography of the American Jewish
population, in recognition of which he holds an
appointment as Corresponding Member of the
Institute for Contemporary Jewry at The Hebrew
University. His publications include <u>Patterns of</u>
<u>Mobility, 1910-1950</u>; <u>Jewish Americans: Three</u>
<u>Generations in a Jewish Community</u>; <u>Urbanization,</u>
<u>Migration, and Fertility in Thailand</u>; "American
Jewry, 1970: A Demographic Profile."

   Arcadius Kahan, Ph.D., is professor of economics and history at the University of Chicago. He
has been a fellow at the Russian Research Center
at Harvard University; Senior Research Fellow at
the Russian Institute, Columbia University, and
held a Guggenheim fellowship. Dr. Kahan has also
been a visiting professor at the London School of
Economics, the Hebrew University in Jerusalem, and
Helsinki University. His many publications include <u>Economic History of the Jews</u> (with Salo
Baron) and <u>Industrial Labor in the</u> U. S. S. R.
(with Blair Ruble).

   Samuel Z. Klausner, Ph.D., is professor of
sociology at the University of Pennsylvania and
Director of the Center for Research on the Acts of
Man in Philadelphia. He has been a Ford Foun-
dation Area Research Fellow, program director for
Columbia University's Bureau of Applied Social
Research Program in Psychiatry, Religion and

Alcohol, and editor of the Journal for the Scientific Study of Religion. His many published books include Psychiatry and Religion; Religion in the United States; and The Study of Total Societies. He was president of the Association for the Sociological Study of Jewry between 1975 and 1977, and is the current editor of its journal.

Everett Carll Ladd, Jr., Ph.D., is professor of political science and director of the Institute for Social Inquiry at the University of Connecticut, and executive director of the Roper Center. He has held fellowships from the Rockefeller, Ford, Woodrow Wilson, and Guggenheim foundations, as well as from the Hoover Institution and the Social Science Research Council. Dr. Ladd has numerous publications. Among his books are Ideology in America; American Political Parties; Transformations of the American Party System (with C. H. Hadley); Political Parties and Political Issues with C. D. Hadley); and Where Have All the Voters Gone?

Sol Tax, Ph.D., is professor of Anthropology at the University of Chicago where he was also associate dean of the social sciences between 1948 and 1953. His principal research has been with North American Indians (since 1931) and among modern Maya Indians in southern Mexico and Guatemala. Dr. Tax was president of the International Congress of Anthropological and Ethnological Sciences (1968-73), editor of the 29th International Congress of Americanists between 1949 and 1952, American Anthropologist (1953-56), Current Anthropology (1958-74), Viking Fund Publications in Anthropology (1959-68). From 1968 to 1973 he was organizer and editor of World Anthropology, resulting in 100 published volumes. Dr. Tax holds honorary memberships in the Royal Anthropological Institute of Great Britain, and the national societies of Chile, Hungary, and Slovakia. He has received citations and medals from the governments of Czechoslovakia and Santander, Spain.

Chapter I

TOWARDS A DEFINITION OF A JEW AND IMPLICATIONS OF GENERAL SYSTEMS THEORY FOR THE STUDY OF JEWISH LIFE

JOSEPH B. GITTLER

The burden of this chapter consists in explicating the nature and meaning of a Jew and then relating the definition of the Jew to general systems theory. The argument will encompass the following objectives and propositions. First, Jewish studies and the study of Jewish life assume a scientific approach. Second, the scientific approach requires appropriate and valid definitions of terms and concepts. Third, given the variety of extant definitions of the Jew, the discussion in this chapter will suggest the definitional criterion of per genus et differentiam. Furthermore, this criterion will enable us to denote Jews in the United States as an ethnic group by differentiating it from other basic types of human social groups, and as an ethnic minority group, from other non-minority ethnic groups. Ethnic groups and ethnic minority groups will then be characterized by a set of antecedant-primary and derivative-secondary sets of components. The elements that make up the Jewish ethnic minority group involve an idealization of these components. Jews participate in and identify with these components in varying ways and by different degrees. The degree of participation and identification is related to the perception of the values of one's reference group. Finally, we shall endeavor to suggest the possible significant roles that general systems theory may play in the study of Jewish life.

DEFINING A JEW

When embarking on a logical scientific definition of a Jew, we are confronted by a plethora of
meanings and characterizations. It appears that
definitions of the Jew are many and varied. Few
people tend to agree on any precise meaning.
Dissidence outweighs concurrence; for what, or
who, is a Jew remains debatable among scholars,
journalists, and politicians.

The history and diversity of definitions are
long and extensive. A Jew has been defined as part
of "a religious community,"[1] as a religious community that continued to live (after the destruction of Jerusalem) "within a shell as it were,
composed of petrified forms of communal institutions and customs."[2] The Jew has been defined, as
well, as a member of a "religious group,"[3] as one
who professed to have definite Jewish religious
preferences,[4] and as a person who adheres to
Judaism as a religion and voluntarily with the fellowship connected with Judaism.[5] He is one "who
gives up his faith (in the formal sense of the
word)... [but] remains a Jew."[6]

The Jews are "relics of the Syriac civilization."[7] By Halakhah, they are the offsprings of
Jewish mothers or are converts to Judaism.[8] They
are individuals whose parents had "Jewish religious
affiliation."[9] Jews are descendants of the Hebrew
people,[10] members "of a scattered group of people
that traces its descent from the Biblical Hebrews
or from post-exilian adherents of Israel,"[11] or, as
people "belonging to the worldwide group constituting a continuation through descent or conversion
of the ancient Jewish people and characterized by a
sense of community,"[12] but with "a name of oppro-
brium or reprobation."[13] Jews are those with a
common heritage, a common history, and common traditions,[14] and people with a common destiny.[15] A
Jew is one who believes "in the spiritual values
that are latent in Jewish history"[16] and is "a sin-
gular example of an old entity which clings to its
identity."[17] He is one who feels his "uncondi-
tional solidarity with the persecuted and exter-
minated. I am a Jew because I feel the Jewish
tragedy; because I feel the pulse of Jewish history...."[18] Jews are a group with a peculiar
"collective psyche forged in the diaspora...;"[19]
they are a psychological type.[20] They are Jews
when "they have experienced 'in their hearts' that
they are Jews...."[21] They have been defined as
subscribers and transmitters of the Judaic

religion.[22] They have been referred to also, as
possessors of an obsession.[23] The Jew is one who
thinks of himself as a Jew and says that he is a
Jew and identifies himself as a Jew.[24] He is one
who replies affirmatively to one or more of the
following questions: Was I born Jewish? Am I
Jewish now? Was my father born Jewish? Was my
mother born Jewish?[25] He is a person whose name is
Jewish,[26] whose mother tongue was Yiddish,[27] whose
children are absent from school on the Jewish holiday of Yom Kippur, and one who is buried by a
Jewish undertaker in a Jewish cemetery.[28]

The Jews are a people or peoplehood, "a people
in time," members of a nation,[29] a nationality,[30]
"a group of nations,"[31] or a "magic nation."[32]
Jews display "that spirit of stubborn clannish-
ness;"[33] they are members of a tribe[34] and persons
identifiable by their physiognomy.[35]

The Jew is considered to be a marginal
person,[36] "a cultural hybrid."[37] He is "doubly
alienated,"[38] a "stranger,"[39] and a pariah.[40]

Jews are defined as being Zionists and as
members of a voluntary association.[41] There are
"gastronomic" Jews.[42] The Jew is one who is not a
"non-Jew."[43] He is "one who doesn't ask, 'Who is a
Jew?'"[44] Jews and Jewishness have been referred to
as a mystique[45] and as a sub-culture.[46] Jews,
finally, are an ethnic group.[46]

Possibly numerous other definitions could be
discovered, only to add to the "tangle of tan-
gles." Perhaps if a contemporary Plato were exposed to all of these, he would exclaim, as he did
in his Seventh Epistle: "No intelligent man will
ever dare to commit his thoughts to words... " and
that "if he should be betrayed into so doing then
surely not the Gods but mortals have blasted his
wits,"[47] -- anticipating echoes of contemporary
semiotics, logical positivism, logical atomism and
language philosophy which try to make thought
through language clear and meaningful in the human
approach to knowledge and reality. Wittgenstein,
considered by many as the father of linguistic
philosophy and who was the author of Tractatus
Logico-Philosophicus, formulated what has become
the basic guiding principle of his philosophical
school: "Whatever can be said at all can be said
clearly." And in the last sentence of the
Tractatus he warns that "whereof one cannot speak,
thereof one must be silent." Logical thought and
scientific reasoning are frequently misled by un-
examined language. Therefore, if definitions are
to be useful in the logico-empirical process, they

must be clear and precise and avoid vagueness,
ambiguity, homonomy, and equivocation. A definition is valid to the extent that it directs
specific inquiries. A definition in scientific
inquiry is valid to the extent that it sets the
path for logical inference and empirical verification. Words obtain their useful meanings only
within particular contexts and frames of reference.

It appears safe to assume that there is no
superior way of knowing humans and their worlds
than the scientific way. If verification of belief
and assertion are the essences of truth, science
has gained credence. "Certainly, whatever enlightenment we possess about ourselves and the world has
been achieved only after the illusion of a
'metaphysical wisdom' superior to 'mere science'
had been abandoned."[48] Any progress that humans
have manifested in their accumulation of knowledge
has meant a veering away from the approaches of
wishful thinking, artistic subjectivity, metaphysical rationalism, and theological revelation. For
the goals of science comprise objectivity, confirm-
ability, logicality, empiricism, and systematiza-
tion. Scientific definitions should therefore be
consistent with the tenets of scienticity.

As I have said, the variety of definitions of
the Jew appears endless. The list I have given
above includes only some of the definitions, reflecting the difficulties in comprehending a common
social reality. However, lack of agreement and
divergent definitions of common terms, thwarts the
growth of a reliable body of knowledge. Definitions commonly held are essential for progress in
science. Lack of agreement in the definition of
terms has been a pronounced problem in the social
sciences, a greater problem than one finds in the
natural sciences. The comparative youth of the
social sciences surely contributes to this discrepancy.

Some agreements in the definitions of the Jew
are apparent: a socio-cultural unit, a distinctive
entity, common ties of background, and cultural
homogeneity. However, variance and vagueness out-
weigh commonality and clarity.

Fortunately, there are guidelines and rules to
help in the formulation of definitions. Knowledge
hinges on our ability to take a perceptual experience, however complex and rich it may be in qualities and feelings, and interpret it through the
construction of concepts and propositions. There
cannot be science without concepts. The earlier
notion that pure empiricism is the gateway to

scientific knowledge confuses the sensory image
with the comprehension of the sense datum. It is
the task of science to symbolize the total realm of
the given through the discovery of relationships
connecting the clearly given with the obscurely
given. "Knowledge of the facts cannot be equated
with the brute immediacy of our sensations."[49] The
Baconian myth of a tabula rasa distorts the view
that facts "do not speak for themselves." As John
Dewey, Morris Raphael Cohen, Kurt Lewin, Alfred
North Whitehead, Herbert Blumer, and many others
have repeatedly remarked, perceptions become facts
only within a prior frame of reference. Concepts
are "fashioners of percepts." Concepts are constructs which give perceptual experiences an
"understandable character."[50] Pure sense experience does not give us knowledge.

Every scientific judgment, therefore, is composed of concepts. Concepts obtain their meanings
through the process of definition. A definition
communicates the meaning a concept is intended to
convey. Scientific concepts must be defined in
terms that are commonly acknowledged by scientists.

While the origin of a concept springs from the
symbolization of an observed event, the accumulation of concepts permits the definition of one concept in terms of another. In this way a new, un-
known term can be defined in terms of the known. A
definition is intended as a rule by which a given
symbol can always be eliminated through the substi-
tution of other symbols. Not only must a substi-
tution of any expression for the definiendum lead
to understanding, it must also be equivalent in
meaning to the definiendum. Two expressions are
equivalent in meaning when they can replace each
other in every proposition in which they occur
without changing either the truth value of the proposition or its capacity to yield other propositions in deduction. It is in this respect that
definitions become tools of scientific analysis.

In science, the purpose of a definition is to
aid in the adequate exposition of the subject
matter in question and in the formulation of principles by relating given facts with conceptually
ordered facts. Through assumption of precise and
unambiguous meanings, scientific concepts become
the elements of scientific propositions and hypotheses.

The process of definition is a problem of
logical analysis rather than one of empirical
inquiry. The major purpose of definitions is to
reveal the meanings of concepts in terms of

familiar concepts and thus establish hypotheses or
theorems in conjunction with other propositions in
the field under investigation. Definitions are
logical instruments which ultimately tend to direct
and channelize the path of empirical research.

In defining the Jew, I would like to borrow
from the traditional Aristotelian principle of per
genus et differentiam. Definition by this mode is
not without its critics. I shall reserve the discussion of the polemics for a subsequent section of
this chapter.

In traditional Aristotelian logic a concept is
defined in terms of its generic characteristics,
which are common to all the concepts (and things)
of the same class (genus), plus its differentiam,
which distinguishes one thing (or concept) from
others within the same genus.

This method of definition is based on the
logical methods of classification and division. A
class of items which is called a species is coor-
dinated with others under a wider class which is
their genus. This wider class in turn is a species
of a still wider genus, and so on.

Applying this modus operandi to the definition
of the Jew, it is obvious that Jews are a special
kind of collectivity. Jews are clearly not an
aggregate, nor a race, nor a clan, tribe, herd,
species, pack, phylum, category, drove, pride, or
cluster. The Jew as a collectivity comes closest
to what the sociologist has characterized as a human social group, -- but a particular kind
(species) of human social group (genus), that is,
an ethnic minority group. This classification
refers to Jews in the United States.

Following the method of the per genus et differentiam system of definitional classification and
division, we can clarify the meaning of "ethnic
minority group" by illustrating its relations to
other terms in its species as well as to items in
its more inclusive genus by the following schematic
diagram. The species consisting of "ethnic" groups
is classified together with the species "social
class," "caste," "age," and "sex" groups under the
genus "unorganized human social groups." The species of unorganized human social groups in turn, is
classified with the species "organized human social
groups" under the genus "social collectivity," and
so on.

I would like to offer the following definitions
in conformity with the genus and differentiam
system. A collectivity includes a number of items
or individuals. A social collectivity comprises a

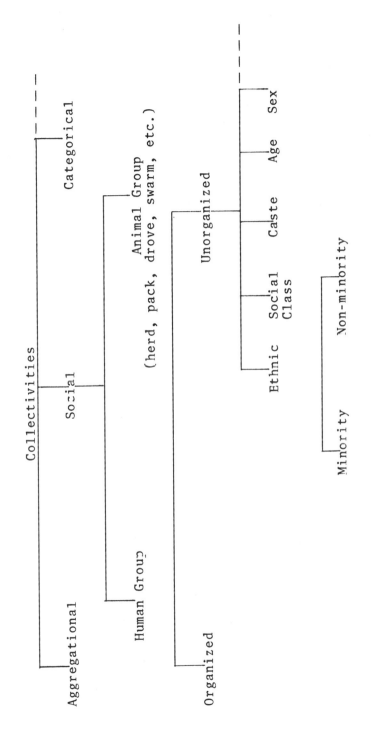

number of individuals in interaction. A human
social group is a type of collectivity. This consists of a number of individuals interacting with
each other in relation to and participating in, a
distinctive set of commonly held symbols (interests, values, and characteristics). The interaction and participation consist of a persistent
pattern operating on a plane of overt and behavioral affiliation through an observable process of
affiliating, participating, and acting together, or
possessing observable common symbols (interests,
values, and other common characteristics). They
are operating on a plane of covert identification,
through personal identification, a feeling of
belonging with other members of the group and to
common symbols (interests, values, and other common
characteristics). They also are operating on a
plane of societal designation, by others referring
to and considering the individual as belonging to a
particular group and set of symbols. An organized
human social group is a group of individuals with
an internal structure; that is, members of the
group possess roles, statuses, positions, and
offices functioning in relation to a set of symbols
and values. An unorganized human social group is a
group that is devoid of an internal structure but
whose members are related to and participate in a
system of symbols and values. (By system is meant
an interrelation of symbolic items to form a
subcultural distinctive structure).

An ethnic group, therefore, constitutes an
unorganized human social group whose members participate in a distinctive set of commonly held
symbols on:

1. A plane of overt and behavioral affiliation
   and association. For example, members of
   the group might wear distinctive clothes,
   speak a particular language, eat a
   distinctive cuisine, and verbally avow
   affiliationwith these characteristics.
2. A plane of covert identification. This
   recognizes an intrapsychic, subjective,
   internalized oneness with a set of symbols,
   such as a feeling for and a consciousness
   of being part of a language, tradition, or
   religion. Identification takes place on a
   cognitive, informational, epistemic level
   and on an attitudinal affective level.
3. A plane of societal designation. This
   consists of being considered, branded,
   referred to, or denoted by others as

Jews. This designation may be covertly
believed or overtly acted upon.

Thus, this mode of defining an ethnic group
"classifies out" organized human-social groups of
the formal type, such as nation, smaller governmental entities, clubs, business firms, organized
religious congregations, and, those of informally
organized social groups, such as family kinship
groups, neighborhoods, and juvenile gangs.

An ethnic group also needs to be distinguished
from other groups of the same unorganized human
social group species such as age, sex, race, and
class groups. Age and sex groups may manifest
their own distinctive subculture and set of symbols. Ethnic symbols may include or overlap with
age and sex symbols.

Race constitutes a biological entity. If a
racial group is viewed within a social context, it
becomes synonymous with the concept of ethnic
group, that is, an unorganized human social group
whose members participate in a set of common symbols on the three planes and ways mentioned previously.

A social class group is an unorganized human
social group which obtains its designation because
of a superordinate-subordinate ascription and differentiation. An ethnic group may be a social
class group; some are. However, insofar as ethnic
groups do not coincide with class groups, -- that
is, ethnic groups are not necessarily identified by
the property of superordinacy-subordinacy, -- they
can be conceptually differentiated from social
class groups. All Jews, for example, participate,
in varying degrees, in several aspects of their
subculture. Jewish holidays such as Yom Kippur,
for example, have a generic and at least a minimal
meaning for all Jews -- from the secularized to the
extreme orthodox, from the impoverished Jew on
welfare, to the affluent suburban upper-middle
class Jew. Ethnicity tends to cut across Jewish
class strata in selective, but significant
symbolic-cultural ways.

Two crucial problems remain when we consider
ethnic groups in the United States. How do we
identify and select ethnic groups, and how do we
classify each selected set of ethnic symbols
according to certain standardized ethnographic
categories?

According to our criteria, an ethnic group in
the United States consists of those individuals
acting in relation to, identifying with, and being
referred to by others as related to one or more

aspects of an endemic symbolic set. Membership in
an ethnic group can be thought of as functions of
attribute, quality, and duration. To illustrate, a
member of the Jewish-American ethnic group is a
Jewish-American, dependent on his speaking Yiddish
or Hebrew. And if he speaks either of the languages, he is a Jewish-American to the extent that
he has used the language over a period of time.
Ethnic behavioral traits (such as language usage)
increase in complexity when correlated with items
of ethnic identification and societal ethnic
designation. The techniques for determining the
degree of an individual's ethnicity are yet to be
developed.

In answer to the second question, what are
categories of ethnic symbolic sets? I would
suggest the following categories as cultural and
symbolic concomitants of ethnic groups in the
United States. These categories are based on the
studies and descriptions of and references to
ethnic groups in the United States.

Members of an ethnic group possess the
following common characteristics:

1. Historic and ancestral national (including
    geographical) origin
2. Institutionalized group structure and/or
    set of group mores, group ways and group
    lore in:
    (a) Language (including body language) and
         literature
    (b) Family surnames
    (c) Marriage, family relations, kinship
         relations, and life cycle of the
         individual
    (d) Religion and philosophy
    (e) Politics
    (f) Education
    (g) Economic life
    (h) Dress
    (i) Cuisine
    (j) Fine and performing arts
    (k) Crafts
    (l) Voluntary associations
    (m) Play and games (recreation)
3. Set of psychological and physiological
    attributes
4. Social disorganization and social deviance.

While endemic behavior, identification, and
societal designation constitute definitions of an
ethnic group in each of these categories, a
distinction should be made between the antecedant,
differentiating, and primary set of categories of

ethnicity, and the <u>consequent, derivative, and</u>
<u>secondary</u> set of categories.
        The first set, unique to ethnicity, includes
the categories of ancestral and national origin,
language and family surnames. The latter set
includes the remaining categories, which, while
applicable to ethnic groups, may be involved in the
characterizations of other unorganized human social
groups such as class, sex, age. Only the specific
and precise descriptive attributions will distinguish the ethnic from the non ethnic, although the
categorical types may be applicable to both. Thus,
middle class Americans and Ukranian-Americans or
Jewish-Americans may be characterized by the way
they dress. Specific Ukranian-American dress,
however, would tend to be different from a generic
middle-class mode of dress <u>per se</u>.
        I believe it is clearly apparent that an indi-
vidual does not possess or manifest all of the
ethnic characteristics. Nor do individuals comprise any one of the items and elements to the same
degree. Thus, Einstein did not consider himself a
religious Jew, at least, not a devoutly religious
Jew. His language usage was neither Yiddish or
Hebrew. His dress and clothes, while sometimes
idiosyncratic perhaps, could not be characterized
as Jewish. I do not know anything about his food
habits. On what basis, then, was he a Jew? I
submit that it was primarily on the basis of
lineage, history, self-identification with Jews and
Jewish symbols as well as being designated a Jew by
outsiders.
        Earlier, we referred to Isaac Deutscher who
thought of himself as a Jew, even though he
considered himself an atheist, a Marxist, and an
internationalist. He eschewed Zionism and was
hostile to all forms of nationalism, including
Israel. He nevertheless declared in one of his
books that he was a Jew because he felt "the Jewish
tragedy as my own tragedy; because [he felt] the
pulse of Jewish history...."[51]
        Spinoza, Heine, Marx, Trotsky, and Freud were
sometimes referred to as non-Jewish Jews.
Tchaikovsky often referred to the two brothers and
pianist prodigies, Nicholai and Anton Rubenstein,
as baptized Jews. There is an organization that
calls itself "Jesus Jews." Among religious Jews we
find the extreme orthodox Hasidim who believe and
follow the precepts that Judaism was divinely inspired and communicated by God to Moses and whose
laws are literally, directly, and permanently binding upon Jews by divine fiat. Their observances

and devotionals are usually emotional and mystical. Hasidim consider themselves disciples of
charismatic rabbis.

At the opposite pole of the Jewish religious
continuum, we find Reform Judaism which rejects the
idea of permanently binding religious laws and
practices divinely transmitted. Torah law, both
written and oral, is conceived as a "growing consciousness of God and of moral law." Eternal validity to any given formulation of Jewish belief is
denied. Reform Judaism asserts the validity of
change.

One should also mention that within Jewish
religious orthodoxy there are variations. The
orthodoxy which is known as the Lithuanian pattern
emphasizes Torah study to the virtual exclusion of
all else, seeks to carry out practical religious
observances in great detail, stresses intellectual
comprehension of religious teaching through logical
discourse, and frowns upon secular learning.

Neo-orthodoxy of the Samson Raphael Hirsch
School seeks to combine Torah with "the way of the
world," by which is meant the values of Western
civilization. A more positive attitude towards
secular learning is exemplified. In this group are
the majority of orthodox synagogues in the United
States and Great Britain.

All this should lead to the recognition that
the pure or real Jew (the so-called 100 percent
"Jew") is a conceptualized type. The actual Jew
may adhere to just one or more phases of one or
more Jewish religious varieties, or one or more
phases of the Jewish ethnic way of life (language,
history, food, art, or customs) and to any extent
described above. Every pure type is a conceptualized, ideal construct often required for the
understanding of the real and the concrete.

I recall Alfred North Whitehead's statement:
"The paradox is now fully established that the
utmost abstractions are the true weapons with which
to control our thought of the concrete fact."
Science has always invented abstract ideal entities
and pure types in order to understand the given and
actual reality. The kind of affiliation and
identification, and the degree of affiliation and
identification will vary directly with reference
group membership (affiliative and identifiable) and
inversely with the quality and degree of a person's
acculturation and assimilation into the outer
culture and groups. Following the direction of our
considerations thus far, an ethnic minority becomes
a species of the genus ethnic group.

The denial to certain groups of the expected
rewards and "goods" of society converts members to
minority group status. An ethnic minority is
therefore an unorganized human social ethnic group
whose members, because of their symbolic-cultural
characteristics, "are singled out from the others
in the society in which they live for differential
and unequal treatment and who regard themselves as
objects of collective discrimination and prejudice. The existence of a minority in a society
implies the existence of a corresponding dominant
group with higher social status and greater privi-
leges. Minority status carries with it the
exclusion from full participation in the life of
the society."[52] Thus, Jewish-Americans, consist of
those individuals who, because of their Jewishness,
experience acts of social discrimination and
attitudes of psycho-social prejudice.

Minority groups are, therefore, something more
than statistics. Numbers are not necessarily
significant in determining minority group status.
They may affect the status but they do not
determine it. For example, there are counties in
the Southern part of the United States where
Negroes substantially outnumber whites. In South
Africa, there are fewer whites than those of other
races. In other parts of the world, a handful of
whites dominate millions of nonwhites. Obviously
we are indicating a pattern of social positions
involving differential orders of prestige, power,
and privilege, rather than a numerical relationship.

Because of the characteristics that members of
a minority group possess and share, and of which
the dominant group disapproves, the minority is
placed in a subordinate position. Expected privi-
leges are withheld; equal status is denied. The
minority group thus becomes a disadvantaged
group. Its members are set apart from other
groups. Being a member of a minority group is a
stigma brought on by the exercise of hostility,
prejudice, and discrimination by dominant group
members.

In an earlier section of this chapter we
alluded to the polemics surrounding the per genus
method of definition. Definition by genus and
differentiam is not the sole technique for scientific definition. There is denotative definition
which consists of definition by examples of objects. This method has serious limitations.[53]

Synonymous defining is another technique, but
it has limited applicability in science. A third

technique, operationalism, came into prominence
during the twentieth century. It was introduced by
P. W. Bridgman and consisted of defining terms by
the operations involved in a given situation
referred to by the term. The operationalist proceeds on an instrumentalist basis, accurately
describing the modus operandi pursued in the name
of the definiens. An operationalist defines his
terms by his measurements of "operations." For
him, public opinion is what public opinion polls
measure.

Much opposition has emerged against crass
operationalism,[54] but some followers of operationalism temper their attitude by a qualified neo-
operationalism. They suggest that operationalism
best serves the social sciences when the nature of
social reality and "social stuff" are taken into
account. Sociological concepts, for example, must
refer to the nature of social reality if they are
to be valid in sociological science. By "social
stuff" we mean the basic ontological character of
social reality that must be taken into account in
defining social objects or the concepts that refer
to them. Thus, neo-operationalism tends to include
complementarily, the traditional Aristotelian
classificatory logic of definition.[55]

Definition by genus and differentiam is not
without its criticisms. Modern symbolic logic
objects to the existentiality implicit in
Aristotelian definition. "A definition is strictly
speaking, no part of the subject in which it
occurs. For a definition is concerned wholly with
the symbols, not with what they symbolize.
Moreover, it is not true or false, being the
expression of a volition, not of a proposition."[56]
The nominalism however of modern symbolic
logic is not as different from traditional "real"
definitions as might appear from this citation.

The opposition to the classificatory logic of
Aristotle propounded by the logical positivists
(and the operationalists) is directed against the
metaphysical inherence of his logical system. It
is true that the traditional logic of Aristotle is
intimately connected with his metaphysics. He
thought of logic as an instrument for discovering
the true relation between the general and the
particular. For Aristotle, the general was the
cause of particular occurrence and change. The
perceived particular follows from the general,
which is known only in conception. Logic therefore
becomes the propaedeutic by which the particular is
proved and deduced from the general. As a judgment

or proposition is proved or deduced, by being concluded from more general judgments through Aristotle's famous syllogistic procedures, so a concept
is deduced or derived by being formed from a more
general concept. This deduction of the concept is
what he calls "definition."

Some logical positivists view with disdain not
only Aristotle's metaphysics but everyone's
metaphysics. For them it appears senseless to try
to say something about what is not matter of fact,
and the only way to avoid senselessness is either
to explain the use of symbols or to say something
verifiable about the matter-of-fact.[57]

We do not have any argument with the positivists in their repudiation of traditional ontology when it purports to search for the "absolute,"
and the "ultimate." By their very nature, propositions about absolutes become unverifiable assertions and bear no scientific value. There is,
however, a difference between propositions about
the absolute and ultimate reality, and assumptive
propositions about a finite, specific reality
capable of implying testable propositions about
various phases of that reality. The social uni-
verse for us, consists of those predicables about
which any other series of predicables would not be
scientifically tenable.

There is an objection by modern logicians and
many of the philosophical neo-realists, to interpret the concepts of genus and species in terms of
substance and attribute rather than function and
variable. However, they do recognize that the essential feature of an analytical or nominal definition (in contradistinction to the Aristotelian
"real" definition) is a construction of a logical
system (a system of interrelated propositions
logically deducible, one from another, and all of
them the logical outcome of some basic, primitive
premises or assumptions) which is interpreted in
terms of the field of knowledge to which the
definiendum belongs. Then, one might ask, how can
the basic terms in a given system of knowledge be
defined except in terms of undefinables (which, to
be meaningful, must be identified with the existential even though the existential may not be
sensorially experiencable), or in the form of basic
premises (which again must refer to reality)? "In
practice, the distinction between verbal and real
definitions is never so sharp, and even in definitions which seem altogether verbal there is
generally some reference to the analysis of what

the words stand for."[58] Some have even questioned
the nominalness of the nominal definitions.[59]

The definitional process, even if we seek to
adhere to the guiding principles of logic, is not
without its difficulties. The genus and differentiam principle clearly furnishes a more secure
basis for definition than definitions springing
from the common everyday usage of terms and concepts or from individual stipulative definitional
choices. Bertrand Russell, considered by many, if
not the father, certainly one of the earliest
proponents of symbolic logic and logical atomism,
remarked to me: "We may criticize or suspect the
Aristotelian view of classification and division,
but we cannot suppress or eliminate it."

We might conclude the matter of definitions by
summarizing the guidelines for defining. Practically every textbook on logic lists the following
set of rules. They were first suggested by
Aristotle in his Topica:[60]

1.   A definition should give the essence of the
     thing defined, rather than its accidental
     properties.
2.   A definition should give the genus and
     differentia of the thing defined.
3.   One should not define by synonyms.
4.   A definition should be concise.
5.   One should not define by metaphors.
6.   One should not define by negative terms.

GENERAL SYSTEMS THEORY APPLIED TO THE STUDY
OF JEWISH LIFE

General systems theory came into wide prominence after World War II. It appears that A. Lotka
in his Elements of Physical Biology, published in
1925, was the first to advance the laws for a
general system. However, the term and program of
general systems theory were introduced in a publication by Ludwig von Bertalanffy, one of the
world's foremost biologists, in 1947. Joined by
Kenneth Boulding, an economist, J. G. Miller, a
psychiatrist and psychologist, W. R. Ashby, a bac-
teriologist, The Society of General Systems was
organized in 1955.

In the last three decades the movement has
attracted additional scholars from practically
every intellectual field and discipline -- philosophy, sociology, anthropology, physics, communication science, computer science, information
theory, operations research, cybernetics, and

educational curriculum study. Extensive discussions developed and numerous publications were
released. (A selected bibliography is listed in
the relevant footnote references of this
chapter[61]).

If we peruse the literature on system and
general systems, the following terms and concepts
recur frequently and in numerous publications:

Function	Social system
Structure	Culture system
Relation	Interaction
Form	Transaction
Organization	Organicism
Pattern	Isomorphism
Universals	Molar analysis
Teleology	Homeostasis
Events	Sociostasis
Dynamics	Information
Wholeness and holism	Cybernetics
Unity of science	Entropy
Interdiscipline	Equifinality
Interdependence of sub-	Humanocentrism
systems	Levels of integration
Action system	Reductionism
Personality system,	

All are intimately connected with the generic
concept of system. For my purposes, I will
therefore confine myself to the definition and
nature of system and general systems only. The
distinctions among the aforementioned terms must
await another time and place.

Employing the per genus principle, we can
define system as the perspective that conceives of
reality as an interrelation of elements rather than
an aggregation of separate objects and parts. The
focus is more on relation and structure and less on
things and disparate elements. The system approach
approximates John Dewey's "unfactured observation"
concept. A system constitutes a totality.[62]

A system differs from an aggregate and a
category. In a system, persons, things, and ideas
are interlinked to form a structure and figura-
tion. In an aggregate, the parts are added; in a
category, the parts are merely similar and independent. A system is greater than the aggregate of
its parts. A society and a group are more than the
sum of individuals, just as a culture is more than
the sum of its traits. Both status and role
presupposes configuration and system.[63] Anthropologists have widely recognized that it is

inadvisable, if not actually impossible, to attempt
to understand a cultural element without simulta-
neously considering its larger context. I recall
Polyani stating in his The Tacit Dimension: "It is
a mistaken belief that since particulars are more
tangible than their structure and system, knowledge
of them offers a truer conception of things." The
system perspective offers a world of organized
complexity rather than a world of "simultaneous
plurality," to employ a phrase of Leibnitz.

Relationships in a system are as real as the
things that compose the system. The unity of a
group is not in the identity of its members but in
their relationships. Connectiveness and organization are the traits of a system. The system
perspective can be "traced in part to the recent
concern of several disciplines to treat their subject matter -- whether the organism, the species,
or the social group -- as a whole, an entity in its
own right with unique properties understandable
only in terms of the whole, especially in the face
of a more traditional reductionistic or mechanistic
focus on the separate parts and a simplistic notion
of how these parts fit together."[64]

General systems extends the notion to an
intersystem perspective. Its emphases are on
interdisciplines, on the integration of the disciplines, and ultimately on the unity of the
sciences. It recognizes that the larger macro-
intersystem relationships are necessary for the
adequate understanding of any one system. One
might colloquialize by asserting that Jews exist
because non-Jews exist; if there were no non-Jews
there would be no Jews; and vice-versa. Either is
because of the other's being. The reality of the
intersystem accounts for the reality of a system.
Just as the individual is known through another, a
group is known through another group. An "I"
obtains its identity through a "thou"; a "we"
obtains its realization through a "they" (Echoes of
Martin Buber, George Herbert Mead, Charles Cooley,
and Morris Raphael Cohen.) Just as there is a
correlation of organs in the body, so there is a
correlation of organisms in the "world of life."
Nature and human life are not arranged into disciplines. That which applies to a system applies
therefore to general systems -- relation, integration, commonality and unity.

Anti-Semitism cannot be understood by certain
personality traits or even economic conditions but
rather only as an integrative structural approach
linking prejudiced personalities to a total

socio-cultural configuration. Kurt Lewin once
claimed that there could be no equality for the
individual Jew unless his Jewish group were
equal. Minority group status and cultural marginality need to be studied in the context of interaction with, and the degree of integration into,
the dominant culture system.

Acculturation and assimilation of Jews cannot
be understood except as they interact with persons
of diverse ethnic backgrounds and as they become
involved in the life of the larger community.
Sociologists and psychologists who have concerned
themselves with the study of Jewish life in the
United States, have recognized the conflict individual Jews experience between their Jewish ethnicity and the motivations towards assimilation.[65]

Knowledge of the factors making for intermarriages among all ethnic groups may be necessary for
the understanding of Jewish-non-Jewish intermarriages. It may even be impossible to discover
"Jewish factors" that are responsible for intermarriages among Jews without the perspective of
general inter-ethnic factors.

Speaking Yiddish or not speaking Yiddish can
be explained through a group or intergroup context,
such as an individual's presence at the YIVO
Institute of Jewish Research on 86th Street in New
York City, and the same individual in the presence
of a chemistry laboratory group at the university. Language maintenance and language usage can
be understood only from an intergroup configuration
and perspective.

Studies of Jewish generation groups without
relating them to earlier and later Jewish
generations are almost meaningless. Jewish life in
the United States cannot be adequately understood
as a separate entity. Nor can any segment or
subdivision of Jewish life be understood in terms
of a separate entity. It is difficult to
comprehend Jewish occupational involvement without
its relation to Jewish social mobility; social
mobility without ethnic goals and values of Jews;
Jewish goals and values divorced from the goals and
values of an industrialized, urbanized America.
The general systems perspective looms significant
in the approach to the study of Jewish life in the
United States.

The Jewish symbolic system and Jewish subsys-
tems may interrelate with each other and with
outside systems by assuming common attributes and
elements, or combining diverse and separate
attributes of different systems into a common

integrative systemic design and structure. One
system or sub-system may be totally included into a
larger system, or some elements may be common among
several systems while other elements are separate. One system may lead into another as when
Judaism touches Christianity. There may be a relationship where diverse entities and systems are
contained in a larger system, or systems can con-
verge to form a new system.

The intersystem relationships are more
suggestive than comprehensive. Further explora-
tions are required to determine the efficacy and
the applications of a number of concepts and
related hypotheses that have emerged in general
systems theory including the concepts of: closed
and open systems; intersystem transformations;
ethnic boundaries; John Dewey's transactionalism;
homeostasis and sociostasis; controlled (cyber-
netic) systems and uncontrolled systems; detector,
selector, and effector functions of a system;
systems in equilibrium and systems in disequi-
librium; idiographic and nomethetic analysis;
static and dynamic equilibrium; and negative
(equilibrating) and positive (non-equilibrating
feedback.[66] The possibilities abound.

It should not be construed that the idea of
systems is novel. Only its expansion, development
and emphases are of recent provenance. The
earliest philosophers debated problems of the one
and many, the particular and the universal, change
and permanence, same and other, the concrete and
the abstract. The Cartesian dualism of separate
mind and matter has departed from the arena of
serious philosophical discourse. Contemporary
philosophy has markedly recognized process, relation, and form as essential features of reality.
Immanual Kant's observation epitomizes this notion
in his assertion: "Gedanken ohne inhalt sind leer,
Anschauungen ohne Begriffe sind blind."[67] Even
Leibnitz, the monadic idealist recognized relations, which is very difficult for a philosophical
idealist to do.

More recently, Alfred North Whitehead advanced
his "fallacy of misplaced concreteness," and often
spoke of the "essential relatedness of all
things." Bertrand Russell often denied the existence of particulars; only universals existed. He
referred to events and relations as facts, and
considered that things differ only in respect of
arrangement and context. John Dewey defined
experience as a relationship between one part of
existence and another. Both Dewey and Russell

assailed the fragmentalization of subject matter
and the separation of the disciplines. Emmanuel
Mesthene observed a reconciliation between pragma-
tism and logical positivism.[68]   Hadley Cantril
argued that there can be "no 'person' except for
his 'environment', nothing 'subjective' except for
what is 'objective', nothing 'personal' except for
what is 'social.'"[69]   Morris Raphael Cohen has
written that "empirical facts are generally resul-
tants of opposing and yet inseparable tendencies
like the north and south poles".[70]

All logic, especially symbolic logic, has been
referred to as a logic of relations. Russell and
Whitehead's Principia Mathematica reduced mathe-
matics to logical relations. Members of the Vienna
Circle promulgated the unity of science and issued
a series of publications under the inscription of
the International Encyclopedia of Unified
Science. Contributors included Rudolf Carnap,
Herbert Feigl, Carl G. Hempel, Joseph Woodger, Otto
Neurath, Joergen Joergensen. Nearly all philosophers of science have frequently viewed the goal of
science as maximization of system and integration.

In physics, contemporary notions acknowledge
wholeness, organization, and dynamics. Classical
mechanics regarded space, time, and mass as independent variables. Einstein established that space
and time are interdependent and that both are dependent on the velocity of light. Heat, light, and
sound as elements of our experience are all found
to be modes of motion in their physical correlates. Different kinds of energy are found to be
transformations of but one energy.[71]   Tradtional
physics does not encompass the feedback processes
of a system in the notion of causality; contemporary physics does.

Modern systems research has also pervaded the
biological, psychological, and social sciences.
General systems approach has reflected itself in
the numerous and increasing inter-disciplinary
programs and in the hybridization of the disciplines: biochemistry, social psychology, bio-
physics, social psychiatry, engineering physiology,
sociobiology, and so on. The quest for relationships, integration, and unifying conceptualizations
has become a fact of contemporary empirical
science. Their implications for the study of
Jewish life is here thus proposed and submitted.

NOTES

1. Solomon Zeitlin, "Who is a Jew? A Halachic-Historic Study," The Jewish Quarterly Review, vol. 49, no. 4 (April 1959) p. 262; E. Bevan and C. Singer, The Legacy of Israel (New York: Oxford University Press, 1953), p. 514.
2. Arnold J. Toynbee, A Study of History, Volume 12: Reconsiderations (New York: Oxford University Press, 1961), p. 296.
3. Roberta T. Ash, "Jewish Adolescents' Attitudes Toward Religion and Ethnicity," Adolescence, vol. 4, no. 14 (Summer 1968) p. 245; "Religion forms part of all that is Jewish, even of the thoroughly secularized life of modern Jews," Erich Kahler, The Jews Among the Nations (New York: Frederick Ungar Publishing Co; 1967), p. 7; Marshall Sklare and Mark Vosk, The Riverton Study (New York; American Jewish Committee, 1957, p. 21; Jack Rothman, Minority Group Identification and Intergroup Relations: An Examination of Kurt Lewin's Theory of Jewish Group Identity (Research Institute for Group Work in Jewish Agencies, 1965), p. 128.
4. Leonard W. Ferguson, "The Sociological Validity of Primary Attitude Scale No. 1: Religionism," The Journal of Social Psychology, vol. 23 (1946), p. 199.
5. The American Council for Judaism, An Approach to An American Judaism (New York: The American Council for Judaism), pamphlet, p. 3.
6. Albert Einstein, "Just What Is A Jew?" in Saul L. Goodman, ed., The Faith of Secular Jews (New York: Ktav Publishing House, 1976), p. 113.
7. Arnold J. Toynbee, op. cit., p. 293.
8. Norman Lamm, "Who Is A Jew?" Jewish Life, vol. 37, no. 5, (May-June, 1970), pp. 6-16; Baruch Litvin, compiler, and Sidney B. Hoenig, ed; Jewish Identity: Modern Responsa and Opinions (New York: Philipp Feldheim, Inc., 1965).
9. George Psathas, "Ethnicity, Social Class, and Adolescent Independence from Parental Control," American Sociological Review, vol. 22, no. 4 (August 1957), p. 417.
10. "Jew," in The American Heritage Dictionary of the English Language (Boston: Houghton Mifflin Co., 1969).
11. "Jew," in The Random House Dictionary of the English Language (New York: Random House, 1968).
12. "Jew," in Webster's Third New International Dictionary of the English Language: Unabridged

(Springfield, Mass.: G. and C. Merriam Co;
1971).
13. "Jew," in The Oxford English Dictionary
(Oxford: Oxford University Press, 1933).
14. Ash, op. cit., pp. 246, 263, 279; "A definition
of the Jewish people must needs correspond to
the aggregate of the concepts expressed by the
three group names: most ancient, ancient, and
modern. The only description applicable to it
is 'the historical nation of all times,' a
description bringing into relief the contrast
between it and all other nations of modern and
ancient times...." S. M. Dubnow, Jewish
History: An Essay in the Philosophy of History
(Philadelphia: The Jewish Publication Society
of America, 1927), p. 10; "...c'est un peuple
tout composé de frerès, et, au lieu que tous
les autres sont formés de l'assemblage d'une
infinité de familles, celui-ci, quoque si
étrangement abondant, est tout sorti d'un seul
homme, et, étant ainsi tous une même chair, et
memberes les uns des autres, [ils] composent un
puissant Etat d'une seule famille. Cela est
unique..." Blaise Pascal, Pensees (Paris:
Libraire Hachette Et Cie, 1904), sect. IX, 620.
15. "The Jewish people is not an abstract notion or
just a collective name for myriads of isolated
and scattered individuals in various
countries. It is a conglomerate whose
actuality, will and common destiny are not open
to question...." David Ben Gurion, Israel
Government Yearbook, 1952-1953 (Jerusalem: The
Government Printer, 1953), p. 34.
16. Schmuel Niger, "What I Believe As A Jew," from
Yisrael: Folk un Land (Chicago: L. M. Stein
Publishing Co; 1952), p. 7. Translated from
Yiddish by Saul L. Goodman, ed., The Faith of
Secular Jews (New York: Ktav Publishing House,
1976), p. 87.
17. Erikson, Erik H., Childhood and Society, second
edition, (New York: W. W. Norton and Co;
1963), p. 354.
18. Isaac Deutscher, The Non-Jewish Jew And Other
Essays (Oxford: Oxford University Press,
1968), p. 51. It should be mentioned that Mr.
Deutscher referred to himself as a Jew even
though he considered himself an atheist, a
Marxist, and an internationalist (p. 56).
19. Robert Greenblatt, "Out of the Melting Pot Into
The Fire," in James A. Sleeper and Alan L.
Mintz, eds., The New Jews (New York: Random
House, 1971), p. 39.

20. Anton Lourie, "The Jew as a Psychological Type," American Imago, vol. 6, no. 2 (1949), pp. 122-155; "Jews May be defined as persons 'with distinctive traits of temperament and aptitude....'" Thorstein Veblen, Essays in Our Changing Order (New York: Viking Press, 1964), p. 222.

21. Isidore Chein, "The Problem of Jewish Identification," Jewish Social Studies, vol. 17 (July, 1955), p. 219.

22. Raphael Loewe, "Defining Judaism: Some Ground-Clearing", The Jewish Journal of Sociology, vol. 7, no. 2 (1965), p. 158.

23. Gerald Abrahams, The Jewish Mind (Boston: Beacon Press, 1961), p. 32.

24. Simon N. Herman, Jewish Identity: A Social Psychological Perspective (Beverly Hills, Calif.; Sage Publications, 1977), pp. 39-61; Brewton Berry, Race Relations (Boston: Houghton Mifflin Co., 1951), p. 55; Michael Selzer, "Who are the Jews? A Guide For the Perplexed Gentile-And Jew," Phylon, vol. 29 (fall, 1968), p. 232.

25. Fred Massarik, "National Jewish Population Study: A New U. S. Estimate," in Morris Fine and Milton Himmelfarb, eds., American Jewish Year Book, 1974-1975, vol. 75 (Philadelphia: The Publication Society of America, 1974), pp. 296-313.

26. Erich Rosenthal, The Jewish Population of Chicago, Illinois (Chicago: The College of Jewish Studies, 1952); Meyer Greenberg, "The Jewish Student at Yale: His Attitude Toward Judaism," in YIVO Annual of Jewish Social Science, vol. 1 (New York: Yiddish Scientific Institute - YIVO, 1946), pp. 214-240.

27. Ira Rosenswaike, "The Utilization of Census Mother Tongue Data in American Jewish Population Analysis," Jewish Social Studies, vol. 33, nos. 2-3 (April-July 1971), pp. 141-159; Ira Rosenswaike, "Estimating Jewish Population Distribution In U.S. Metropolitan Areas in 1970," Jewish Social Studies, vol. 36, no. 2 (April 1974), pp. 106-117; U. S. Bureau of the Census, 16th Census of the United States, 1940, Population: Nativity and Parentage of the White Parentage of the White Population: Mother Tongue (Washington, D.C., 1943), p. 1.

28. The author recalls a report of a research study that estimated the Jewish population in Chicago by employing this definition of Jews, but he

has been unable to track down the published
reference.
29. Solomon Zeitlin, "Who Is A Jew? A Halachic-
    Historic Study," The Jewish Quarterly Review,
    vol. 49, no. 4, April 1959, p. 242.
30. Simon Dubnow, "The Doctrine of Jewish
    Nationalism," in Saul L. Goodman, ed., The
    Faith of Secular Jews (New York: Ktav
    Publishing House, 1976), p. 178; "Jews are a
    nationality with a historic culture whose
    central characteristic is the Yiddish
    language," Saul L. Goodman, op. cit., p. 9.
31. Michael Selzer, "Who are the Jews? A Guide for
    the Perplexed Gentile-and Jew," Phylon, vol. 29
    (fall 1968), p. 231.
32. Nathan Rotenstreich, "The Revival of the Fossil
    Remnant-or Toynbee and Jewish Nationalism,"
    Jewish Social Studies, vol. 24 (1962), p. 138.
33. Thorstein Veblen, Essays in Our Changing Order
    (New York: Viking Press, 1964), p. 220.
34. Erich Kahler, The Jews Among The Nations (New
    York: Frederick Ungar Publishing Co; 1967), p.
    9.
35. Leonard D. Savitz and Richard F. Tomasson, "The
    Identifiability of Jews," American Journal of
    Sociology, vol. 64 (1958-1959), pp. 468-475;
    Leo A. Goodman, "Quantitative Methods for the
    Study of Identifiability," American Journal of
    Sociology, vol. 65, (1959-1960), pp. 246-257.
36. Everett V. Stonequist, The Marginal Man: A
    Study in Personality and Culture Conflict (New
    York: Russell and Russel, 1961), pp. 140-156;
    Thorstein Veblen, op. cit., pp. 222, 226.
37. Ibid., p. 80.
38. Thorstein Veblen, op. cit., chapter on: "The
    Intellectual Preeminence of Jews in Modern
    Europe," pp. 219-231; Allen Guttman, The Jewish
    Writer in America: Assimilation and The Crisis
    of Identity (New York: Oxford University
    Press, 1971).
39. Georg Simmel, Soziologie (Leipzig: Duncker und
    Humblot, 1908), pp. 685-691; Kurt H. Wolff, ed.
    and trans., The Sociology of Georg Simmel
    (Glencoe, Ill.: The Free Press, 1950), pp.
    403, 407-408.
40. H. H. Gerth and C. Wright Mills, trans. and
    ed., From Max Weber: Essays in Sociology (New
    York: Oxford University Press, 1946), p. 189.
41. The American Council for Judaism, An Approach
    To Judaism" (New York: The American Council
    for Judaism, 1953), p. 3.

42. Isidore Chein, "The Problem of Jewish Identification," Jewish Social Studies, vol. 17 (July, 1955), p. 219.
43. Michael Selzer, op. cit., p. 233.
44. Norman Lamm, op. cit., p. 6.
45. Ernest Van Den Haag, The Jewish Mystique (New York: Stein and Day, 1969).
46. Jews have been denoted as a subculture and ethnic group by numerous writers.
47. Epistle VII, Sections 343, 344. Translations by Walter Hamilton, Plato (New York: Penguin Books, 1973), p. 138 and Wilbur Marshall Urban, Language and Reality (New York: The Macmillan Co., 1939), p. 53. Many discussions and arguments have ensued over the years relative to the authenticity of Plato's Epistles. Of the letters attributed to Plato, thirteen are in existence. During the nineteenth century Plato's letters were generally dismissed as forgeries. The seventh and eighth of his epistles, however, are now recognized as genuine. The others remain in doubt (see Paul Friedlander, Plato (Princeton, N.J.: Princeton University Press, 1958), p. 236; R. G. Bury, Plato, vol. 7 (Cambridge, Mass.: Harvard University Press, 1961), p. 39; G. C. Field, Plato And His Contemporaries (New York: Haskell House Publishers, 1974), pp. 197-201.
48. Ernest Nagel, Sovereign Reason (Glencoe, Ill.: The Free Press, 1954), p. 31. It is not to be construed that the virtues of science devalues the worthiness of the non-sciences. Each has its purpose to fulfill in its own way.
49. Morris R. Cohen and Ernest Nagel, An Introduction to Logic and Scientific Method (New York: Harcourt, Brace and Co., 1934), p. 391.
50. Herbert Blumer, "Science Without Concepts," The American Journal of Sociology, vol. 36 (1931), pp. 515-533. See also John Dewey, Logic: The Theory of Inquiry (New York: Henry Holt and Co., 1938), p. 228; Kurt Lewin, Field Theory in Social Science (New York: Harper and Row, 1951), chapter 2; Morris R. Cohen and Ernest Nagel, op. cit., p. 391; Morris R. Cohen, Studies in Philosophy and Science (New York: Henry Holt and Co., 1949), p. 52-53; Kasimir Ajdukiewicz, "The Scientific World-Perspective," in Herbert Feigl and Wilfrid Sellars eds., Readings in Philosophical Analysis (New York: Appleton-Century-Crofts, 1949), pp. 182-188; C. G. Hempel, "Fundamentals

of Concept Formation in Empirical Science," in
International Encyclopedia of United Science,
vol. 2, no. 7 (University of Chicago Press,
1952).
51. Isaac Deutscher, op. cit., p. 51.
52. Louis Wirth, "The Problems of Minority Groups,"
In Ralph Linton ed., The Science of Man in the
World Crisis (New York: Columbia University
Press, 1945), p. 347. See also M. F. A.
Montagu, "On the Phrase 'Ethnic Group' in
Anthropology," Psychiatry, vol. 8 (1945), pp.
27-33.
53. I. M. Copi, Introduction to Logic, third
edition. (New York: The Macmillan Co., 1968),
pp. 107-110.
54. R. M. MacIver, Social Causation (Boston: Ginn
& Co., 1942); F. S. C. Northrup, The Logic of
the Sciences and the Humanities (New York:
Macmillan Co., 1947); A. C. Ramsperger,
Philosophies of Science (New York: F. S.
Crofts, 1942); M. R. Cohen, Preface to Logic
(New York: Harper and Bros., 1936).
55. R. Abelson, "Definition," The Encyclopedia of
Philosophy, vol. 2 (New York: Macmillan Co.
1967). This article analyzes several of the
more recent philosophical theories on
definition, especially as they are developed
and influenced by advancements in symbolic
logic.
56. A. N. Whitehead and B. Russell, Principia
Mathematica (Cambridge: Cambridge University
Press, 1910), p. 11.
57. A. J. Ayer, Language, Truth and Logic, (New
York: Oxford University Press, 1936); H.
Feigl, "Logical Empiricism," in D. D. Runes,
ed., Twentieth Century Philosophy (New York;
Philosophical Library, 1943), pp. 371-416; D.
M. Emmet, The Nature of Metaphysical Thinking
(New York: The Macmillan Co., 1946, p. 3:
"Our minds seem impelled to seek or create
significance in their world as a whole in terms
of concepts originally formed to express
relations within experience. But, we ask, what
warrant have we to suppose that the world views
which results are more than that, the product
of the mind's own impulse towards the creation
of forms in which the imagination can rest, and
a feeling of significance be enjoyed?... May
not such world views, whether metaphysical or
theological, prove in the end to be simply word
patterns, drawn by developing the implications
of ideas, such as the idea of 'Being',

'Perfection', ideas which have indeed the power
of evoking emotional response, but which are
none the less merely ideas, and do not say
anything about reality, transcending
appearance."

58. Morris R. Cohen and Ernest Nagel, op. cit., p.
232.

59. R. W. Eaton, General Logic (New York: Charles
Scribner's Sons, 1931), p. 300; C. K. Ogden and
I. A. Richards, The Meaning of Meaning (New
York: Harcourt Brace and Co., 1930), p. 110.

60. Raziel Abelson, "Definition," in The
Encyclopedia of Philosophy, vol. 2 (New York:
The Macmillan Co., 1967), p. 322.

61. Kenneth F. Berrien, General and Social Systems
(New Brunswick: Rutgers University Press,
1968); Walter Buckley ed., Modern Systems
Research for the Behavioral Scientist
(Chicago: Aldine & Co., 1968); Walter Buckley,
Sociology and Modern Systems Theory (Englewood
Cliffs, N.J.: Prentice-Hall, 1967); William
Gray, Frederick J. Duhl, and Nicholas D. Rizzo,
eds., General Systems Theory and Psychiatry
(Boston: Little, Brown, 1969); George J. Klir,
An Approach to General Systems Theory (New
York: Van Nostrand Reinhold, 1970); George J.
Klir, ed., Trends in General Systems Theory
(New York: John Wiley and Sons, 1972); Ervin
Laszlo, Introduction to Systems Philosophy (New
York: Gordon and Breach, 1971); M. D.
Mesarovic, ed., Systems Theory and Biology (New
York: Springer-Verlog, 1968); Ludwig von
Bertalanffy, General Systems Theory (New
York: Braziller, 1968); Ludwig von
Bertalanffy, Robots, Men and Minds (New York:
Braziller, 1967). See also bibliographical
references in Ervin Laszlo, The Relevance of
General Systems Theory (New York: George
Braziller, 1972), pp. 193-205.

62. Piaget has formulated several propositions
governing the properties of a system. See Jean
Piaget, "The concept of Structure," in
Scientific Thought: Some Underlying Concepts,
Methods and Procedures (Paris: Unesco, 1972),
p. 35.

63. "One cannot treat the father as an isolated
object and analyze the relation [of his son] to
him, without treating him as part of the
nuclear family as a social system," Talcott
Parsons and Robert F. bales, Family:
Socialization and Interaction Process (Glencoe,
Ill.: The Free Press, 1955), p. 92.

64. Walter Buckley, ed., Modern Systems Research
    For the Behavioral Scientist (Chicago: Aldine
    Publishing Co., 1968), p. xxiii.
65. Nathan Glazer, American Judaism (Chicago:
    University of Chicago Press, 1957), p. 9.
66. See Alfred Kuhn, The Logic of Social Systems
    (San Francisco: Jossey-Bass Publishers, 1974).
67. "Form without content is empty; content without
    form is blind."
68. Emmanual G. Mesthene, "Toward Reunion in
    Philosophy: Pragmatism and Logical Positivism
    Reconciled," Commentary, vol. 24 (1957), p. 70.
69. Hadley Cantril, "Toward A. Humanistic
    Psychology, Etc; vol. 12 (1955), p. 80.
70. Morris R. Cohen, A Preface to Logic (New
    York: Meridian Books, 1956), p. 87.
71. Ray H. Dotterer, Philosophy By Way of The
    Sciences (New York: The Macmillan Co., 1929),
    p. 105.

Chapter II

JEWS IN THE UNITED STATES:
PERSPECTIVES FROM DEMOGRAPHY*

SIDNEY GOLDSTEIN

At a time when the demographic as well as the
social and perhaps even the economic structure of
the Jewish community is undergoing rapid change,
the need for continuous monitoring of these changes
and an assessment of their implications for the
future become crucial. Changes in size, composition, and distribution, as well as in the patterns
and levels of births, deaths, and population movement have tremendous significance for the local as
well as the national community. Knowledge about
these demographic factors is clearly essential for
purposes of planning whether a community should
provide certain services, where facilities should
be located, how they should be staffed, and who
would be able to bear the burden of funding them.
Furthermore, the demographic structure of the
Jewish community also has great significance for
its social, cultural, and religious viability,
whether these are judged by the ability to support
an educational system, organized religious life, or
to provide a sufficient density of population to
insure a sense of community identification.
     Because the socio-demographic structure of the
Jewish community, like that of the larger American
community, is both a product and a cause of change,
it is vital to have data available to document the
changes, and to assess their implications for the
future. Unfortunately, however, such data on
American Jewry are often lacking.[1] The absence of
a question on religion in the United States
decennial census precludes tapping the wealth of

information that would otherwise be available in
the census for analytic purposes on religious
characteristics of the population for local communities and even for local neighborhoods within
those communities. The need for comprehensive data
on religious identification is documented clearly
by the fact that perhaps the best single source of
information available on the religious size and
composition of Jews and other religious groups remains that collected by the Bureau of the Census in
the March, 1957 Current Population Survey.[2] Because answers to that survey were voluntary, the
Bureau could include a question on religion. But
1957 is long past and much has happened to the
American population and to the American Jewish population since then. The 1957 data, relatively rich
though they are, therefore can serve mainly as a
bench mark against which changes can be measured
rather than as an indication of the current situation. Unfortunately, we have few new sets of
comprehensive data.

The National Jewish Population Study was an
important and promising attempt to design and
conduct a nationwide survey representative of the
United States Jewish population. As a report in
the American Jewish Year Book indicates, "The
study, sponsored by the Council of Jewish Federations and Welfare Funds, now has completed data
collection and other tasks prerequisite to analysis
and constitutes a repository of information that
will require 'mining' and interpretation for many
years to come."[3] It remains largely just that. To
date, relatively few published reports on the number and basic characteristics of the Jewish population have appeared. This overview will make use
of the limited National Jewish Population Study
information that is available, but in the absence
of a comprehensive evaluation of the basic data,
even these limited data must be used with caution.

Other nationwide demographic statistics containing information on religious identification are
available from various surveys undertaken by public
opinion polls and other organizations.[4] Some of
these surveys have been used particularly to gain
insights on American Jewish fertility, but because
they include too small a number of Jews, detailed
analysis of these data for such purposes is greatly
restricted.[5]

Aside from the 1957 Current Population Survey
and the data from the National Jewish Population
Survey, locally sponsored community surveys still
provide the best data on the characteristics of

Jews. These studies differ considerably in
quality, depending in particular on the manner of
selecting the sample population, but also on the
quality of the interviewers, the response rates,
and the sophistication of the analysis. Since some
of the surveys rely exclusively on the lists of
families available to the local federation, serious
doubts are raised about how representative the samples are. They are usually strongly biased in
favor of individuals and families who contribute to
fund raising efforts. In some communities, the
federation has made a concerted effort before undertaking a survey to insure coverage of donors and
nondonors as well as of both affiliated and unaffiliated families. The success of such attempts
varies both with community size and with the ease
of identifying unaffiliated households. In the
limited instances where these efforts have been
successful, the resulting samples provide a good
basis for studying the entire population; in other
cases, the findings about the extent and nature of
Jewish identification, intermarriage, and demographic characteristics and behavior are probably
seriously biased by the omission of individuals and
families who are highly assimilated.

Beyond these concerns the findings from
community surveys must be used with great caution
for generalizing to the national community, since
other considerations affect how representative the
local sample will be for such broader purposes.
Most of the surveys conducted in local communities
have been for moderate-sized places with Jewish
populations of 25,000 or less; Boston, Los Angeles,
Washington, Detroit, Baltimore, and San Francisco
are exceptions. Legitimate questions must be
raised about the extent to which findings based on
moderate-sized communities are typical of the total
American Jewish population. Yet, assessment of
these studies suggests that they display impres-
sively similar patterns for the varied locations
that have been surveyed.[6] Variations can generally
be explained by the nature of the community itself,
-- that is, whether it is an older community or a
newer suburban area, and in which region of the
country it is located. The relatively high degree
of homogeneity that characterizes the patterns of
these communities suggests that the underlying
demographic profile of American Jewry as a whole
probably does not deviate significantly from that
depicted by already existing sources, incomplete as
they are. The fact that the findings which are
available to date from the National Jewish

Population Study also conform to the general
patterns provides some additional basis for confidence in the community studies as well as in the
National Jewish Population Study itself.

In undertaking this review, the focus, within
the limits of available information, will be on the
major aspects of concern to the demographer: size,
composition, distribution in space, and the components of change (fertility, mortality, and migration).   The presentation would not be complete,
however, without some attention to intermarriage.
Throughout the discussion, the implications of the
current situation for future patterns of growth and
identification will be explored.

POPULATION GROWTH

At no time in American history has there been
a complete enumeration of the American Jewish population.   Whether referring to the population in
1790 or in the 1970s, the statistic is an estimate
and therefore subject to some question.   For example, for 1972 the American Jewish Year Book reported a total Jewish population of 6,115,320, but in
1974 it cited a considerably lower number,
5,732,000.   The drop reflected the findings of the
National Jewish Population Survey, and particularly
the reassessment of Greater New York's population,
which had been reported at 2,381,000 between 1962
and 1973 by the American Jewish Year Book, but
which was estimated by the National Jewish
Population Survey to be only 1,998,000 as of
1971.[7]   As the last American Jewish Year Book
stressed, at least two factors continue to make
even the most recent estimates problematic: the
difficulty in documenting the extent of the shift
to the "sun-belt" states and continued doubts about
the accuracy of the New York City estimates which
may still be too high.[8]

Even the National Jewish Population Study
estimate of 5,800,000 total American Jewish population in 1971 needs qualification.   The statistic
refers to the population residing in Jewish households, exclusive of the institutional population,
and as such includes both Jews and non-Jews.   If
non-Jews are excluded, again based on information
gathered in the National Jewish Population Survey,
the total number of Jewish residents in households
is 5,370,000 persons.   If added to that is an
estimated 50,000 Jews in institutions, the total
population in 1971 would be 5,420,000 persons,

still some half million less (a 10 percent differential) than the previous estimates used by the
American Jewish Year Book. This is far too great a
range of difference to allow strong confidence in
the estimates which have been provided.[9]
     A set of annual estimates of the American
Jewish population for the period 1940 to 1975 by
Ira Rosenwaike,[10] based on use of the 1957 Bureau
of the Census estimates, indicates that the Jewish
population in 1970 in the United States was
5,500,000, very close to the estimate emanating
from the National Jewish Population Study.
Rosenwaike estimated a 1975 population of
5,619,000, only 69,000 greater than in 1970. This
estimate takes account of levels of fertility,
mortality, and immigration, but does not
incorporate estimates of losses resulting from
intermarriage and assimilation. While all estimates are subject to question, the close corre-
spondence between the 1970 estimate and the figure
given in the National Jewish Population Study and
the small growth since then, points to the strong
likelihood that the total population in 1970 was
well below the six million mark and that it has
remained so. The American Jewish Year Book
estimate that the 1979 Jewish population totaled
5,860,900 conforms to this expectation.[11]
     The Jewish population of the United States has
clearly experienced a tremendous growth between the
time of the formation of the United States and the
1970s. From a community estimated to number only
slightly above 1000 in 1790, the Jewish population
had passed the one million mark by the end of the
next century. Over three-quarters of that growth
occurred, however, in the last two decades of the
century, reflecting the onset of massive immigration from Eastern Europe in the 1880s. Between
1881 and 1902 almost 800,000 Jews had entered the
United States. By the beginning of the twentieth
century, Jews constituted 1.4 percent of the total
American population (Table 1). Immigration continued to augment the Jewish population even more
substantially in the first several decades of the
twentieth century; between 1902 and 1924, over 1.5
million Jews had immigrated and all but a small
percentage remained in the United States, in contrast to high return rates among other ethnic
groups. By 1927, Jews were estimated to number 4.2
million persons. The fourfold increase in an interval of less than three decades was far greater
than the increase of the total population of the
United States; during the same interval the

Table 1:   JEWISH POPULATION GROWTH IN THE UNITED
           STATES, 1790-1970

Year	Number	Percent of Total United States Population
1790[b]	1,200	0.03
1818[a]	3,000	0.03
1826	6,000	0.06
1840	15,000	0.1
1848	50,000	0.2
1880	230,000	0.5
1888	400,000	0.6
1897	938,000	1.3
1900	1,058,000	1.4
1907[b]	1,777,000	2.0
1917	3,389,000	3.3
1927	4,228,000	3.6
1937	4,771,000	3.7
1950[c]	5,000,000	3.5
1960	5,531,000	3.1
1970	5,870,000	2.9
1975	5,732,000	2.7
1979	5,860,900	2.7

[a]Estimates for 1818-1899 are based on "Jewish
  Statistics," American Jewish Year Book, vol. 1
  (1900), p. 623.
[b]Estimates for 1790 and 1907-1937 are from
  Nathan Goldberg, "The Jewish Population in the
  United States," in The Jewish People, Past and
  Present, vol. 2 (New York: Jewish Encyclopedia
  Handbooks, 1955), p. 25.
[c]The 1950-1979 estimates are taken from the
  AmericanJewish Year Book, vols. 70-80 (1969-
  1980).

American population grew by only about 60 percent. Reflecting this differential rate of growth,
Jews more than doubled their proportion of the
total population from the 1.4 percent in 1900 to
3.6 percent in 1927.
     Thereafter, the imposition of immigration
quotas slowed the rate of growth. Often over-
looked, however, is that between 1925 and World War
II about 250,000 Jews immigrated to the United
States, and that another 320,000 did so between the
end of the war and 1975. Despite its reduced volume compared to the peak period between 1881 and

1924, immigration has therefore continued to be an
important component of growth. Without it, the
American Jewish population today would be substantially smaller in size, particularly given the low
rates of natural increase, losses through intermarriage and assimilation, and a small loss through
emigration, especially to Israel and Canada.[12]
What is interesting is that despite this immigration, only half a million persons are estimated to
have been added overall to the Jewish population
between 1927 and 1937 and only one-quarter million
more by 1950. Such slow growth, with comparatively
minor exception, has persisted to the present, and
the Jewish population has increased at a much
slower rate than the population as a whole. Whereas the total United States population increased by
just over three-fourths in the 50 years between
1930 and 1980, the Jewish population grew by only
about one-third in this same interval.
     Estimates of the net effects of international
migration on the growth of the Jewish population in
the 1970s suggests that net immigration has contributed about 8000 persons per year to Jewish population growth in the United States.[13] If estimates
of the near-equal number of births and deaths during this period are correct, net immigration may
thus have accounted for as much as 60 percent of
the small growth of the American Jewish population
between 1970 and 1975. By contrast, in the early
1950s net immigration is estimated to have accounted for only one-fifth of total growth. With the
increase in the influx of Russian Jews in the
1970s, amounting to approximately 58,700 persons
between 1975 and 1979,[14] supplemented by what may
be a substantial immigration of Israelis, immigration undoubtedly has persisted as the most important component of growth.
     Reflecting the long-term reversal in rates of
growth between the Jewish and the total population,
the proportion of Jews in the total population,
after peaking at 3.7 percent in 1937, has undergone
steady decline to 2.7 percent in 1979, about the
same percentage as in approximately 1910. Given
the low Jewish birthrate, the losses sustained
through intermarriage and assimilation, and what
may well be higher levels of mortality due to the
aging of the population, there seems little prospect of a reversal in the slower rates of growth
that have come to characterize recent years. If
anything, the decline in the growth rate is likely
to persist and may even become negative in the not
too distant future.

In fact, consideration of the joint impact of
these forces has led to dire predictions about the
virtual extinction of the American Jewish population within the next 100 years. One forecast suggests, "When the United States celebrates its
tricentennial in 2076, the American Jewish community is likely to number no more than 944,000
persons and conceivably as few as 10,420."[15] While
this prediction is overly pessimistic, in the
absence of a drastic reversal in ongoing patterns,
a decline does seem probable; the projections by
Lieberman and Weinfeld of a Jewish population of
three to four million by the end of the twenty-
first century seems much more likely.[16]

Yet the decline in relative numbers may not be
very significant in view of the fact that Jews have
never constituted a numerically large segment of
the American population. Despite their small
numbers, Jews are generally considered the third
major religious group in the country. There seems
little reason to expect that this situation will
change, even should the Jewish percentage of the
total population decline further. As long as Jews,
both as a group and individually, continue to play
significant roles in the cultural, educational,
political, and economic life of the country, more
important factors than sheer numbers may be influencing the position of the Jewish community within
the total American community. These factors include changes in their geographical concentration,
as well as in their representation in selected
socioeconomic strata of the population. Only when
the combination of changes in total numbers are
accompanied by significant changes in distribution
and composition which are deleterious to the prominent role which Jews have played on the American
scene will the change in numbers itself take on new
significance.

MORTALITY

Better health and longer life have characterized the Jewish population in the Western world
from at least as early as midseventeenth century.[17] Factors contributing to this favorable
differential have included the positive effect of
religious observance on health conditions; the
relatively longer exposure which Jews have had to
"civilized" environments and urban settings, resulting in higher levels of immunity against certain contagious diseases; and the higher than

average socioeconomic status which Jews have enjoyed, permitting them thereby to obtain more and
better medical attention and to live in a better
environment. Because of the low mortality levels
and the generally good health conditions which have
characterized American society in recent years,
minimum attention has been paid by Jewish scholars
to the mortality experience of the American Jewish
population. In part this also reflects the difficulty of obtaining the necessary data in the
absence of direct information on religion on death
certificates. No study on Jewish mortality levels
appears to have been conducted since 1970. The few
studies undertaken before 1970 were limited both
because of their restriction to a small number of
communities and because they were cross-sectional
and did not, therefore, provide trend data that
might be useful for projections.

Although the specific findings differed somewhat among communities, the general conclusion
seems warranted that as recently as the 1960s, some
differences existed between Jews and the total
white population in age specific death rates, life
expectancy, and survival patterns, generally more
so for males than for females.[18] Jewish age specific death rates were below those of the white population at younger ages, possibly because of a combination of the conditions already outlined which
have lowered the susceptibility of Jews to contagious diseases. The particularly lower mortality
among Jewish babies under one lends support to this
interpretation. Older Jews have a higher mortality
than the total white population, which may reflect
the possibility that, given the better medical
attention they receive at earlier ages and their
better ability to survive contagious diseases, more
Jews with physically impaired lives survive until
later years when the effects of chronic diseases
produce higher death tolls. Data for Providence,
Rhode Island, for the cause of death support such
an interpretation.[19]

Again, it is necessary to use caution in
interpreting these data, both because of their
limited coverage of the American Jewish population
and because of their outdated character. It is
especially important to recognize that the cross-
sectional character of the data provides no basis
for projecting future patterns, particularly about
the mortality experience of older persons. In the
United States in general, minimal changes in mortality are expected. The fact that relatively
small differences already existed between Jews and

non-Jews in the 1960s and that these have most
likely diminished still further as the socioeconomic environment of Jews and non-Jews and their
utilization of health services become more similar
probably means that future mortality will be even
more similar than that observed here. Certainly,
the differences observed for the 1960s are not
large enough to account for the overall differences
in the rate of natural increase of the Jewish population compared to the total population. At the
same time, the aging of the Jewish population means
that the number of Jewish deaths is likely to
rise. To the extent that this happens, the rate of
natural increase is likely to decline in the absence of a corresponding rise in births and especially if the birthrate should decline. Given these
patterns, whatever differential in natural growth
characterizes Jews and non-Jews in the future will
be largely attributable to variations between them
in levels of fertility.

FERTILITY

The available evidence clearly indicates that
throughout their history in the United States, Jews
have had a lower birthrate than non-Jews. Yet only
in very recent years has lower fertility become an
openly discussed concern of the Jewish community.
In part, this reflects the fact that Jewish fertility, like that of the larger society, has recently
declined to a point where continuation at its current levels would lead to zero population growth or
possibly even negative population growth--reflec-
ting situations wherein births are either equal to
or below the number of deaths, thereby leading to
stability or decline in population size in the
absence of reenforcement from international migration. For the Jews, this threat of population decline is particularly serious since it can be exacerbated by losses resulting from intermarriages
and assimilation.
Despite the injunction to be fruitful and
multiply, Jews have had the smallest families of
virtually every ethnic and religious group. As
early as the late nineteenth century, available
evidence pointed to a Jewish birthrate which was
lower than that of the non-Jewish population; this
differential, although narrowing, has persisted to
the present.
In the Rhode Island Census of 1905, the only
state census that obtained information on religion

and related it to family size, the average family
size of native-born Jewish women was 2.3, compared
to an average of 3.2 for native-born Catholics, and
2.5 for native-born Protestants.[20]   Studies in the
1930s found Jews not only to have lower fertility
but also more to use contraceptives, to plan pregnancies, and to rely on more efficient methods to
achieve that goal.[21]   The 1941 Indianapolis fertility study, a milestone in demographic research in
the United States, found the fertility of Jews,
controlling for age differences, to be 25 percent
lower than for Protestants, whereas that of Catholics was about 15 percent higher.[22]

     The results of the 1957 population survey
conducted by the United States Bureau of the Census
also confirmed the lower fertility of Jews.[23]   The
cumulative fertility rate (children ever born) of
Jewish women 45 years of age and over was 2.2, compared to 3.1 for Catholic women and 2.8 for Protestant women.   Lower fertility also characterized
Jewish women at younger ages.   Moreover, controlling for area of residence, the fertility rate for
Jewish women in urban areas was 14 percent below
that of all urban women.

     Beginning in the 1950s, a series of surveys
were undertaken to investigate the fertility behavior of the American population.   Although Jews
constituted only a small portion of each of the
samples in these surveys, the data clearly pointed
to lower Jewish fertility.   The 1965 Growth of
American Families study showed that the average
number of children born by that year to women under
age 44 was 2.3 for Protestants and 2.8 for Catholics, compared to only 2.1 for Jews.[24]   By the end
of childbearing, Jews also expected to have a
smaller total number of children, only 2.9, than
either Protestants or Catholics, 3.0 and 3.9 respectively.   The similarity between the Protestant
and Jewish expected averages is particularly noteworthy in view of the earlier observed differences,
but expectations may not be fully realized.   In a
1970 study, Westoff and Ryder found that among
women 35 to 44 years of age, those at the end of
reproduction, sharp religious differentials existed.[25]   Restricting the comparison to white women,
Catholics averaged 3.6 children compared to only
2.9 for Protestants, and 2.1 for Jewish women, a
level equivalent to zero population growth.   The
authors also made a distinction between wanted and
unwanted children.   Reflecting their successful and
high level of fertility control, only 3 percent of

the Jewish children were reported as unwanted, by
far the lowest percentage of all religious groups.
        Although focussing on a somewhat different
population, and using a follow-up approach to their
orginal sample rather than an independent cross-
section of the population in successive rounds of
interviews, the Princeton fertility studies of 1957
and 1960 reached the same conclusions as those reported by Growth of American Families.[26] Jews,
when compared to Protestants and Catholics, desired
fewer children and more successfully planned their
pregnancies.
        Since the late 1960s, a new set of statistics
allows national comparison of the current fertility
of Jews and non-Jews.[27] The data collected in the
National Natality Surveys of 1967, 1968, and 1969
by the National Center for Health Statistics are
based on follow-up interviews with samples of mothers of legitimate births reported on birth certificates in those three years. By combining the data
from the three years, it was possible to assemble a
sample of 167 Jewish women who gave birth during
that period; they constituted 2 percent of the
total sample. Omitted are all childless married
women, all mothers of illegitimate children, and
all women who did not have a child during 1967-
1969. The latter restriction means that the respondents are younger than all married women and
they probably average somewhat more children than
the total married.
        Use of these data does have the advantage of
allowing assessment of current fertility, whereas
most of the surveys focus on cumulative fertility. In conjunction with the estimates of Jewish
women by age from the National Jewish Population
Study, a variety of basic fertility measures could
be computed; these were, in turn, compared with
those of the United States white population. It
must be stressed that the fertility rates calculated represent only very crude estimates since
they are subject to wide sampling errors. However,
even when these sampling errors are taken into
account, the evidence clearly documents the low
fertility of Jews.
        During 1967 to 1969, the crude birthrate for
total American whites was 16.8, but only 9.6 for
the Jewish population (middle estimates will be
used throughout the text discussion). Because the
age composition of the Jewish and total population
is quite different, a better comparison of Jewish
and total fertility can be made if age is controlled. As the data in Table 2 show, with the

exception of the 25-29 age group, Jewish fertility
is consistently below that of the total white
population and usually substantially so. Probably
reflecting the later age of marriage of Jewish
women, related in part to their tendency to stay in
school longer, the birthrate of Jewish women aged
15-19 is only 7.2 per thousand, compared to 59.9
per thousand for the total white population. This
differential narrows in the next age group, but the
birthrate remains very low for Jewish women. Because of the delay in marriage and consequent delay
in fertility, the age specific fertility rate for
Jewish women in the 25-29 year age group was actually slightly above that of the total white population. About half of all Jewish births occurred to
women aged 25-29, and almost three-quarters of
total fertility is completed by age 29. Corresponding percentages for the total white population
are only 25 percent and 63 percent, respectively.
The Jewish fertility rate drops precipitously for
women aged 30-34, and continues the decline for
higher age groups.
     The cumulative effect of these age differences
leads to an estimate of an average of 1468 children
per thousand Jewish women at the end of their
reproductive cycle, assuming that the specific patterns of 1967-1969 persisted. This contrasts to
2388 for the total white group. To the extent that
2.1 is the average number of births per woman required for replacement level, these data make it
very clear that, unless there are drastic errors in
either the birth data or the base population data,
Jewish fertility levels were already below replacement during the late 1960s, whereas those for
the total whites in those years were still above
replacement level. The tremendous differential
between the two, approaching the ratio of 2:1, is
substantial enough to confirm that the difference
in the crude rate is not strictly a matter of age
composition but also reflects a very real difference in fertility behavior between Jews and the
total population.
     Replacements can be measured more clearly
through use of the net reproduction rate which
shows the number of daughters which would be born
to a thousand women passing through their reproductive years, subject to both current age specific
fertility rates and current mortality patterns. In
general, a net reproduction rate of a thousand indicates that the women will produce enough daughters exactly to replace themselves; a rate below a
thousand is indicative of inadequate replacement;

Table 2: COMPARATIVE MEASURES OF FERTILITY OF JEWISH AND TOTAL WHITE
UNITED STATES POPULATIONS, 1967-1969

	Jewish Population*			United States White Population
	Low Population Base	Medium Population Base	High Population Base	
Crude birthrate	9.9	9.6	9.2	16.8
General fertility rate	48.1	46.2	44.5	82.3
Total fertility rate	1527.5	1467.5	1412.5	2388.0
Net Reproduction Rate	722.5	694.2	668.2	1143.6
Age specific birthrates				
15-19	7.5	7.2	6.9	55.9
20-24	63.2	60.8	58.4	164.1
25-29	153.0	147.0	141.5	141.0
30-34	60.3	57.9	55.8	73.7
35-39	17.5	16.8	16.2	34.0
40-44	4.0	3.8	3.7	8.9

* Based on population estimates from National Jewish Population Study, 1970-71,
and on fertility estimates from the 1967-1969 National Natality Surveys.
Low population estimate is 5,550,000.
Medium population estimate is 5,775,000.
High population estimate is 6,000,000.

conversely, a rate above a thousand indicates more
than adequate replacement. Based on the assumption
that Jewish mortality and that of the white population of the United States are quite similar, the
net reproduction rate for Jews is shown to be
between 668 and 722 per thousand compared to 1144
per thousand for the total white population. The
net reproduction rate thus confirms what has already been indicated by the other measures, that
the replacement level of Jews is both far below
that of the total white population and also considerably below the level needed to insure growth if
the rates of 1967-1969 persist.

The restriction of the National Natality
Survey data to women actually having children
during the specified years argues for the exploitation of complementary data which allow assessment
of cumulative fertility. Some limited insights
into this can be obtained from data available from
the National Opinion Research Census annual surveys. By combining the data from the 1972 through
1975 surveys, it was possible to obtain 89 ever
married Jewish women in all age groups over 18.[28]
These women had averaged 2 children up to the time
of the survey, compared to 2.7 for both Protestants
and Catholics. Among women aged 40-49, the age
group at the end of childbearing, corresponding
averages were 2.4, 3.4, and 3.6 for Jews, Protestants, and Catholics, respectively. The pattern of
lower Jewish fertility is reflected dramatically in
the parity data. About equal percentages of all
religious groups were childless, but 70 percent of
the Jewish women had no more than two children,
compared to only 53 percent of the Protestants and
52 percent of the Catholics. By contrast, 16 and
17 percent, respectively, of Protestant and Catholic women had 5 or more children, compared to only
1 percent of the Jews. Regardless of the index
used, therefore, the National Opinion Research
Center data, which reflect cumulative fertility
behavior rather than current performance or expected future levels, point to consistently lower
Jewish fertility compared to that of non-Jews.

The evidence available from 15 Jewish community studies encompassing the period 1953-1976 also
points to lower Jewish fertility (Table 3). These
data measure fertility by comparing the number of
children under five years of age per 1000 women
aged 20-44. Particularly noteworthy is the observation that five of the seven communities which
took surveys before 1960 reported child-women
ratios above 500, whereas none of the surveys taken

since 1960 has done so; and the ratios for three of
the four communities surveyed in the 1970s display
the lowest of all, below 400, and in the case of
Greater Kansas City only 231. That this low
fertility is typical of the national scene is indicated by the National Jewish Population Study data
for 1970-1971 which reveal a child-woman ratio for
Jews of only 352, some 27 percent below the 1970
national average of 485 for the white 1970 urban
population.

Also using data from the National Jewish Population Study, Della Pergola has undertaken what
constitutes one of the most comprehensive assessments yet completed of fertility patterns among the
Jewish population of the United States as a
whole.[29] The large sample size, consisting of 5311
ever married females age 15 and over, allows much
more in-depth study, despite some concerns about
the coverage of the National Jewish Population
Study, than any other national sample. The
exploitation of the retrospective fertility history
information collected in the survey enhances the
richness of the analysis undertaken. The findings
of the analysis, basically confirm the insights
gained in other studies.

Throughout the period covered by the analysis,
Jewish fertility was consistently lower than among
total whites, varying from the ratio of 69 Jewish
births per 100 white births in about 1930 to a high
of 87 in 1945, and declining thereafter to only 68
in 1965 when the total Jewish fertility rate was
again below replacement level. As Della Pergola
notes, "Jewish fertility levels basically followed
over time the general fluctuations of the total
whites, but patterns of response to period societal
change were relatively earlier, sharper, and faster
as appropriate to a nearly perfectly contracepting
population. The most recent cohorts were unmis-
takably directed towards increasingly lower fertility."[30] This is true even though young ever
married women indicate an expectation to slightly
surpass replacement levels; these expectations seem
unrealistically high, given other patterns
observed.

Della Pergola also noted considerable variation in fertility levels of different marriage and
birth cohorts, but these generally occurred within
the boundaries of lower fertility. But Della
Pergola also suggests that there may be a 'minimum'
level below which families are unwilling to lower
their fertility, providing societal circumstances
are not too exacting. What seems to vary more

Table 3:   JEWISH CHILD-WOMAN RATIO: NUMBER OF
            CHILDREN UNDER AGE FIVE TO NUMBER OF
            WOMEN AGED 20-44 IN SELECTED COMMUNITIES

Community	Year	Fertility Ratio
New Orleans, La.	1953	496
Lynn, Mass.	1955	528
Canton, Ohio	1955	469
Des Moines, Iowa	1956	596
Worcester, Mass.	1957	525
New Orleans, La.	1958	510
Los Angeles, Calif.	1959	560
South Bend, Ind.	1961	494
Rochester, N. Y.	1961	489
Providence, R. I.	1963	450
Camden, N. J.	1964	480
Springfield, Mass.	1966	418
Columbus, Ohio	1969	444
Dallas, Texas	1972	304
Minneapolis, Minn.	1972	436
Houston, Texas	1975	342
Greater Kansas City	1976	231
National Jewish Population Study	1971	352
U.S. white urban population	1960	635
U.S. white urban population	1970	485
U.S. white metropolitan population	1975	360

Sources: Sidney Goldstein, "American Jewry,
      1970:   A Demographic Profile," The American
      Jewish Year Book, 1971, vol. 72 (Philadel-
      phia: The Jewish Publication Society of
      America, 1971); Betty J. Maynard, The Dallas
      Jewish Community Study (Dallas: Jewish
      Welfare Federation, 1974).   Judith B. Erickson
      and Mitchel J. Lazarus, The Jewish Community
      of Greater Minneapolis (Minneapolis: Federa-
      tion for Jewish Service, 1973; Sam Shulman,
      David Gottlieb, and Sheila Sheinberg, A
      Sociological and Demographic Survey of the
      Jewish Community of Houston, Texas(Houston:
      Jewish Community Council of Metropolitan
      Houston, Inc., 1976); The Jewish Population
      Study of the Greater Kansas City Area (Kansas
      City: Jewish Federation, 1977).

among cohorts than the absolute differences in
average number of children born, which generally

varies within a range of one child, is the tempo of
childbearing which is affected by age of woman at
marriage, duration of marriage, and societal
circumstances.

The detailed analysis leads Della Pergola to
conclude that "long-term American cycles of socio-
demographic change stimulated a multi-faceted
Jewish demographic response. This included, during
the more adverse years, non-marriage, later marriage, more frequent childlessness, fewer children
per mother, longer birth intervals, and later
termination of childbearing. After World War II,
trends were quite similarly reversed for the different components of Jewish family formation,
although relatively late marriage and low fertility
generally characterize the entire period."[31]

A final set of data, whose major attrac-
tiveness is its currency and national coverage, but
which includes only a small number of Jews, is the
National Survey of Family Growth sponsored by the
federal government.[32] The results of the first
survey, conducted in 1973-1974, showed that for the
white population of the United States the number of
children ever born was 2180 but for Jews only 1914
(Table 4). If the comparison is in terms of total
children expected, the Jewish average of 2356 per
thousand was 15 percent below the total white
average of 2783. Perhaps more significant, Jewish
women aged 20-24 expected to have 1569 children per
thousand women, a number 32 percent below the 2313
expected by all white women, and well below replacement level. Only among women aged 35 and
older was the average number of children expected
above replacement level; yet even these averages
were only 0.4 to 0.6 children above replacement
level, and well below the averages of the total
population.

Lower Jewish fertility is also reflected by
the fact that only 15 percent of all Jewish women
aged 15-29 were pregnant, seeking to become pregnant, or in a postpartum status at the time of the
survey, compared to 23 and 26 percent, respectively, of the white Protestant and Catholic married women in the same age range.[33] These data
indicate, too, the high levels of fertility control
characterizing Jews: 91 percent of all currently
married Jewish women 15-44 years of age were practicing contraception or were sterilized at the time
of the 1973 survey. This level contrasted to 79

Table 4: TOTAL NUMBER OF CHILDREN EVER BORN AND TOTAL BIRTHS EXPECTED PER 1000 CURRENTLY MARRIED WOMEN AGED 15-44, BY AGE AND RELIGION IN THE UNITED STATES, 1973

Religion	15-19	20-24	25-29	30-34	35-39	40-44	All Ages
			Children Ever Born				
Protestant	482	928	1670	2548	2993	3169	2158
Catholic	471	888	1773	2727	3273	3546	2359
Jewish	*	*	994	2058	2510	2733	1914
Other, none	*	1035	1025	2103	2471	2510	1467
All women	479	921	1651	2575	3054	3251	2180
			Births Expected				
Protestant	2246	2260	2402	2798	3088	3198	2710
Catholic	2790	2514	2650	3138	3476	3632	3057
Jewish	*	1569	2094	2058	2583	2771	2356
Other, none	2020	2117	2002	2553	2680	2586	2557
All Women	2376	2313	2445	2879	3183	3297	2783

*Figure does not meet standards of reliability.

Source: Gordon Scott Bonham, "Expected Size of Completed Family Among Currently Married Women 15-44 Years of Age: United States, 1973," Advancedata (from Vital and Health Statistics of the National Center for Health Statistics), vol. 10 (August, 1977).

percent of the white Protestant women and 73 percent of the white Catholic women.

The low levels of Jewish fertility observed in
these various studies strongly suggest that Jews
continue to have highly favorable attitudes toward
family planning and to be highly successful in the
use of contraceptives. In a period of generally
declining fertility, the fertility of the Jews may
be lower still. Goldscheider and Uhlenberg have
argued that the "characteristics" approach, which
attempts to explain the lower Jewish fertility by
the social and economic characteristics that distinguish Jews from non-Jews, falls short of supply-
ing a full explanation for the differential.[34] He
maintains that attention must also be given to the
minority position of Jews and to the crosscultur-
ally shared Jewish values that have helped to
account for lower Jewish fertility in the past and
in widely different societies. Perceptions of
discrimination, feelings of insecurity, and values
particularly conducive to fewer children may continue to contribute to lower Jewish fertility.

Thus, although Jewish fertility may foreshadow
the patterns of other groups as we move into the
era of the perfect contraceptive population, Jews
may still continue to be characterized by lower
levels of fertility because of other social-psycho-
logical factors associated with the still unique
position of Jews in the larger society. That the
already low Jewish fertility levels have evidently
declined even further as part of the national pattern suggests that the motives for small families
reflect a complex combination of factors involving
both conditions unique to the Jews and those shared
with the larger population. Even though Jewish
community leaders have spoken out against zero population growth and in favor of higher Jewish fertility in order to compensate for losses through
intermarriage and in order to avoid declines in
aggregate numbers, American Jews have shown little
evidence of reversing their exceptionally low
fertility levels.

At the same time, it seems apparent that, as
among the general population, the number of Jewish
singles has increased in recent years. In part
this reflects higher levels of enrollment in college and graduate school, later age at marriage,
changes in life style that involve more frequent
sharing of households while unmarried, and higher
divorce rates. This comparatively new development
has implications both for fertility levels and for
the vitality of the Jewish family which has been a

mainstay of the community's strength and survival. To date, the community and its institutions continue to experiment with various methods to cope with the means by which to insure maintenance of Jewish identification on the part of this segment of the population.[35]

It will be interesting to observe, if general fertility levels should rise in the next decade as some experts predict,[36] whether Jews participate in the upward swing. Past patterns suggest that, if they do, it will not be to the same extent as the general population. As Cohen has recently suggested, the combination of factors helping to explain the low Jewish birthrate (including higher divorce and separation rates; later age at marriage and possible rises in levels of celibacy; increased extrafamilial activity; higher educational levels; greater secularism; and higher rates of intermarriage) should serve to reenforce the low fertility levels.[37]

For the immediate future, and most likely for the longer run as well, available evidence points to birth levels among Jews which are inadequate to insure growth, especially when viewed in conjunction with possible losses through intermarriage and assimilation. There seems little prospect that the total Jewish population of the United States is likely to rise above six million in the foreseeable future. The chances are much more likely that it will stabilize or move toward five million, and possibly go even lower. Moreover, the losses in population resulting from zero or negative growth take on added significance because they will also produce changes in the age composition of the Jewish population, reducing the percentage of youths and increasing that of aged. Before turning to questions of composition, attention needs to be given to the other components of change: intermarriage, assimilation, and migration.

INTERMARRIAGE

In contrast to the recent concern about levels of Jewish fertility, interest in the levels and impact of intermarriage on Jewish identity and demographic survival has a much longer history. Particular importance was attached to intermarriage, now so much because it was seen as a threat to the demographic maintenance of American Jewry, but rather because it was viewed as an index of loss of Jewish identification and a threat to the social

and religious cohesiveness of the community. Yet,
if marital assimilation takes place at a high rate,
the Jewish group faces demographic losses both
through the assimilation of the Jewish partner in
the marriage and through the loss of children born
to such a marriage. Thus, it is not surprising,
particularly in the face of earlier evidence that
the Jewish group had been remarkedly successful,
compared to other groups, in maintaining religious
endogamy - that a variety of evidence suggesting an
increasing rate of intermarriage has set off alarm
bells in the Jewish community.

Regrettably, the quality of information on the
rates of intermarriage and on the impact of intermarriage on identity is still poor; we still lack a
clear picture of the overall situation. The
evidence that is available suggests that the level
of intermarriage and its impact varies considerably
depending on the size, location, age, and social
cohesiveness of the particular community. Compli-
cations are also introduced by the manner in which
intermarriage is measured. Studies relying exclusively on current religious identification of
marriage partners run the risk of undercounting
intermarriage, since those partners to a mixed
marriage who have changed their religion in conjunction with the marriage would not be identified
as having intermarried. This problem can be compounded by fairly loose definitions of who is
regarded as a Jew. At the other extreme, the rates
of intermarriage may be inflated if the criteria
for religious identification rely upon the ancestry
of individuals rather than relying on their
personal life histories.

Despite these measurement problems, the
evidence clearly points to an increased rate of
Jewish intermarriage. A number of communities
surveyed in the late 1950s and 1960s showed levels
of intermarriage between 5 and 10 percent, levels
which differed only minimally from those observed
in communities surveyed in the 1930s. The March
1957 sample survey conducted by the Bureau of the
Census found that only 3.8 percent of married persons reporting themselves as Jews were married to
non-Jews and that 7.2 percent of all marriages in
which at least one partner was Jewish were intermarriages.[38] Both these statistics are probably
somewhat low, since no information was collected on
the earlier religion of the marriage partners. Yet
the 1950s and 1960s also produced studies that
revealed intermarriage rates as high as 17 percent

in New York City, 37 percent in Marin County,
California, and 54 percent in Iowa.[39]
  Eric Rosenthal's analysis of intermarriage
among the Jewish population of Washington, D.C. in
1956[40] aroused serious anxieties concerning the
threat which intermarriage represented to the demographic survival of the Jewish population. The
anxiety grew out of his observation that the rate
of intermarriage increased from 1.4 percent among
foreign-born husbands, to 10.2 percent among second
generation men, up to 17.9 percent of husbands of
third or more generations. The possibility that
these generation differentials reflected a trend
toward rising levels of intermarriage were reinforced by data emanating from other community
studies, such as Providence and Springfield,[41] even
though the levels of intermarriage were lower than
those for Washington. The 1965 Boston survey also
suggested a sharp rise in the level of intermarriage among the very youngest segment of the population; in contrast to a 3 percent level of intermarriage among couples in which the age of the
husband was 51 and over, 20 percent of the couples
in which the husband was 30 years old or younger
were intermarried.[42] Interestingly, the 1975
Boston survey also found 3 percent of couples in
which the age of the husband was 50 and over to
have been intermarried but the rate had risen to 26
percent of those under 30 years of age.[43] The
sharpest increase occurred in the intermediary age
groups. In contrast to 7 percent of those with the
husband between ages 31 and 50 who were intermarried in 1965, 22 percent of those in the 30-49 age
range in 1975 were intermarried. The lesser rise
for the youngest age group may reflect the high
percentage in that age group who are still unmarried and that intermarriage occurs somewhat later.
  The National Jewish Population Study provided
the first nationwide set of comprehensive data on
Jewish intermarriage patterns.[44] Since it ascertained the religious identity of the marriage
partners at the time they met, it allowed fuller
assessment of intermarriage than did the census
data. The study found that 9.2 percent of all
Jewish persons married at the time of the survey
were intermarried. This level was not unusually
high; what was "shocking" about the findings was
the analysis of intermarriage in terms of marriage
cohorts. This analysis determined that the level
of intermarriage rose from 2 percent of those individuals who had married between 1900 and 1920, to 6
percent of those marrying between 1940 and 1960,

and increased precipitously thereafter to 17 percent of the marriage cohort of 1960-1965, and to
the unusually high level of 32 percent of those
marrying in the five years preceding the survey.
    In the absence of a full evaluation of the
National Jewish Population Study survey data and of
supporting evidence from independent sources at-
testing to the validity of this very high level of
intermarriage, its exactness must be questioned.
There seems little doubt, however, that the finding
does justify the conclusion, based on reports by
rabbis, newspapers, and other sources, that the
level of intermarriage has risen very substantially
in recent years. This is undoubtedly related to
the increasing proportion of the population that is
now third generation, that has moved away from
older areas of dense Jewish population to newly
developed, more integrated areas within both the
cities and suburbs; it may be related to the very
high proportion of Jewish youth enrolled in colleges and universities, to the entrance of Jews
into occupations and social groups which earlier
had been closed to them, to the generally greater
freedom and integration which Jews have enjoyed in
American society in recent years, and to the increasing secularization and weakening of tradition
among younger Jews. Whether these conditions will
lead to still further increases in intermarriage or
whether a plateau may have been reached around
which the experience of individual communities will
fluctuate has not been ascertained. To answer this
question, comparativee data of the type emanating
from the Boston study are needed.
    Whether the effects of intermarriage on demo-
graphic growth are serious may largely be determined by the extent of conversion to Judaism on the
part of the non-Jewish partner to the marriage, as
well as on the extent to which children born to the
marriage are raised as Jews. Obviously, counts
such as this for purposes of measuring the demographic outcome may not do justice to the effect of
intermarriage on Jewish identification per se and
on religiosity, which constitute other significant
dimensions of the question of intermarriage.
Considerable evidence does exist indicating that a
substantial part of the threat of high levels of
intermarriage to demographic survival is reduced by
the comparatively high rates of conversion to
Judaism as well as of children being raised as
Jews.
    When attention was given to these questions as
part of the 1963 Providence survey, for example, it

was found that of all the intermarried couples, 42 percent had experienced the conversion of one partner to Judaism thereby creating religious homogeneity within the family unit.[45] Even more significant, perhaps, the proportion of persons converting consistently increased with decreasing age, a finding consistent with that of many other studies. The 1975 Boston survey did not find as high a level of conversion; those data indicate only about 10 percent of all the intermarriages of males 30-49 years of age at the time of the survey resulted in a conversion of the non-Jewish partner.[46] The National Jewish Population Study found that in 27 percent of the intermarriages in which the husband was originally Jewish, the wife converted; however, among those couples in which it was the wife who was originally Jewish, only 2.5 percent of the husbands converted.[47] However, an interesting finding of the study is that a very substantial percentage of non-Jewish partners in intermarriages identify themselves as Jews even though they have not officially converted. This was true of 46 percent of the non-Jewish wives and 44 percent of the non-Jewish husbands.

The same questions can be raised from the point of view of the religion in which the children of intermarriages are reared. According to the 1963 Providence survey, 78 percent of the 280 children born to intermarried couples were being raised as Jews. This contrasted very sharply to the 70 percent of the children of mixed marriages being raised as non-Jews according to Rosenthal's Washington survey. The National Jewish Population Study found a high proportion of children of intermarriage being raised as Jews, 63 percent of the children of Jewish fathers, and 98 percent of Jewish mothers.

Overall, therefore, the evidence suggests that although the rate of intermarriage has increased sharply, a substantial proportion of these intermarriages result in the conversion of the non-Jewish spouse to Judaism and an even larger number result in the non-Jewish spouse identifying as Jewish. Moreover, the rate of conversion seems to be higher among the very groups having a higher intermarriage rate. Furthermore, a significant proportion of children from such marriages are evidently being raised as Jews. Finally, evidence from several studies indicates that the fertility patterns of intermarried couples come to closely reflect those who are not intermarried, whereas older groups had a much stronger tendency to have

significantly lower fertility.[48]   Taken together,
these changes suggest that the net effects of
intermarriage on the overall size of the Jewish
population may not be as serious as the rates of
intermarriage themselves suggest. The effect of
intermarriage on Jewish identification and religiosity may be a different matter, and these concerns can certainly have long-run implications for
the demographic variables.

Reflecting the continuing concern with the
impact of intermarriage on Jewish demography and
identity, the American Jewish Committee during
1976-77 sponsored an eight-city study focussing on
intermarriage and the Jewish future, directed by
Egon Mayer.[49]   Defining intermarriage broadly as a
marriage between any individual born Jewish and one
who was not, the study population encompassed 446
intermarried couples in Cleveland, Dallas, Long
Island, Los Angeles, New York City, Philadelphia,
San Francisco, and Westchester. Given the ad hoc
character of the selection of the respondent
couples (largely through reliance upon local informants) and a large lack of responses, the results
cannot be regarded as representative of all intermarried couples. Furthermore, the absence of any
control groups of Jewish homogamous marriages precludes direct comparisons with the characteristics
of those who have not intermarried as well as cal-
culation of the rates of intermarriage.

Typical of previous findings, two-thirds of
those who have intermarried consisted of a Jewish
man and a non-Jewish woman. Interestingly, the
ratio was lower in the younger age group, suggesting that higher rates of intermarriage may come
to characterize women as their educational and
occupational patterns more closely resemble those
of men. The effect of the women's liberation movement and the lack of Jewish husbands when many men
are intermarrying may also lead to a closer balance
in the ratio of male and female intermarriage
rates. If this does not happen, it could well lead
to a growing proportion of Jewish women who remain
unmarried due to the lack of available Jewish
spouses.

In this study, just over one-quarter of the
non-Jewish born respondents had converted to
Judaism, whereas only 3 percent of the Jews had
converted out. The finding that rates of
conversion were highest in the youngest age group
(one-third of those aged 20-29 compared to one-
fourth of those aged 30-49, and only one-fifth of
those aged 50-59) again lends support to earlier

evidence that higher rates of conversion prevail
among groups with the highest intermarriage
rates. About 80 percent of the Jewish spouses in
marriages in which the other spouse had converted
considered their children Jewish, compared to about
one-third of the Jewish spouses in mixed marriages.

Overall, the study concludes that intermarriage represents a threat to Jewish continuity, as
evidenced by the low conversion rate, the low level
of Jewish conduct and practice in mixed marriages,
the low proportion of children regarded as Jewish,
and the fact that most of the children are not
socialized as Jews. On this basis, and particularly since the sample is biased in favor of those
marriages known to the Jewish community, the author
concludes that intermarriage clearly results in
losses rather than in additions to the Jewish population. Strong stress is therefore placed on the
need for outreach programs designed to provide more
formal and informal opportunities to enhance the
Jewish content of the family life of the intermarried and especially to strengthen the likelihood
that children will identify as Jews. Most provoc-
ative is Mayer's suggestion that a new category of
"naturalized" Jew be established to allow those who
have not converted to identify more formally with
the Jewish people and thereby confer a since of
legitimacy to the non-converted spouse as a way of
strengthening the Jewish identity of the family.

Together, the results of the varied studies
reviewed here confirm that the problem of intermarriage warrants considerable concern in both the
policy and research areas. That it is receiving
such attention is evidenced by recent calls by such
community leaders as Rabbi Alexander Schindler of
the Reform movement to reverse the practice of
centuries and begin a drive to convert the "un-
churched" to Judaism.[50] He especially argues for
conversion of the non-Jewish partner in an impend-
ing marriage and to remove the "not-wanted signs"
that make non-Jewish spouses feel alienated. It
needs to be stressed, however, that from a demographic perspective, attention to intermarriage certainly should not exclude concern for the impact of
fertility and population redistribution on the size
of Jewish population and on the quality of Jewish
identification. Concurrently, the Jewish community
needs continuously to recognize some truths about
intermarriage expressed by Marshall Sklare some
years ago:

A more realistic confrontation is
necessary, and that requires a much larger

body of research than we now possess on
the current rate of intermarriage in the
country as a whole. It also requires much
more information about the Jews who intermarry and about the causes and consequences of their doing so. So, too, there
is a need for studies to evaluate the various methods in use to combat intermarriage, particularly those involving Jewish
education. And demographic research will
have to be done at regular intervals so
that a reliable trend-line can be
established.[51]

ASSIMILATION

Attempts to assess the demographic impact of
intermarriage on Jews are difficult, attempts to
evaluate the impact of assimilation are almost impossible. To some extent, the problem is illustrated by the experience of the National Jewish
Population Study. To qualify, a household for inclusion in the study at least one person within it
was required to be "Jewish." By intent, a broad
definition of Jewish was used.[52] The respondent
had to provide an affirmative reply, for himself or
for one or more household members, to at least one
of the following questions: Was person born
Jewish? Is person Jewish now? Was person's father
born Jewish? Was person's mother born Jewish?
Clearly, a more narrow or Halakhic definition would
exclude certain households, some of whose members
may, however, satisfy sociological (idealogical or
behavioral) definitions of Jewishness.
It was on the basis of a broad definition of a
Jewish household as one including one or more Jewish persons that the National Jewish Population
Study reached the estimate of 5,800,000 Jews in
1971. But as noted earlier, if non-Jewish persons
in such households, including non-Jewish spouses
and children not being raised as Jews are excluded,
the total number of Jewish residents in households
is reduced to 5,370,000, almost a 10 percent reduction.
The use of a "loose" definition has particular
implications for the study of intermarriage. In
his assessment of intermarriage, using the National
Jewish Population Study data, Massarik distinguishes between "typical intermarriage" in which
either the husband or the wife was Jewish at the
time the couple met and "marginal intermarriage" in

which one or both partners expressed no preference
concerning religious viewpoint at the time of
initial meeting, noted the existence of some Jewish
familial or ancestral roots, but affirmed either
only vague relatedness to Jewishness or none at
all.[53] Massarik's analysis does not indicate the
numerical division between these groups, but it
could well be that the high rates of intermarriage
he noted are partially a function of the inclusion
of "marginal intermarriages" in the total.

The problem encountered by the National Jewish
Population Study and comparable surveys clearly
document the difficulties in determining for survey
purposes who constitutes a Jew; the Halakhic definition is too simple for the sociologist and demographer, particularly for analyses of assimilation. Yet, the possibility is very limited of
identifying clearly those individuals who were born
Jews but who do not identify themselves or live as
Jews; even the study may not have succeeded in
identifying a representative sample of such persons
in its survey, despite the wide net that was thrown
out.

Some limited insights have come from studies
of college students who have "dropped out" from
Judaism. A study of 1961 Jewish seniors found that
about 13 percent had apostatized, while in 1969, 21
percent of the graduates reported no religious preference.[54] Comparison of freshmen in the 1965
survey with freshman covered in 1972 shows a rise
in the number who expressed no religious preference
from 13 to 18 percent. However, it is not at all
clear whether such individuals, if approached in a
general population survey would or would not report
themselves as Jewish, and therefore these data have
only very limited value. All that one can conclude
is that the same general conditions in society
which have led to a rise in intermarriage also
probably lead to a substantial number of dropouts
and provide little basis for believing that the
rate will decline in the foreseeable future.

Another study designed to assess assimilation
was undertaken in Los Angeles.[55] Based on 413
respondents selected from a canvas of 5000 households, the analysis concluded that intermarriage, a
reduced birth rate, and the decline of Jewish
neighborhoods were contributing to the assimilation
of nearly a half-million Jews in Los Angeles. That
was compounded by declining rates of affiliation
and involvement in Jewish religious and secular
organizations. The authors also find that "at the
same time, the picture that emerges from the survey

is a vibrant people whose closest personal associations are with other Jews in their family, friendship, and occupational groupings." They further
note that "one of the most significant changes in
Jewish life in the last generation is the way in
which Jews act out their Jewishness. Whereas only
18 percent see being Jewish as primarily religious,
61 percent perceive of Jews as an ethnic-cultural
group." This was seen as "a dramatic shift from
formal religious involvement to ethnic and cultural
commitment." As a result, the challenge for Jewish
leaders is seen as the need to adapt their institutions to the increasingly informal expressions that
are becoming more common.

Overall, one can raise the questions whether
assimilation is, in fact, an especially new phenomenon in Jewish history. We know that crusades, in-
quisitions, and pogroms all took a heavy toll of
the Jewish population, but these in themselves were
probably inadequate to account for the tremendous
loss in numbers that must have occurred if only
16.7 million Jews were alive just before the holocaust; many were also lost through assimilation and
intermarriage.[56] Yet then, as now, any attempt to
approximate the losses sustained through "dropouts"
would be sheer guesswork. It is likely to remain
so for many years to come.

MIGRATION AND POPULATION REDISTRIBUTION

Jewish history might easily be written in
terms of migration and resettlement, from the days
of Abraham's move to Canaan to the more recent
exodus from the Soviet Union. Yet, in the United
States, the large majority of immigrants arriving
between 1880 and 1924 tended to be quite stable
geographically. They settled in comunities, often
the ports of entry, where there was a need for
their labor in industries with a growing demand for
their products, as in the garment industry. Sub-
sequently, many immigrants went into business for
themselves and, while socially and economically
mobile, they and often their children remained in
the same city all their lives. This pattern now
seems to be undergoing a significant change.

Because Jews are increasingly third and fourth
generation and more highly educated than ever before, they now enjoy the widest possible range of
occupational choices ever open to them. But the
kinds of education which Jews are seeking and the
kinds of jobs for which their high education

qualifies them very often require geographic
dispersion, movement away from family and out of
centers of Jewish population concentration.   The
problem is exacerbated by the fact that many high
level jobs require repeated movement so that
inddividuals and families have no opportunity to
plant deep roots in any single Jewish community.

Regional Distribution

Estimates indicate that in 1900, 57 percent of
American Jewry lived in the Northeast, in contrast
to 28 percent of the total American population; and
virtually all of the Jews in the Northeast were in
New York, Pennsylvania, and New Jersey (Table 5).
New York alone accounted for about 40 percent of
the national total.   The North Central region
accounted for the next largest number of Jews--
about one-fourth--with most concentrated in
Illinois, Ohio, Indiana, Wisconsin, and Michigan.
By contrast, one-third of the total United States
population lived in this region in 1900.   Compared
to the general population, Jews were also
underrepresented in the South, where 14 percent
were located, largely in Maryland.   Florida at that
time had only 3000 Jews.   The proportion of the
Jews in the West in 1900 was identical to that of
the general population, just over 5 percent.
The continued mass immigration from Eastern
Europe during the first decades of the twentieth
century resulted in a fourfold increase in the
Jewish population of the country between 1900 and
1930; and it became even more concentrated in the
large cities of the Northeast, especially New
York.   By 1930, the Northeast region contained 68
percent of the American Jewish population and most
of it lived in New York.   The other regions of the
country all contained smaller proportions of the
Jewish population than they had in 1900, with the
sharpest change occurring in the South.   The Far
West continued to be the region with the smallest
percentage of Jews, although the proportion of the
total American population living in the western
states doubled between 1900 and 1930.   Jews had
clearly not yet joined the western movement on the
same scale as had the rest of the population.
By 1979, the pattern had changed considerably,
reflecting both the cutoff of large-scale immigration and increasing internal mobility.   Jews in
large measure seem to have followed the pattern of
redistribution characterizing the population as a
whole; in fact, they may even be doing so to an

exaggerated degree. For example, between 1930 and
1979, the percentages of Jews living in the
Northeast declined from 68 to 58 percent. These
were larger percentage decreases in absolute points
than those characterizing the general population
(see Table 5). The drop was even more substantial
for the North Central States where Jews decreased
from 20 percent of the national total in 1930 to
only 12 percent in 1979. In contrast, both the
South and the West contained growing proportions of
the total United States Jewish population, reflecting the strong participation of Jews in the shift
to the Sun Belt and to the western states. Between
1930 and 1979, the South's share more than doubled,
and that of the West tripled. The growth of the
Jewish population in the South is illustrated by
the experience of the Orlando metropolitan area.
In 1966, it included only 600 Jews; by 1977 the
Jewish population of Orlando had reached 11,000,
and it is projected to rise to over 20,000 by
1985.[57] Although the South and the West continued
to contain proportionally fewer Jews than members
of the general population, the differences in distribution had considerably narrowed.

      Thus, by 1979 the greater mobility of Jews had
resulted in patterns of distribution throughout the
country that resembled somewhat more closely those
of the general population. These similarities are
likely to become accentuated in the future as Jews
increasingly enter occupations whose nature requires mobility because of the limited opportunities available in particular areas, as family ties
become less important for the third generation Jew
than they have been for the first and second generation, and as more Jews no longer feel it necessary
to live in areas of high Jewish density. In an
ecological sense, therefore, the population will
become a more truly "American population," with all
that this implies regarding opportunities for
greater assimilation and less numerical visibility.

      At the same time, the Middle Atlantic
subregion, and the New York area in particular,
remains a very large and obviously dynamic center
of American Jewry. Over half of the American
Jewish population was still concentrated in the
Middle Atlantic States in 1979, and two out of
these three million persons lived in Greater New
York. Yet even here changes are occurring. The
estimates of Jewish population prepared by the
American Jewish Year Book show a decline in the

Table 5: DISTRIBUTION OF TOTAL UNITED STATES AND JEWISH POPULATION, BY REGIONS, IN 1900, 1930, 1968, and 1979 (BY PERCENTAGES)

Region	1900 Jewish[a]	1900 United States	1930[c] Jewish	1930[c] United States	1968[d] Jewish	1968[d] United States	1979[e] Jewish	1979[e] United States
Northeast	56.6	27.7	68.3	27.9	64.0	24.2	57.9	22.5
New England	7.4	7.5	8.4	6.6	6.8	5.7	6.6	5.6
Middle Atlantic	49.2	20.3	59.9	21.3	57.1	18.5	51.3	16.9
North Central	23.7	34.6	19.6	31.4	12.5	27.8	11.9	26.7
East North Central	18.3	21.0	15.7	20.5	10.2	19.8	9.6	18.9
West North Central	5.4	13.6	3.9	10.9	2.3	8.0	2.3	7.8
South	14.2	32.2	7.6	30.7	10.3	31.2	15.8	32.4
South Atlantic	8.0	13.7	4.3	12.8	8.1	15.0	13.5	15.9
East South Central	3.3	9.9	1.4	8.0	0.7	6.6	0.7	6.4
West South Central	2.9	8.6	1.9	9.9	1.5	9.6	1.7	10.1
West	5.5	5.4	4.6	10.0	13.2	16.8	14.3	18.4
Mountain	2.3	2.2	1.0	3.0	0.9	4.0	1.8	4.7
Pacific	3.2	3.2	3.6	7.0	12.2	12.8	12.5	13.7
Total United States Percent	100.0	100.0	100.0	100.0	100.0	100.0	100.0	100.0
Number (in 1000s)	1058	75,994	4228	123,203	5,869	199,861	5861	218,059

[a]"Jewish Statistics", American Jewish Year Book, vol. 1 (1900), pp. 623-624.
[b]U.S. Bureau of the Census, 1960 Census of Population, vol. 1, Characteristics of the Population (Washington, D.C.: Government Printing Office, 1961), pp. 1-16.
[c]H. S. Linfield, "Statistics of Jews," American Jewish Year Book, vol. 33 (1931), p. 276.
[d]Alvin Chenkin, "Jewish Population in the United States," American Jewish Year Book, vol. 70 (1969), p. 266.
[e]Alvin Chenkin and Maynard Miran, "Jewish Population in the United States, 1979," American Jewish Year Book, vol. 80 (1980), p. 163.

Jewish population of Greater New York from 2.38 million in 1972 to just under two million in 1979.[58] In part, this may reflect an artifact of the system of estimating the population; but in part it may also reflect the impact of changing rates of natural increase and migration from the New York area. The American Jewish Year Book statistics show a decline in the Jewish population of New York City from 1.84 million in 1972 to 1.23 million in 1979, and even this is considered an overestimate with one million probably being a more realistic statistic. This decline reflects both the change in enumeration procedures, partly related to the estimates derived from the National Jewish Population Study, and the impact of changing distribution patterns. There seems little doubt, however, that the concentration of Jews in the Northeast corridor focussing on New York is likely to undergo substantial change in future years as increasing numbers of Jews leave this section of the country.

This process of dispersal is documented by an analysis of the changing geographic distribution of American Jews between 1952 and 1971, based on data from the American Jewish Year Book.[59] The heavy residential concentration of the Jewish population is demonstrated by the fact that only 504 of the 3093 populated counties of continental United States contain at least 100 Jews, and most of these are metropolitan counties and most are in the Northeast. More interesting, however, is that the highest growth in Jewish population between 1952 and 1971 occurred in counties outside those of traditional residence. In all, 77 counties were added to the list of counties containing 100 or more Jews; 37 of these are in what the authors refer to as "new areas" and 10 more are in California and Florida. In contrast, areas of high concentration in 1952 displayed moderate or little growth. Concurrently, therefore, the changes point to higher rates of dispersal and continued growth associated with urbanization and metropolitanization. Overall, while still remaining highly concentrated compared to other religious groups, the evidence on changing residence patterns leads the authors to conclude that Jews locate in counties with high degrees of denominational pluralism regardless of the size of the Jewish community, and that this suggests that Jews "feel 'accepted' in America and are less concerned about venturing out into more traditionally conservative culturally homogeneous enclaves."[60]

Suburbanization

The redistibution of population is occurring
concurrently in a number of ways, including regional changes as well as shifts within and between
metropolitan and nonmetropolitan areas. Throughout
its history in the United States, the Jewish population has been overwhelmingly concentrated in urban
places. At the time of the 1957 census survey,
about nine out of evey ten Jews lived in urbanized
areas of 250,000 or more persons.[61]
     Within the urban and metropolitan areas, Jews
tended to live in a limited number of neighborhoods, but this pattern is also undergoing
change. For example, between 1923 and 1970 radical
shifts in distribution occurred in New York City
alone.[62] Although very approximate estimates,
these data illustrate the pattern of development
that has probably characterized other areas of
Jewish concentration. In 1923, 39 percent of the
1.9 million Jews living in New York City resided in
Brooklyn, and 37 percent lived in Manhattan; less
than 3 percent lived in Queens. By 1970,
Manhattan's share of the New York City Jewish
population had declined to only 14 percent, that of
Queens had risen to 31 percent, while Brooklyn
increased its dominance to 42 percent. Concurrently, the proportion of the total living in the
Bronx declined from 20 to 12 percent. Even more
significant, the percentage of Jews in the Greater
New York area living in the city proper, in contrast to the suburban counties, declined from 82
percent of the total in 1957 to 64 percent by
1970. By 1979, the American Jewish Year Book
estimated only 61 percent of Greater New York's
Jewish population to be living in the city proper,
and the real figure may be 50 percent or less.[63]
     Similar patterns emerge from the limited data
available for such metropolises as Chicago and
Detroit; and the same pattern characterizes moderate sized communities. In 1970, for example, only
17 percent of the Jews of Greater Providence, Rhode
Island, were living in the old urban areas of the
central city, in contrast to 45 percent in 1951;
the proportion living in the suburbs had grown from
11 to 36 percent.[64] The comparative data from the
Boston 1965 and 1975 surveys show similar patterns.[65] Both the city and the older suburbs
experienced population declines while the newer
outer suburbs gained, resulting in an increased
dispersal of the population. Suburbanization is
also clearly evidenced in Minneapolis. In the 1957

survey, 66 percent of the population was found to
be living in the city and 34 percent in the
suburbs.[66] By the 1971 survey, the pattern had
been more than reversed, with 23 percent in the
city and 77 percent in the suburbs.

Overall, therefore, the developing pattern
seems to be one of ever greater dispersion and a
more general integration. As a result, Jewish
institutions may become located at quite widely
separated points within a metropolitan area, and
many communities find it increasingly difficult to
decide upon a central location for those institutions serving the community as a whole. In the
past, residential clustering has been an important
variable in helping to perpetuate Jewish values and
the institutions important to the functioning of
the community. In metropolitan areas with large
Jewish populations, such clustering undoubtedly
will continue both within the central cities and in
some of the suburbs. But greater dispersal and
greater integration seem likely to become more
common in the future, assuming greater importance
in explaining changes in the extent and character
of ties to Judaism and making it increasingly difficult from both a financial and an organizational
perspective to provide services to the total population. The impact of both suburbanization and the
more general dispersal of the population throughout
the United States on the assimilation process needs
to be fully recognized. In particular, much more
research is necessary to ascertain how communal
orientation varies among Jews living in cities and
suburbs of differing Jewish density and size, and
what significance the various activities available
to Jews and the patterns of interaction and experience of Jews with non-Jews have for the larger
question of Jewish identification and survival.

Small-Town Jewry

Because the vast majority of America's Jews
live in large metropolitan areas, until recently
little attention has been given to the situation of
Jews in those small towns, where the Jewish
community itself typically numbers no more than a
few thousand families and often less. Since World
War II many of these small communities have had
great difficulty retaining their population, Jewish
and non-Jewish. Like their neighbors, Jews have
left to seek better educational, occupational, and
social opportunities in larger cities. Many of
those who remained small town residents tended to

minimize their Jewishness and often assimilated or
intermarried. On the whole, small town life was
generally viewed as isolating the Jew both from his
co-religionist and from the non-Jewish community in
which he was often regarded as a "stranger."[67]
    Yet, beginning with the 1970s and consonant
with what seems to be an emerging trend among the
American population as a whole of movement from
metropolitan areas to small towns and rural places,
including locations which had earlier lost population, a number of small Jewish communities are once
again gaining population. Some Jews are now
seeking the tranquility and slower pace of small-
town life and, at the same time, seem to be developing a more active identification with Judaism in
their new surroundings. Jewish life in small towns
is beginning to be viewed as having positive as
well as negative effects on its members. Despite
the limited communal services that are available in
such places, the strong desire of many small-town
Jews to maintain their identification may result in
"more Judaism per square Jew in the small town than
in the big city."[68]
    Although levels of identification are not
easily measured, the demographic effects of both
the old and the new trend of movement first away
from and, more recently, to small Jewish communities is evident in communities such as Charleston,
West Virginia.[69] In 1959, the city included 1626
Jews; by 1975 the Jewish population had declined to
1118, of which only 703 persons had been in
Charleston 16 years earlier. The decline in popu
lation resulted from both an excess of deaths over
births and more out-migrants than in-migrants. It
was further compounded by a high rate of intermarriage. By 1977, despite continuing high intermarriage rates, the community's migration losses had
been reversed and it was gaining population.
    The 1977 Annual Report on Charleston's Jewish
Population, the nineteenth in this unique series,
was one of the most optimistic to appear. As its
introduction states:

        In our report of a year ago we stated that
        there were indications, however slight,
        'that we are on our way upward (demograph-
        ically) instead of downward, ...' We
        are pleased to report that this year's
        study reveals that Charleston's Jewish
        population is definitely on its way up-
        ward. In this past year, more newcomers
        (90), moved to our community than in any

year since 1959 when we began these
studies. Our losses through moving, (49),
were less than in any of the past 18
years. The good news, then, is that fewer
are leaving and more are coming.[70]

The importance of such a reversal is further evidenced in the fact that the gain through migration
was more than enough to compensate for losses
through a surplus of deaths over births and through
intermarriages, accounting for all of the increase
experienced in the community's total size from 1121
to 1151 during 1976-77.
    The reports on Charleston issued since 1977
have been less optimistic. The 1978 report shows a
gain of only two persons, and the 1979 analysis
reported a resumption of the decline in total population size, from 1158 to 1086.[71] This reversal
reflected in part the continuing excess of deaths
over births; it also resulted from the removal from
the 1979 population count of those individuals who
had been counted for a number of years even though
they had left the community. Nonetheless, despite
this record cleansing operation, in both 1978 and
1979 Charleston gained Jews through migration.
Such a migration of Jews to Charleston is probably
being experienced by a number of small communities
and could be crucial in either maintaining or creating the critical mass requisite to initiation and
maintenance of the institutional facilities essential for continued Jewish identification. Migration may thus constitute the "blood transfusion"
which greatly enhances the chances of small community survival.

Internal Migration

    Among the demographic concerns which have
received the least attention and research are the
extent and character of Jewish migration within the
United States. For such an analysis, national data
are essential, but, except for the recent information available from the National Jewish Population
Study, no such data exist. Our insights on Jewish
migration patterns have, therefore, been largely
restricted to what can be gleaned from local Jewish
community surveys.
    Judged both by the percentage of population
who have been born outside the community of residence and by the length of time that individuals
have resided in the area in which they were

enumerated in community surveys, high levels of
population mobility have come to characterize
American Jews. The 1963 Detroit study found that
only one-third of the total Jewish population of
Detroit were born in the city; 28 percent were
foreign-born; and 36 percent had moved to Detroit
from other places in the United States, half from
other locations in Michigan.[72] A similar picture
emerged for Camden, New Jersey, where one-third of
the residents had been born in the Camden area, and
as many as 60 percent had moved from other places
in the United States, probably reflecting the
younger age of the Camden population.[73]

The 1975 Boston survey found that only 30
percent of the respondents living in Boston in 1975
had also been living in the city in 1965.[74] Although the 1965 survey provided no basis for anticipating the decline of Newton and Brookline, both
those older suburbs experienced heavy out-
migrations and a population decline in the number
of Jews. Of those Jews who lived in the city of
Boston in 1965 and still resided in the Boston area
in 1975, more than half remained in the city itself. However, this stable core was supplemented
by a considerable influx from outside the Boston
area and there was some shifting in residence within the area by those living in it in both 1965 and
1975.

In Dallas, the 1972 survey found that only 35
percent of the population was born in Dallas, and a
high percentage of these were children.[75] Over
half the Jewish population had moved to Dallas from
other parts of the United States, and an additional
14 percent were foreign born. Consistent with the
patterns of regional redistribution noted earlier,
23 percent of the migrants to Dallas who had been
born in the United States had originated in the
Northeast, and 27 percent in the North Central
States. Similarly, the 1976 Greater Kansas City
survey found that "not only are the majority of the
household heads not born in Kansas City but there
is little tendency for this proportion to increase
among the younger people."[76]

Given these illustrative data, it was not surprising that the National Jewish Population Study
found that only 62 percent of the Jewish population
aged 20 and over in 1970 were still living in the
city in which they had resided in 1965.[77] One out
of every five adult Jews had changed the city or
town of his residence while remaining in the same
county or metropolitan area; and an additional 3
percent had changed areas within the same state;

but 10 percent of the total adult population had
actually moved to a different state within the
five-year interval. These high mobility levels are
even more dramatic for Jews in the peak migration
ages of 25-39 years. As the data in Table 6 show
just under half of persons aged 25-29 and 35-39
resided in the same city in 1970 as 1965, and only
four out of every ten persons between the ages of
30-34 did so. Moreover, for those 25-29 years old,
interstate migration accounted for the single
largest group of mobile persons, almost one in four
in this age group. Even for those aged 30-34,
almost one in five moved between states. The
higher percentage in this age group moving within
the same county or metropolitan area is related to
their life cycle stage of family formation and
expansion.

Residential stability rises quite dramatically
above age 40 and peaks at the ages 55 -64, among
whom three-fourths reported themselves as living in
the same city in 1970 as they had in 1965; a large
proportion who moved did so only within the same
general area. For persons aged 65 and over the
stability rate remains comparatively high, although
it declines somewhat as a result of retirement, the
breakup of families through the death of one of the
spouses, or the departure of children from home.
Yet the fact that 30 percent or more of the persons
65 and over had made some kind of residential move
within a five-year period indicates that geographic
mobility must be incorporated into community planning processes. The need to do so is especially
crucial for the younger age groups among whom both
much more movement occurs and more of it involves
longer distances requiring clear breaks with former
communities and integration into new ones.

The continuation of a large degree of movement
is apparent from preliminary tabulations of the
National Jewish Population Study data based on
questions about plans to move.[78] Of the total population, 16 percent indicated plans to move within
at least five years. Again, sharp age differentials characterize this aspect of mobility: 61
percent of those 25-29 years of age indicated they
planned to move, and 11 percent expected to do so
immediately; 47 percent among those aged 20-24
years also planned to move. These mobility intentions are related to the family formation and
career stages of persons in these age groups. The
greater stability of older ages is evidenced by the
sharp decline in the percentage planning to move
among those aged 30 to 34--29 percent--and a

Table 6: MOBILITY: CURRENT RESIDENCE BY PLACE OF RESIDENCE IN 1965, BY AGE (TOTAL FOR EACH AGE GROUP = 100 PERCENT)

Age Group	Same City As 1965	Different City, Same General Area In 1965*	Different Area, Same State As 1965	Different State From 1965	In Foreign Country In 1965
20-24	60.2	28.3	1.3	8.0	1.7
25-29	48.0	21.3	2.6	22.8	4.2
30-34	41.6	30.8	2.9	18.8	4.5
35-39	48.6	28.7	11.7	7.1	3.5
40-44	62.2	22.1	1.6	12.0	1.5
45-49	66.8	16.6	1.3	11.9	1.0
50-54	67.2	17.7	3.0	6.5	5.1
55-59	75.3	13.6	2.0	3.4	5.4
60-64	76.1	12.4	1.7	4.8	1.5
65-69	70.1	14.8	0.7	10.9	2.6
70-74	70.2	17.5	0.7	8.2	2.3
75-79	69.9	17.6	3.7	4.0	2.7
80 and over	62.7	24.6	1.5	5.2	2.6
Total**	61.6	20.0	3.1	8.9	2.5

Note: Horizontal details may not add to 100 because of "no answer."
*Same county or same standard metropolitan statistical area.
**Includes 6 percent of the individuals under 19 for whom no detailed data are shown above.

Source: National Jewish Population Study, Mobility. (New York: Council of Jewish Federations and Welfare Funds, 1974).

further decline to only 19 percent of those 35-39, following which the percentage varies irregularly within a narrow range of 15 and 19 percent through age 70, following which even greater stability seems to set in.

Further evidence of changing Jewish mobility patterns is available through information collected on the residence of the children of family units surveyed, permitting comparison of place of residence of children in relation to that of their parents. Lenski has noted that one of the best indicators of the decreasing importance attached to family and kin groups of modern Americans is their willingness to leave their native community and migrate elsewhere.[79] Since most migration is motivated by economic or vocational factors, he suggests migration serves as an indicator of the strength of economic motives compared to kinship ties. In modern society the removal of economic rewards out of the hands of kinship and extended family groups lessens the dominance of Jewish families over the economic placement of its young. The change in kinship relations coupled with more fluid labor markets thus contributes to higher mobility rates.

If this interpretation is correct, data available for both Providence and for northern New Jersey suggest that kinship ties among Jews have been weakening. In the 1963 Providence survey only one-third of sons aged 40 years and over were living outside Rhode Island compared to just over half of the sons between ages 20-39.[80] Moreover, a higher proportion of the younger group were living further away. Accentuation of this trend is suggested by the fact that almost two-thirds of sons under age 20 living away from their parental home resided outside the state. Although fewer daughters lived away from their parental community, the basic age pattern was the same as for males. In northern New Jersey, about one-fourth of both sons and daughters living outside of their parental home remained in the same general area, and an additional quarter were living in other parts of New Jersey.[81] But about 25 percent were living in parts of the United States outside of New Jersey, New York, and Pennsylvania, pointing to a fairly substantial dispersal of family members.

Together, these data support the assumption that the American Jewish community is becoming increasingly mobile and that such mobility must be taken into account in any evaluation of Jewish life in the United States. Such mobility affects not

only the size of a particular community but also
the characteristics of its residents if the migration process is selective of age, education, occupation, and income. At the same time, migration
may have an important effect on the migrants, as
well as on community institutions. To the extent
that community ties within the Jewish population
are expressed through membership in synagogues and
temples, enrollment of children in educational programs, and participation in local organizations and
philanthropic activities, the high degree of population movement may disrupt patterns of participation or weaken the loyalities they generate.
More seriously, they may result in the failure of
families and individuals to identify with organized
life in the local community. Sociological research
has suggested, for example, that recent migrants to
a community are much less active in its formal
structure than are long-time residents.[82] Although
their participation eventually increases, the
adjustment has been shown to take five years, and
migrants may never reach the same level of participation as persons who grew up in the community. If
a significant proportion of migrants know in advance that their residence in a community is not
likely to be permanent, the stimulus for active
participation and affiliation may be even weaker.

     Mobility is not a new facet of Jewish life,
and at a number of points in Jewish history it may
have served to strengthen the Jewish community and
indeed to insure its very survival. Such mobility
may still serve a positive function in selected
situations. Small Jewish communities may benefit
considerably from the influx of other Jews who are
attracted by nearby universities or new economic
opportunities.

     More often, migration may have a deleterious
effect on the community and the migrant. Especially when there is repeated movement, the individual's ties to Judaism and the Jewish community
may be weakened; this, in turn, may affect the
strength of the formal community structure as an
increasing proportion of individuals fail to develop strong loyalties to local institutions. For
all too long local Jewish communities have assumed
that most Jews remain residentially stable for a
lifetime and that they are therefore willing and
obligated to support local organizations. This may
no longer be true for many Jews. An increasing
number may be reluctant to affiliate with the local
community, not so much because they do not identify
with Judaism but because they anticipate that they

will not remain in the local area long enough to
justify the financial and other investments
required. The situation is undoubtedly complicated
further by the dispersed residential patterns which
Jews adopt and by their high degree of social integration into religiously heterogeneous groups. All
of this suggests the need for greater concern with
the role of migration in the future of American
Judaism. Indeed, the rising rates of intermarriage
may largely be only a by-product, along with other
undesirable consequences, of increased mobility and
weaker ties both to the family and to the community. Given high mobility rates, there is a press-
ing need to view the Jewish community in national
terms, in addition to a local perspective, so that
the official affiliation of individual Jews to
Jewish institutions can be easily transferred from
one community to another, thereby facilitating
maintenance of Jewish identity.

SOCIO-DEMOGRAPHIC COMPOSITION OF THE POPULATION

While size and density are crucial variables
in the strength and vitality of any segment of the
population, the particular composition of the
population with respect to a wide range of demographic, social, and economic variables also significantly affects the group's current vitality and
future survival. To the extent, for example, that
one's generation in the United States affects the
strength of ties to traditional Judaism, the changing proportion of native-born and foreign-born
individuals in the Jewish community takes on great
relevance. Rising levels of education and changing
patterns of occupational careers also have direct
effects on the levels of population movement, the
degree of integration into the social and residential structures of the larger community, and the
likelihood of intermarriage. Age structure is a
crucial variable, because the sociodemographic
structure of the population as well as the processes of birth, death, and migration are closely
affected by it. In the growing attention, both in
research and planning, that has been given to the
Jewish population, the size of the total population
and the dynamics of change have received priority. Too little attention has been given to composition and the impact that changing composition may
have. The discussion which follows attempts to
review the major composition variables briefly,
with a view to describing the present

sociodemographic characteristics of the American
Jewish population, likely changes in the future,
and the implications that such changes may have.

Generation Status

Of all the demographic characteristics of the
Jewish population, perhaps the one with the
greatest relevance for its future is the changing
status of the Jews, that is, how many are foreign
born, how many are children of foreign-born
parents, and how many are third-or older-generation
Americans. In the past, a major factor in the
continued vitality of the American Jewish community
has been the massive immigration of Jews from the
ghettos of Eastern Europe. Now, for the first time
in the community's history, third generation Jews
face the American scene without massive outside
reinforcement. At the same time, Jews enjoy much
greater freedom than ever before, so that in
several respects the Jewish community in the United
States is increasingly an American Jewish community. Although this emergent pattern has been
somewhat modified by the influx of Jews from both
the Soviet Union and Israel, the full extent to
which the upsurge in this immigration affects the
demographic composition and particularly the
sociological character of American Jewry, especially of the populations in those communities
where they are settling, remains to be documented.
Every community study which has collected data
on generation status documents the diminishing
proportion of foreign born and the rise in third
generation Jews. These studies show the percentage
of American-born Jews as well above 70 percent and
becoming increasingly higher.[83] In Boston, for
example, between the 1965 and 1975 surveys, the
percentage of foreign born declined from 22 to 12
percent of the total.[84] By contrast, those with
American-born parents rose from 20 to 49 percent.
Evidence of change is even sharper, judged by the
generation composition of different age groups.
Over 80 percent of those under age 40 in Boston
were born of American-born parents, but this was
true of only 2 percent of those aged 65 and over.
The same general pattern emerges from the
National Jewish Population Study which found 23
percent of the heads of household in the Jewish
population to be foreign born, and one out of every
five was already third generation.[85] The distribution would favor American-born individuals much

more strongly if the data referred to the population as a whole.

Assessment of the demographic, social,
economic, and religious characteristics of three
generations in the Jewish community suggests that
the community's future depends to a great degree on
how its members, now increasingly third generation,
react to the freedom to work for integration into
the American social structure. Whether they are
reversing or accelerating certain trends toward
assimilation, initiated by their second generation
parents or by the small number of older third-
generation Jews, needs careful monitoring.

Research has suggested that the geographic
dispersal and deconcentration of the Jewish
population marked for many not only a physical
break from the foreign born but symbolized the more
dramatic disassociation of American-born Jews from
the ethnic ties and experiences that had served as
unifying forces for the earlier generation.[86] The
degree of identification with Judaism of the third
generation Jews who participate in this dispersal
has become a key issue. The residential changes
are taking place concurrently with sharp increases
in the amount of secular education and with an
opening up to Jews of career opportunities in the
professions and at high executive levels of business. All of these factors increase the amount of
interaction between Jews and non-Jews and contribute to the high intermarriage rates and to redi-
rections of the religious system.

Yet, these trends toward assimilation have
been counterbalanced by a tendency toward increased
Jewish education for the young as well as by increases in certain religious observances which are
seen as better fitting into the American scene.
The religious change among three generations of
Jews is undoubtedly a complex process involving the
abandonment of traditional forms and the development of new forms of identity and expression
which are seen by many Jews as more congruent with
the broader American way of life. Analysis of the
Providence community in 1963 suggested that, evolving out of the process of generational adjustment,
the freedom to choose the degree of assimilation
has been exercised in the direction of Jewish identification.[87] Whether that pattern holds for the
nation as a whole and whether it has changed since
the Providence survey are major questions that
argue strongly for fuller exploitation of existing
data and collection of new information on the

interactions among generation change, demographic
variables, and Jewish identity.

Age Composition

Of all demographic variables, age is regarded
as the most basic. The significant impact of age
on the generation status of the Jewish population
as well as on fertility and migration have already
been noted. Age composition also has obvious
implications for communal institutions. Until the
National Jewish Population Study, the only source
of information on the age composition of Jews
nationally was the 1957 Census Survey. It clearly
indicated that the Jewish population was, on the
average, older than the general white population of
the United States. The median age of the Jewish
group was 36.7 years compared to 30.6 for the total
white population. This substantial differential
results from sharp differences in the proportion
under 14 years of age and in the 45-64 age
category. The youngest group constituted only 23
percent of the Jewish population, compared to 28
percent of the total white population; this
reflected lower Jewish fertility. By contrast,
only 21 percent of the total white population but
28 percent of the Jews were between 45 and 64 years
of age in 1957 (Table 7). Both the Jewish and the
total white populations had quite similar proportions in the 65 and over age category, 10 and 9
percent, respectively. On the whole, data on the
age of individuals available from individual communities confirm that the age of the Jewish group
is older than that of the total population.
The data from the 1971 National Jewish Population Survey indicate that Jews continue to differ
from the general population in age composition.
Whereas 28 percent of the national population was
under age 15 in 1970, only 23 percent of the Jewish
population was in this age category, virtually
identical to the 1957 differential which refers to
those under age 14. By 1970, both the Jewish and
the general population had more persons aged 65 and
over, 11 and 10 percent, respectively. But this
differential is understated, since the Jewish
institutional population was not covered directly
in the National Jewish Population Study. If they
are included, the proportion of aged Jews rises to
12 percent. The effects of the declining birthrate
are clearly evidenced in the decreasing percentage
of Jewish children in the youngest age groups.

Table 7: PERCENT DISTRIBUTION OF JEWISH POPULATION BY AGE IN SELECTED COMMUNITIES AND THE UNITED STATES

Community	Date of Study	Age Distribution				
		Under 15	15-24	25-44	45-64	65 and Over
Washington, D.C.	1956	30	9	38	18	5
Worcester, Mass.	1957	27	11	26	26	10
Los Angeles, Calif.	1959	27	12	25	28	8
Rochester, N.Y.	1961	25	12	24	26	13
St. Joseph, Ind.	1961	30	14	24	24	8
Pittsburgh, Pa.	1963	27	14	25	26	8
Providence, R.I.	1963	25	14	24	27	10
Detroit, Mich.	1963	31	11	25	25	8
Milwaukee, Wis.	1964	24	15	23	28	10
Camden, N.J.	1964	30	13	23	28	6
Springfield, Mass.	1966	24	16	21	27	12
Boston, Mass.	1966	23	17	25	24	11
Flint, Mich.	1967	29	10	30	23	8
Columbus, Ohio	1969	27	13	23	28	9
Houston, Texas	1976	25	14	30	22	9
Greater Kansas City	1976	15	15	22	29	19
United States Jews	1957[a]	23	12	28	28	10
United States Whites	1957[a]	28	14	28	21	9
United States Jews	1971	23	18	22	25	11
United States whites	1970	28	17	24	21	10

[a]For the United States, lowest age categories are "under 14" and "14-24."

Sources: Sidney Goldstein, "American Jewry, 1970: A Demographic Profile," American Jewish Year Book, 1971, vol. 72. (Philadelphia: The Jewish Publication Society of America, 1971); Fred Massarik and Alvin Chenkin, "United States National Jewish Population Study: A First Report," American Jewish Year Book, vol. 74 (1973), p. 271. 1970 U.S. Census of Population.

Whereas 20 percent of the Jewish population in 1970
was aged 10-19, only 12 percent was under ten years
old. If these data are accurate, they point to a
very substantial reduction both in the absolute
number of youngsters in the population and in their
proportion of the total. Such changes have serious
implications for future growth, for educational
program needs, and for the size of a future "reser-
voir" from which adult support and leadership can
be drawn.

The dramatic changes occurring in age composition are illustrated on the community level by
comparative data from surveys taken in the same
community. For example, the 1958 survey of New
Orleans found 11 percent of the population to be
under age five and 15 percent to be age 65 and
over.[88] Reflecting, in part, the effect of lower
fertility and in part the cumulative effects of
migration and lengthening of life, the 1973 survey
found only 6 percent of the population to be under
six years (six was used instead of five as the cut
off in 1973) but 21 percent to be 65 and over.
Clearly there has been a substantial aging of the
community in the 15-year interval.

As demonstrated, the American Jewish community
already has an older age structure than the total
United States white population; over time, because
of its lower fertility and its higher proportion of
individuals in the middle age group, the Jewish
population can be expected to become even older.
The United States as a whole is already facing
serious problems associated with an aging population; but during the next few decades these problems may become even more serious for the Jewish
community. We can look forward to a rise in the
percentage of older Jews from the 11 percent level
observed in 1971 to over 15 percent by the early
1990s.[89] This implies a 40 percent increase in the
number of aged over the 1971 count. Concurrently,
the number of children under 15 will be lower,
reflecting the low birthrates noted earlier.
Changes will also occur in the middle of the age
range as the reduced number of persons born during
the depression years move into the upper middle-age
range. This change may initially create some
serious problems for the community, as the pool of
persons to whom it can turn for leadership and
financial contributions is somewhat reduced.

In short, Jewish communities need to reeval-
uate and reorganize their services to meet the
changing age composition. Equally important, continuous monitoring of the changes in age must be

maintained. The past fluctuations in fertility
will manifest themselves in the magnitude of different age cohorts as they pass through the life
cycle and may lead to temporary rises or declines
in the need for services catering to particular
segments of the community. While recognizing the
general trend toward an aging population, and its
associated problems of housing, financial restrictions, and health impairment, there must also be an
awareness that changes are taking place related to
changes in age, and that the need for schools,
playgrounds, camps, and teenage programs will also
change as the overall age profile varies. Even if
the size of the population were to remain constant,
the shift in age will undoubtedly call for drastic
changes in services, in residential distribution
patterns, and in the ability of the community to
provide the resources needed for strong leadership.

One of the more serious consequences of
changes in the age structure and the resulting
higher proportion of Jewish aged may be increasing
problems of poverty. Lulled by the general afflu-
ence of America's Jews, the Jewish community paid
little heed to its poor until the publication in
1971 of Ann Wolfe's article, "The Invisible Jewish
Poor."[90] As a result of these findings and the
ensuing controversy over the actual number of Jewish poor in America, communal institutions in a
number of cities initiated concerted efforts to
deal with the problem and new research programs
were undertaken to document the subject.

Regardless of whether the number of Jewish
poor in the United States is estimated at 164,000[91]
or 700,000 to 800,000[92] persons, those concerned
with the issue generally agree that a large majority of the poverty striken are over age 60. Descriptions of the Jews who have retired to South
Beach in Miami[93] or of those still left in the
tenements of the Lower East Side in New York[94]
serve as poignant examples. If, as Bertram Gold
states, "Most of the Jewish poor are poor because
of special circumstances--isolated old age, cultural separateness, maladjustment, death of the bread-
winner,"[95] the problems may well become more severe
in the near future. Larger numbers of older persons, coupled with the loosening of family ties and
the greater mobility among American Jews, would
help to create the kinds of situations which foster
poverty. The Jewish community may thus have one
more dimension to add to the services it will be
called on to provide. At the very least, it is an
area which should be closely monitored, with an eye

to alleviating the situation before it becomes more
acute.

Education

Of the Jews who immigrated to America in the
late 1800s and early 1900s a large majority came
because of the supposedly equal opportunities for
social and economic mobility. But lacking secular
education, adequate facility in English, and
technical training, rapid advancement proved an
unrealistic goal for many. For others, both
education and occupational achievement were made
difficult, if not impossible, by factors related to
their foreign-born status and/or their identification as Jews. Frustrated in their own
efforts to achieve significant mobility, many Jews
transferred their aspirations to their children.
First generation American Jews recognized the
special importance of education as a key to occupational mobility and made considerable effort to
provide their children with a good secular education. Reflecting the great value placed by Jews on
education, both as a way of life and as a means of
mobility, the Jews of America have compiled an
extraordinary record of educational achievement.
The limited data available for the period
around 1950 show the education of Jews was higher
than that of the white population, averaging about
12 years and 10 years, respectively.[96] This differential was confirmed on the national level by
the 1957 Census Survey.[97] For the population 25
years old and over, the median number of school
years completed by Jews was 12.3 compared to 10.6
for the general population. Yet, even sharper differences than those conveyed by these statistics
distinguished the educational achievements of Jews
from those of the general population; 17 percent of
the adult Jews were college graduates compared to
only 7 percent of the general population. At the
other extreme of the educational hierarchy, 29
percent of all adult Jews had recieved only an elementary school education compared to 40 percent of
the total population. Various community studies
lent further weight to the strength of the differential and pointed particularly to the rising levels of education among younger Jews, both males and
females.[98] That an estimated 80 percent of those
in the college age group were enrolled in college
emphasized the very high value placed by Jews on
college education. In fact, within the Jewish population, the important educational differential in

Table 8: PERCENT DISTRIBUTION OF YEARS OF SCHOOL COMPLETED BY PERSONS AGED 25 AND OVER OF THE JEWISH AND TOTAL UNITED STATES WHITE POPULATION, BY SEX, IN 1970[a]

Years of School Completed	Males		Females		Both Sexes	
	Jewish	Total White	Jewish	Total White	Jewish	Total White
Less than 12 years	15.2	46.1	16.0	44.9	15.6	45.5
12 years	22.5	28.5	35.3	35.5	29.2	32.1
College:						
1-3 years	17.3	11.1	21.0	11.1	19.2	11.1
4 years	14.9	7.2	13.6	5.7	14.2	6.4
5 or more years	26.5	7.1	10.6	2.8	18.2	4.9
Unknown	3.5	-	3.5	-	3.5	-
Total percent	100.0	100.0	100.0	100.0	100.0	100.0

Sources: For the Jewish population, see Fred Massarik and Alvin Chenkin, "United States National Jewish Population Study: A First Report," American Jewish Year Book, vol. 74 (1973), p. 280.
For the United States white population see U.S. Bureau of the Census, 1970 U.S. Census of Population: General Social and Economic Characteristics, PC(1) C1 (Washington, D.C.: Government Printing Office, 1972), p. 386.

[a]Since the differentials between the Jewish and the total white population change only minimally when age is controlled, the non-standardized data are presented here.

younger groups is between those who had only some
college education and those who went on to postgraduate work. This was further confirmed by
studies of educational expectation among school-age
children. In 1965, 86 percent of the Jewish
students planned to attend college compared to only
53 percent of the general student body.
    The National Jewish Population Study lends
further support to the conclusions based upon these
earlier sets of data (Table 8). Among the male
Jewish population aged 25 and over, only 15.2 percent had not graduated high school. By contrast,
60 percent have had some college education. Of
those aged 30-39 (age-specific data are not shown
in Table 8), who constitute the youngest age cohort
likely to have completed their education, only 4
percent had no high school education and 83 percent
had some college education. In fact, at least 70
percent had graduated college, and 45 percent of
all the males aged 30-39 had done some graduate
work. Although sex differentials are apparent
among Jews, as they are for the total population,
Jews value extensive education for women, particularly among the younger cohorts. Like the men,
very few women (16 percent) had less than a high
school degree, but many more had restricted their
education to a high school level; just over half
reported some college education. Sharp age
differentials are evident, however. Among women
aged 30-39, only 2.4 percent had less than a high
school degree, and as many as 75 percent had some
college education. The sharpest difference between
men and women appears with respect to graduate
work. Of women 30-39 years of age, only 15 percent
reported a graduate or professional degree. The
trend data suggested by age differentials point
clearly, however, to rising levels of graduate work
among the younger women.
    Comparison in Table 8 of the levels of educa-
tion completed by Jews with those reported in the
1970 United States census for the total white population documents the persistence of sharp educational differentials. Just over half of the Jews
but only 22 percent of the non-Jews had some college education; the widest difference characterized
those with some graduate studies, 18 percent of the
Jews compared to 5 percent of all whites. At the
other extreme, only 16 percent of the Jews had less
than 12 years of schooling compared to 46 percent
of all whites. Clearly, Jews continue to be characterized by distinctively higher levels of

educational achievement, and, as the data in Table 8 show, this holds for both men and women.

These data on the changing educational achievements within the Jewish population and the differentials between the Jews and the larger American population have a number of implications for the various demographic developments reviewed in this assessment. First, they clearly confirm the exceptionally high level of education that has come to characterize the Jewish population. Although the differentials between Jews and non-Jews will diminish, particularly if current emphasis on recruitment of minority group members and underprivileged students persists, it will still be some time before college attendance levels among the non-Jewish population reach those achieved by Jews. As a result, some of the educational differences can be expected to persist for a number of decades and indirectly to continue to affect occupation and income differentials. The growing enrollment of women in graduate work and the implications that this has for their developing independent careers has particular significance for both marriage rates and fertility as well as for family stability.

To the extent that education is highly correlated with occupation, the continuing high number of college graduates in the Jewish population will affect its occupational composition, providing, of course, that the opportunities for employment exist which utilize skills developed through education. In the future, even more Jews will likely be engaged in intellectual pursuits and in occupations requiring a high degree of technical skill. Concommitantly, there will also probably be a reduction in the number of self-employed, both because small, private business will not provide an adequate intellectual challenge and because patterns of discrimination which thus far have excluded Jews in large corporations are likely to continue to weaken.

As before, and perhaps increasingly so, the impact of high education will go beyond occupation. In order to obtain a college education, particularly at the postgraduate level, a large proportion of young Jews must leave home. As a result, their ties to both family and community will weaken. Moreover, many of these college-educated Jews will not return permanently to the communities in which their families live and in which they were raised.

A 1973 study undertaken in Savannah, Georgia,
for example, has shown that from 1954 to 1958, half
of Savannah's Jewish college graduates settled in
the city.[99] From 1965 to 1969, only one in five
returned; the Jewish community is losing its college graduates for lack of job opportunities. Thus
education serves as an important catalyst for geographic mobility which eventually leads many individuals to take up residence in communities with
small Jewish populations, to live in highly integrated neighborhoods, and to work and socialize in
largely non-Jewish circles. The extent of such a
development needs to be assessed and future patterns need to be monitored.

Finally, Jews with higher education may have
significantly higher rates of intermarriage and
become more alienated from the Jewish community.
This development involves not only the possibile
impact of physical separation from home and the
weakening of parental control in dating and courtship patterns, but also the general liberalizing
effect a college education may have on religious
values and Jewish identity. It would be ironic if
the very strong positive value which Jews have
traditionally placed on education and that now has
manifested itself in a very high proportion of
Jewish youths attending college turns out to be an
important factor in the general weakening of the
individual's ties to the Jewish community.

Whether the high levels of enrollment in
colleges and in graduate work will persist remains
an open question. If the Jewish population becomes
more generally dispersed and tendencies toward migration increase, a much higher proportion of Jewish youth may be raised in neighborhoods and attend
schools that are less densely Jewish. Some evidence suggests that in such a situation the motivation for higher education is less strong.[100] If
so, a somewhat lower proportion of Jewish youth may
plan to go to college in the future. Still another
factor that may affect enrollment levels is the
perceived employment opportunity open to college
students. If the job market is such that students
are discouraged from continuing their college and
graduate studies, Jews may well be affected more
than other segments of the population, especially
if this situation is coupled with emphasis on
minority group selection in admission to universities and in the hiring practices of large firms.
We need studies to document whether the college
dropout rate has risen for Jews and whether the
more recent Jewish high school graduates are, in

fact, continuing their education. It seems less
likely now than it did one or two decades ago that
a college education will become virtually universal
for Jewish youth. More likely, levels of educational achievement will plateau at the high level
they have already reached or slightly below it.

Occupational Composition

Reflecting in part the high levels of education
attained by the Jewish population, Jews are also
disproportionally concentrated in the upper ranks
of the occupational structure. As part of his
analysis of the social characteristics of American
Jews prepared in 1954 for the tercentenary
celebration of Jewish settlement in the United
States, Nathan Glazer observed that, outside New
York City, the homogeneous character of the
occupational structure of Jewish communities was
beyond dispute.[101] Basing his conclusions on a
number of local Jewish community surveys conducted
between 1948 and 1953, he noted that the proportion
of Jews in the nonmanual occupations ranged from 75
to 96 percent, compared to 38 percent for the
American population as a whole. Even in New York
City, where greater heterogeneity would have been
expected, as many as two-thirds of the employed
Jews were engaged in nonmanual work. Extreme
rapidity has characterized the social and economic
rise of Jews in America. Glazer further noted a
general tendency for the ethnic concentration in a
single occupation to suffer dilution as the natve-
born generation became better educated and more
familiar with occupational opportunities; but, for
the Jews, "this dilution upward becomes a
concentration, for the Jews began to reach the
upper limit of occupational mobility relatively
early."[102] For Jews to reflect the general occupational structure of the United States would, in
fact, require downward mobility for many, and
Glazer concluded that, since this will not happen,
"we may expect the Jewish community to become more
homogeneous in the future as the number of first
generation workers and the culture they established
declines."[103]
Both the data from the fairly large number of
community studies conducted in the 1950s and 1960s,
as well as those from the 1957 Census Survey support Glazer's thesis of an upward shift in Jewish
occupational affiliations. The latter, in particular, had special significance because of its national coverage. It found that three-fourths of

all Jewish employed males were in white collar positions compared to only 35 percent of the total
white male population.[104]   To a very great extent,
this large difference is attributable to the much
greater concentration of Jewish men in professional
and managerial positions. Compared with males,
women in the labor force were much more concentrated in white collar positions, and therefore the
differentials between Jewish women and all women
were less marked than those between Jewish men and
all men. Just over four out of every five Jewish
women were in white collar jobs, compared to just
over half of the total female labor force.

The sharp generation changes in occupational
affiliation reflected in the 1957 data are attested
to by a 1964 B'nai Brith Vocational Service
report.[105]   It found that three-fourths of all
Jewish high school youths hoped to enter professional and technical jobs whereas only one in five
of their fathers actually held such jobs. By contrast, only 3 percent hoped to be business propri-
etors compared to 27 percent whose fathers owned
businesses.

The 1965 and 1975 Boston surveys have particular value in documenting recent changes in occupational composition, although some of the change
may reflect selective in- and out-migration and
changing opportunities in the Boston area.[106]   In
1965, one-third of the employed Jewish males in
Boston were professionals; by 1975 this proportion
had risen to 40 percent. The percentage engaged in
clerical and sales work also rose from 15 to 21
percent. As might be expected on the basis of
developments noted earlier, the proportion engaged
in managerial activities declined from 37 to only
27 percent of the total in 1975. In all, therefore, the percentage of males making their living
in white collar work rose, but the distribution by
specific types of occupations shifted.

Jewish women followed a somewhat different
pattern, with increasing percentages engaged in
both professional and managerial activities. These
changes relate to the rising educational levels of
women and their greater participation in the labor
force. In both 1965 and 1975 in the Boston area,
over 90 percent of all women were in white collar
jobs, contrasted with 70 percent for the non-Jewish
employed women, with most of the differential being
attributable to fewer non-Jews in professional and
managerial positions.

Similar patterns of occupational distribution
were found by the National Jewish Population Survey

(Table 9). Almost 90 percent of all males and
females were employed in white collar positions,
and those in the younger ages are much more heavily
concentrated in professional activities. Only a
very small proportion are engaged in manual work.
Data from the various community surveys also point
to a continuing increase in the proportion of Jews
engaged in white collar work, but within the white
collar group, there appears to be a shift toward
more professionals; either stability or decline
characterizes the managerial and proprietor
group. With the decrease in small businesses, an
increasing proportion of Jewish men may be turning
to executive positions in larger corporations,
instead of operating their own firms as did many of
their parents and grandparents.

Simon Kuznets, in his analysis of the trends
in the economic structure of American Jewry, assessed the various constraints affecting the occupational choices of American Jews. He concluded
that it is evident that changes in these constraints have contributed toward greater concentration of Jews in professional and technical
pursuits; an increase in employees rather than
employers among officials, managers, and within the
professional-technical group; a decline in the
share of industrial blue-collar jobs; and a lesser
concentration in trade, particularly small proprietorships.[107] The reasons he cites are similar to
those mentioned earlier in this analysis.

Change also characterizes the non-Jewish
population. Between the 1957 census survey and the
1970 decennial census, the occupational differentials between Jews and non-Jews seem to be narrowing somewhat, as a result of the noticeable increase in the percentage of non-Jews in white collar jobs. Three-fourths of all Jewish males 14 and
over were already in white collar work in 1957,
compared to only 35 percent of the all white males;
by 1970 this was true of 87 percent of the Jewish
males aged 25 and over covered by the National
Jewish Population Study and 42 percent of all white
males aged 16 and over in the 1970 census. For
females, the data also suggest some narrowing.
Whereas 83 percent of Jewish women were in white
collar work in 1957, and 89 percent in 1970, among
all white women the percentage rose from 55 to 65
percent. More important, perhaps, sharp differences persisted despite the narrowing. For
example, among men, twice as large a proportion of

Table 9: PERCENTAGE OCCUPATIONAL DISTRIBUTION OF THE JEWISH AND TOTAL UNITED STATES WHITE POPULATION, BY SEX, IN 1970[a]

	Males		Females		Both Sexes	
	Jewish	Total White	Jewish	Total White	Jewish	Total White
Professional and technical	29.3	15.0	23.8	16.3	27.4	15.5
Managers, Administrators	40.7	12.0	15.5	3.9	32.2	9.0
Clerical	3.2	7.6	41.7	8.1	16.2	18.4
Sales	14.2	7.4	8.3	36.8	12.2	7.7
Crafts	5.6	21.8	1.5	1.9	4.2	14.4
Operatives	3.9	18.7	2.3	14.0	3.4	17.0
Service	1.2	7.3	3.6	17.4	2.0	11.0
Laborers[b]	0.3	5.7	0.2	0.9	0.3	3.9
Agriculture[b]	-	4.5	-	0.7	-	3.1
Unknown	1.7	-	3.1	-	2.2	-
Total percent	100.0	100.0	100.0	100.0	100.0	100.0

[a]The Jewish population includes persons aged 25 and over; the total white population includes persons aged 16 and over. Since the differentials between the Jewish and the total white population change only minimally when age is controlled, the non-standardized data are presented here.

[b]No separate category for agriculture was included in the National Jewish Population Study data.

Source: For the Jewish population see Fred Massarik and Alvin Chenkin, United States National Jewish Population Study: A First Report," American Jewish Year Book, vol. 74 (1973), pp. 284-285. For the United States white population: U.S. Bureau of the Census, 1970 U.S. Census of Population: General Social and Economic Characteristics, PC(1)-C1 (Washington: Government Printing Office, 1972), p. 392.

Jews were in the professional and technical group
as of all white males. Only 11 percent of Jewish
men were engaged in manual work compared to 58 percent of all white men; for women the difference was
almost as great, 8 percent of Jewish women compared
to 35 percent of all white women.

As differentials between Jews and non-Jews
with respect to educational level diminish and as
discriminatory restrictions on occupational choice
weaken, it seems likely that occupational differentials generally and within the white collar occupations will decline. The major question, as with
education, revolves about the specific direction in
which the youngest generation will move as they
face career decisions. How many of them, motivated
by different values and attracted by new life
styles, will gorego college and attempt to make a
living through manual work or lower white collar
positions? How many of those who are trained for
higher positions, but who are frustrated by their
inability to obtain such work, will opt for blue
collar jobs or seek employment in clerical or sales
positions?

A 1972 assessment of employment prospects for
Jewish youth stressed that Jewish young men and
women face "relatively greater" job hunting difficulties in the near future and should give more
consideration to nonprofessional jobs than they
have in the past due to the projected slower rise
in professional and technical jobs between 1970 and
1980.[108] In his review, Herbert Bienstock called
for more emphasis on vocational guidance and placement and on "attitudinal reconditioning, particularly in terms of value structures relating to nonprofessional job opportunities,"[109] especially as
the latter become more attractive in pay and security than in the past. Although predicting that a
majority of Jews entering the job market would continue to seek white collar jobs, Bienstock, a labor
force expert, also suggested that young Jews might
turn in increasing numbers to self-employment, not
in the old-style shop or small store, but in new
areas where demands for services are likely to
grow.

Only repeated surveys of the kind that have
been undertaken in Boston, but preferably on a more
frequent basis, and more intensive monitoring of
changes occurring both at the attitudinal and the
behavioral level will provide the opportunities to
assess fully the very significant reversals in the
trends of the past that may be occurring at present
or that are likely to occur in the near future. At

the same time, research is needed to ascertain
whether the changing occupational affiliations of
Jews, and particularly their entrance into new
types of professional and managerial responsibili-
ties, leads to increased channeling of self-
identification through the professional or intellectual subsocieties rather than through the Jewish
community and the ways in which such occupational
mobility is related to geographic mobility. The
two together may well provide the organized community with one of its major challenges.

THE CURRENT AND FUTURE DEMOGRAPHIC SITUATION

Assessment of the demographic situation of
American Jewry in 1970[110] pointed to a number of
challenges which the American Jewish community must
face in the closing decades of the twentieth century as a result of the demographic changes that
were then taking place. The low level of Jewish
fertility, coupled with some losses from intermarriage, pointed at best to maintenance of the slow
growth rate characterizing the Jewish population in
the second and third quarters of the twentieth century, and possibly to still slower growth. Concurrently, increasing Americanization seems likely
to continue, as judged by greater geographic dispersion, a higher percentage of third-and fourth-
generation Americans, and narrowing of such key
socioeconomic differentials as education, occupation, and income. All these changes pointed to the
potential for greater behavioral convergence between Jews and non-Jews and corresponding losses in
Jewish identify. However, it was also suggested
that structural separation and continuity of Jewish
identity would persist as American Jews continued
their efforts to find a meaningful balance between
Jewishness and Americanism.
Since the 1970 assessment was undertaken, many
of the patterns that were then emerging have become
further accentuated. By 1977, the Jewish population constituted only 2.7 percent of the American
population, in contrast to the peak of 3.7 percent
reached in the mid-1930s. Jewish fertility levels
seem to have declined even further as part of the
national pattern in the 1970s. If the fertility
rates of Jews persist at the low levels reached in
the 1970s, the American Jewish population is quite
certain to decline in actual numbers (unless there
continue to be compensating additions through
immigration). Even should fertility remain at near

replacement level, the losses resulting from intermarriage and assimilation will compound the effects
of either very low natural increase or negative
growth resulting from an excess of deaths over
births.

Recent estimates of the Jewish population
suggest that although the American Jewish population had approached the six million mark in the
late 1960s, it has not yet passed that milestone
and, given the recent pattern of demographic
growth, is not likely to do so. A realistic assessment suggests that the Jewish population of
America will remain at approximately its present
size, between 5.5 and 5.8 million, through the end
of the century. In the absence of significant
reversals in fertility behavior or in rates of
intermarriage, a decline will set in during the
first decades of the twenty-first century that
could well lead to a reduction of one to two million by the time of the tricentennial. Most of the
social and economic changes characterizing the
United States in general, in combination with the
unique characteristics of the Jewish population
itself, are likely to reenforce the low growth
rates or decline. These include high rates of divorce and separation, later age at marriage and
possible rises in levels of non-marriage, increased
extra-familial activity on the part of women, higher education levels, greater secularism, and growing concern with the environment, and rising costs
of living. Many of these very same factors are
likely to lead to continued high levels of intermarriage. Although its effects on population size
are compensated to a degree by conversions to
Judaism and the rearing of many of the children of
intermarriages as Jews, maintenance of the high
levels of intermarriage reported in recent years
would undoubtedly compound the impact of low fertility on the rate of population growth.

Jews have already become widely dispersed
throughout the United States; this trend is likely
to continue in the future. The available evidence
suggests that as a result of higher education and
changing occupations, lower levels of self-
employment, weakening family ties, and reduced
discrimination, Jews have begun to migrate in increasing numbers away from the major centers of
Jewish population. Even while distinct areas of
Jewish concentration remain and while Jews continue
to be highly concentrated in the metropolitan
areas, the emerging patterns of redistribution
point to fewer Jews in the Northeast, substantial

decreases in central cities, and possibly even some
reduction in the suburban population as Jews join
the movement out of the metropolitan areas, to
smaller urban places, and even to rural locations. Regardless of which particular stream
becomes more popular, the net result is likely to
be a much more geographically dispersed Jewish
population in the decades ahead.

Such greater dispersal means that factors
other than religion will provide an increasingly
important basis for selecting areas and neighborhoods of residence. In turn, the lower Jewish
density will provide the seeds for still greater
acculturation and assimilation. Moreover, to the
extent that Jews increasingly participate in the
pattern of repeated population movement which
characterizes the American scene, additional dangers to the strength of community ties loom on the
horizon.

The decline in relative numbers or even in
total numbers may not be very significant in the
next few decades, since Jews have never constituted
a numerically large segment of the American population. What may be more crucial is the vitality of
individual Jewish communities; and this may be much
more influenced by the size of such communities and
their socioeconomic composition. Only when the
changes in total numbers are accompanied by significant changes in distribution and composition
which are deleterious both to the ability to maintain a vital Jewish community and to foster individual Jewish identification will the change in
numbers itself take on new significance. Because
population movement has special significance for
these concerns, any substantial change in the pattern of residential distribution of Jews and in
their ability to maintain close identity with a
Jewish community takes on special importance.

Operating partly as cause and partly as an
effect of these changing patterns of growth, distribution, and intermarriage are the underlying
changes in population composition characterizing
American Jewry. Perhaps the most striking composi-
tional change has been the reduction in the percentage of foreign born. Indeed, as already noted
in 1970, even the proportion of second-generation
American Jews has begun to diminish as third-and
fourth-generation people become an ever larger
proportion of the Jewish population. The pace of
change would even be faster were it not for the low
levels of Jewish fertility, which, in addition to
contributing to the low rate of population growth,

result in a reduced number of young persons in the
population and an increasing proportion of aged.

Given the zero growth levels of fertility
which the Jewish population seems to have reached,
the average age of the Jewish population is likely
to rise still further and to remain substantially
above the average of the general population. Thus,
a major challenge for the Jewish community in the
future will be the comparatively large numbers of
older persons, a considerable portion of whom will
be widows.

Jews remain unique, despite some evidence of
narrowing of differentials, in having a high concentration of highly educated, numerous white
collar, and high income individuals. The large
proportion of Jews who obtain specialized university training, their tendency to move out of small
family businesses into salaried employment, and
their increasing willingness to seek and take positions away from their community of current residence helps to explain the growing residential dispersal of the Jewish population. The same factors
undoubtedly also contribute to the high rates of
intermarriage, the low level of fertility, and the
growing tendency toward assimilation.

In combination, the current pattern of very
low fertility, high levels of intermarriage, and
lower residential density through population redistribution all serve to potentially weaken the demographic base of the Jewish population in the United
States. Yet, to the extent that Jews retain a comparatively close-knit ethnic-religious identification within the total society, the potential for
continued vitality remains. Stability of numbers
or even declining numbers need not constitute a
fundamental threat to the maintenance of a strong
Jewish community and to high levels of individual
Jewish identity. The risk that this may happen is
obviously present, but this has been true in the
past when even larger numbers obtained. Although
maintenance of numbers is certainly desirable in
the interest of providing a strong base for insur-
ing Jewish identity and vitality, whether or not
the community as a whole should or can do anything
to control the changing fertility levels or the
patterns of redistribution is debatable. To the
extent that mobility and fertility behavior represent reactions to a wide and complex range of social, economic, and normative changes in the larger
American society, they are probably well beyond the
direct and even indirect control of the organized
Jewish community. What is perhaps more important

is that the community undertake and maintain a
fuller assessment of the implications of these
developments and that it be prepared, on the basis
of such assessments, to engage in experimentation
with and development of new institutional forms
designed, at a minimum, to mitigate the negative
effects of population decline and of population
dispersal. Ideally, these efforts should also increase the opportunities for greater participation
of individuals in the organized life of the Jewish
community, and for greater commitment to self-
identification as Jews. In so doing, the community
would help insure that the changes that do occur
still allow for a meaningful balance between being
Jewish and being American.

NOTES

*This report is a revised version of a paper
presented at the Colloquium on Jewish Life in the
United States: Perspectives from the Social
Sciences, sponsored by the YIVO Institute for
Jewish Research, May 28 and 29, 1978. The report
draws heavily on material previously published by
the author in "American Jewry, 1970: A Demographic
Profile," American Jewish Year Book, 1971, vol. 72,
pp. 3-88. The contents of this chapter will be
published also in the forthcoming American Jewish
Year Book, 1981.

1.   An excellent review of the varied efforts
     undertaken between 1818 and 1977 to gather and
     assess statistics on the American Jewish
     population was prepared by Jack Diamond, "A
     Reader in the Demography of American Jews,"
     American Jewish Year Book, 1977, vol. 77, pp.
     251-317. It documents both the recurring need
     for current information on the number,
     distribution, characteristics, and growth
     patterns of the Jewish population in the
     United States and the varied and often
     ingenious efforts to meet the challenges
     created by the general absence of regular,
     official data on the Jewish population.

2.   U.S. Bureau of the Census, "Religion Reported
     by the Civilian Population of the United
     States, March 1957," Current Population
     Reports, Series P-20, No. 79 (1958).

3.   Fred Massarik and Alvin Chenkin, "United
     States National Jewish Population Study: A

First Report," <u>American Jewish Year Book,</u>
<u>1973</u>, vol. 74, p. 264.

4.   As, for example, the annual General Social
     Survey conducted by the National Opinion
     Research Corporation.

5.   Ronald Freedman, Pascal K. Whelpton, and
     Arthur A. Campbell, <u>Family Planning,</u>
     <u>Sterility, and Population Growth</u> (New York:
     McGraw-Hill, 1959); Norman B. Ryder and
     Charles F. Westoff, <u>Reproduction in the United</u>
     <u>States, 1965</u> (Princeton: Princeton University
     Press, 1971); Charles F. Westoff, Robert
     Potter, Jr., and Philip Sagi, <u>The Third Child</u>
     (Princeton: Princeton University Press,
     1963); Charles F. Westoff, Robert Potter, Jr.,
     Philip Sagi, and Eliot Mishler, <u>Family Growth</u>
     <u>in Metropolitan America,</u> (Princeton:
     Princeton University Press, 1961); Pascal K.
     Whelpton, Arthur A. Campbell, and John E.
     Patterson, <u>Fertility and Family Planning in</u>
     <u>the United States</u> (Princeton: Princeton
     University Press, 1966).

6.   Sidney Goldstein, "American Jewry, 1970:   A
     Demographic Profile," <u>American Jewish Year</u>
     <u>Book, 1971</u>, vol. 72, pp. 17-19.

7.   Cf., Alvin Chenkin, "Jewish Population in the
     United States, 1972," <u>American Jewish Year</u>
     <u>Book, 1973</u>, vol. 74, pp. 307-309, and Alvin
     Chenkin, "Jewish Population in the United
     States, 1974," <u>American Jewish Year Book,</u>
     <u>1976</u>, vol. 76, pp. 229-236.

8.   Alvin Chenkin and Maynard Miran, "Jewish
     Population in the United States, 1979,"
     <u>American Jewish Year Book, 1980</u>, vol. 80, p.
     159.

9.   Moreover, given the nature of the sampling
     procedures employed in the National Jewish
     Population Study and resulting potential
     biases, the "official" National Jewish
     Population Study estimate of the U.S. Jewish
     population of 5,780,000 is actually the middle
     of three estimates that range from a low of
     5,560,000 to a high of 6,000,000.   Each of
     these statistics has its own standard error,
     so that the 95 percent confidence limit for
     the respective estimates would be:

High	6,000,000	±	1,175,000
Medium	5,780,000	±	884,000
Low	5,560,000	±	763,000

The wide range encompased by these estimates,
especially when their sampling errors are
taken into account, provides further evidence

of the absence of exact statistics describing
the Jewish population. (Bernard Lazerwitz,
"An Estimate of a Rare Population Group: The
U.S. Jewish Population, "Demography, vol. 15
(August 1978), pp. 389-394.)

10. Ira Rosenwaike, "A Synthetic Estimate of
American Jewish Population Movement Over the
Last Three Decades." Paper presented at the
Seventh World Congress of Jewish Studies,
Jerusalem, August 1977.

11. Chenkin and Miran, op. cit., p. 162.

12. Simon Kuznets, "Immigration of Russian Jews to
the United States: Background and Structure,"
Perspectives in American History, vol. 9
(1975), pp. 35-124; Jacob Lestchinsky, "Jewish
Migrations, 1840-1956," in Louis Finkelstein,
ed., The Jews (New York: Jewish Publication
Society, 1960), pp. 1536-1596; Calvin
Goldscheider, "The Demography of Jewish
Americans: Research Findings, Issues, and
Challenges." Paper presented at Brandeis
University "Planning Conference for Modern
Jewish Studies," Waltham, Mass., October 21-
24, 1979.

13. Rosenwaike, op. cit., pp. 6-7.

14. Personal communication from HIAS, March 11,
1980. The number includes only those Russian
immigrants who were assisted by HIAS.

15. Elihu Bergman, "The American Jewish Population
Erosion," Midstream (October 1977), p. 9.

16. Samuel S. Lieberman and Morton Weinfeld,
"Demographic Trends and Jewish Survival,"
Midstream (November 1978), pp. 9-19.

17. Salo Baron, A Social and Religious History of
the Jews, vol. II (New York: Columbia
University Press, 1937), p. 169.

18. Goldstein, op. cit., pp. 12-15.

19. Sidney Goldstein, "Jewish Mortality and
Survival Patterns: Providence, Rhode Island,
1962-1964," Eugenics Quarterly, vol. 13 (March
1966), pp. 48-61.

20. Calculated from Rhode Island Census of 1905,
"Conjugal Conditions, Maternity Tables,"
Bulletin IV, part one of the annual report for
1907, table VII, p. 551.

21. R. K. Stix and Frank Notestein, Controlled
Fertility (Baltimore: The William and Wilkins
Co., 1940), p. 29; Raymond Pearl, The Natural
History of Population (New York: Oxford
University Press, Inc., 1939), pp. 241-242.

22. Pascal K. Whelpton and Clyde V. Kiser,
"Differential Fertility Among Native White

Couples in Indianapolis," Social and
Psychological Factors Affecting Fertility, I,
Milbank Memorial Fund Quarterly, vol. 21
(July, 1943), pp. 226-271.

23. U.S. Bureau of the Census, op. cit.
24. Ryder and Westoff, op. cit.
25. Charles F. Westoff and Norman B. Ryder, The
Contraceptive Revolution (Princeton:
Princeton University Press, 1977).
26. Westoff, Potter, and Sagi, op. cit., p. 89;
Westoff, Potter, Sagi, and Mishler, op. cit.,
pp. 72-92.
27. Sidney Goldstein, "Jewish Fertility in
Contemporary America," in Paul Rittenband, ed;
Modern Jewish Fertility (Leiden: Brill
Publishers, in press).
28. General Social Surveys, 1972 through 1975,
conducted by National Opinion Research Center,
Roper Research Center, Inc., Williamstown,
Mass.
29. Sergio Della Pergola, "Patterns of American
Jewish Fertility" (Jerusalem: Institute of
Contemporary Jewry, The Hebrew University,
1979), mimeographed paper.
30. Ibid., p. 18.
31. Ibid., pp. 13-14.
32. Gordon Scott Bonham, "Expected Size of
Completed Family Among Currently Married Women
15-44 Years of Age: United States, 1973,"
Advancedata (from Vital and Health Statistics
of the National Center for Health Statistics),
10 (August 1977).
33. Kathleen Ford, "Contraceptive Use in the
United States, 1973," Vital and Health
Statistics, Series 23 (forthcoming).
34. Calvin Goldscheider and Peter R. Uhlenberg,
"Minority Group Status and Fertility,"
American Journal of Sociology, vol. 74
(January 1969), pp. 361-372.
35. Cf., New York Times, April 2, 1976.
36. Ronald Lee, "Demographic Forecasting and the
Easterlin Hypothesis," Population and
Development Review, vol. 2 (1976), p. 459.
37. Steven Cohen, "Renascence or Oblivion." Paper
presented at meeting of Task Force on Jewish
Population, New York, September 19, 1977.
38. U.S. Bureau of the Census, op. cit.
39. Goldstein, "American Jewry, 1970," op. cit.,
p. 28.
40. Erich Rosenthal, "Studies of Jewish
Intermarriages in the United States," American
Jewish Year Book, 1963, vol. 64, pp. 34-51.

41. Sidney Goldstein, The Greater Providence
     Jewish Community: A Population Survey
     (Providence, Rhode Island: General Jewish
     Committee, 1964); Sidney Goldstein, A
     Population Survey of the Greater Springfield
     Jewish Community (Springfield, Mass.: Jewish
     Community Council, 1968).
42. Morris Axelrod, Floyd J. Fowler, and Arnold
     Gurin, A Community Survey for Long Range
     Planning. A Study of the Jewish Population of
     Greater Boston (Boston: Combined Jewish
     Philanthropies of Greater Boston, 1967).
43. Floyd J. Fowler, 1975 Community Survey: A
     Study of the Jewish Population of Greater
     Boston (Boston: Combined Jewish
     Philanthropies of Greater Boston, 1977), pp.
     66-67.
44. Massarik and Chenkin, op. cit., pp. 292-306.
45. Goldstein, The Greater Providence Jewish
     Community, op. cit, pp. 186-187.
46. Fowler, op. cit.
47. Massarik and Chenkin, op. cit., pp. 296-297.
48. Sidney Goldstein and Calvin Goldscheider,
     Jewish Americans: Three Generations in a
     Jewish Community (Englwood Cliffs, N.J.:
     Prentice-Hall, Inc., 1968), pp. 166-169.
49. Egon Mayer, "Patterns of Intermarriage Among
     American Jews: Varieties, Uniformities,
     Dilemmas, and Prospects" (New York: American
     Jewish Committee, 1978), mimeographed report.
50. Alexander Schindler, as reported in the
     Providence, Rhode Island Sunday Journal,
     December 3, 1978.
51. Marshall Sklare, "Intermarriage and the Jewish
     Future," Commentary, vol. 37 (April 1964), p.
     52.
52. National Jewish Population Study, National and
     Regional Population Counts (New York: Council
     of Jewish Federations and Welfare Funds,
     1974), p. 6.
53. Massarik and Chenkin, op. cit.
54. Cohen, op. cit.
55. Neil C. Sandberg and Gene N. Levine, as
     summarized in News from the Committee,
     American Jewish Committee Newsletter 79-960-
     200, November 21, 1979.
56. Roberto Bachi, Population Trends of World
     Jewry (Jerusalem: Institute of Contemporary
     Jewry, The Hebrew University, 1976).
57. Rhode Island Herald, September 1, 1977.

58. Alvin Chenkin, "Jewish Population in the
    United States, 1974," American Jewish Year
    Book, 1976, vol. 76, pp. 232-236.
59. William M. Newman and Peter L. Halvorson,
    "American Jews: Patterns of Geographic
    Distribution and Change, 1952-1971," Journal
    for the Scientific Study of Religion, vol. 18
    (June 1979), pp. 183-193.
60. Ibid., p. 192.
61. U.S. Bureau of the Census, op. cit.
62. Goldstein, "American Jewry, 1970," op. cit.,
    pp. 39-41.
63. Jack Diamond, "How Many Jews in New York
    City?" Congress Monthly (January 1978), pp. 8-
    10.
64. Ibid., p. 42.
65. Axelrod, Fowler, and Gurin, op, cit.; Fowler,
    op. cit., pp. 28-33.
66. Judith B. Erickson and Mitchel J. Lazarus, The
    Jewish Community of Greater Minneapolis
    (Minneapolis: Federation for Jewish Service,
    1973).
67. Eugen Schoenfeld, "Problems and Potentials,"
    in Abraham D. Lavender, ed., A Coat of Many
    Colors: Jewish Subcommunities in the United
    States, (Westport, Conn.: Greenwood Press,
    1977), pp. 71-72.
68. Rabbi Benjamin M. Kahn quoted in New York
    Times, November 25, 1973.
69. See, The Jewish Population of Charleston, W.
    Va., annual reports of 1959 through 1977
    (Charleston, W. Va.: Jewish Population
    Committee, B'nai Jacob Synagogue).
70. Ibid., 19th Annual report, p.1.
71. Ibid., 20th and 21st Annual Reports.
72. Albert J. Mayer, The Detroit Jewish Community
    Geographic Mobility: 1963-1965, and Fertility
    - A Projection of Future Births (Detroit:
    Jewish Welfare Federation, 1966).
73. Charles F. Westoff, A Population Survey
    (Cherry Hill, N.J.: Jewish Federation of
    Camden County, 1964).
74. Fowler, op. cit., p. 29.
75. Betty J. Maynard, The Dallas Jewish Community
    Study (Dallas: Jewish Welfare Federation,
    1974).
76. The Jewish Population Study of the Greater
    Kansas City Area (Kansas City, Mo.: Jewish
    Federation, 1979), p. 12.
77. National Jewish Population Study, Mobility
    (New York: Council for Jewish Federations and
    Welfare Funds, 1974).

78. Ibid., pp. 5-6.
79. Gerhard Lenski, The Religious Factor (Garden City, N.Y.: Doubleday and Co.; Anchor Books, 1963), p. 214.
80. Goldstein, "American Jewry, 1970," op. cit., pp. 51-52.
81. Mervin F. Verbit, Characteristics of a Jewish Community: The Demographic and Judaic Profiles of the Jews in the Area Served by the Jewish Federation of North Jersey (Paterson, N.J.: Jewish Federation of North Jersey, 1971), p. 13.
82. Basil Zimmer, "Participation of Migrants in Urban Structures," American Sociological Review, vol. 20 (1955), pp. 218-224.
83. Goldstein, "American Jewry, 1970," op. cit., pp. 53-57.
84. Fowler, op. cit., p. 16.
85. Massarik and Chenkin, op. cit., p. 276.
86. Goldstein and Goldscheider, op. cit.
87. Ibid., pp. 171-231.
88. Opinions and Attitudes of the New Orleans Jewish Community (New Orleans: Jewish Welfare Federation, 1973).
89. National Jewish Population Study, The Jewish Aging (New York: Council of Jewish Federations and Welfare Funds, 1973), p.1.
90. Ann G. Wolfe, "The Invisible Jewish Poor," in Lavender, op. cit., pp. 137-144.
91. Kaplan, "Comment: The Invisible Jewish Poor, I," in Lavender, op. cit., p. 149.
92. Wolfe, op, cit,, p. 143.
93. Elinor Horwitz, "Jewish Poverty Hurts in South Beach," in Lavender, op. cit., pp. 160-166.
94. Mark Effron, "Left Behind, Left Alone," in Lavender, op. cit., pp. 167-179.
95. As quoted in Rhode Island Herald, February 4, 1972.
96. Ben Seligman and Aaron Antonovsky, "Some Aspects of Jewish Demography," in Marshall Sklare, ed. The Jews (Glencoe, Ill.: The Free Press, 1958), p. 54.
97. Sidney Goldstein, "Socioeconomic Differentials Among Religious Groups in the United States," American Journal of Sociology (May 1969), pp. 612-631.
98. Goldstein, "American Jewry, 1970," op. cit., pp. 63-65.
99. Rhode Island Herald, September 1, 1977.
100. A. Lewis Rhodes and Charles B. Nam, "The Religious Context of Educational

Expectations," <u>American Sociological Review</u>,
vol. 35 (April 1970), pp. 253-267.

101. Nathan Glazer, "The American Jew and the
Attainment of Middle-Class Rank: Some Trends
and Explanations," in Sklare, op. cit., p.
138.

102. Ibid., p. 146.

103. Ibid.

104. Goldstein, "Socioeconomic Differentials," op.
cit.

105. <u>New York Times</u>, June 25, 1972.

106. Axelrod, Fowler, and Gurin, op. cit.; Fowler,
op. cit., pp. 46-47.

107. Simon Kuznets, <u>Economic Structure of U.S.
Jewry: Recent Trends</u> (Jerusalem: Institute
of Contemporary Jewry, Hebrew University,
1972), pp. 17-18.

108. <u>New York Times</u>, June 25, 1972.

109. Ibid.

110. Goldstein, "American Jewry, 1970," op. cit.

Chapter III

JEWISH LIFE IN THE UNITED STATES:
PERSPECTIVES FROM PSYCHOLOGY

MORRIS N. EAGLE

What can a psychologist, in particular a
psychoanalytically oriented clinical psychologist,
offer to the study on Jewish lie in America? For
that matter, what can any psychologist offer in
view of the paucity of psychological research and
information available on this topic?
In my perusal of the literature, not only have
I found relatively little work carried out, but of
the work that has been done, what I have found most
useful and most enlightening are those observations, findings, and insights that are related to
and can be seen in the light of broader principles
and truths. Kurt Lewin's[1] work, for example,
stands out as reflecting these qualities. When he
wrote about Jews in the United States, he applied
general concepts and principles taken from social
psychology. For example, his observation regarding
the positive relationship between marginality and
inner conflict are intended to apply to all people
crossing the margin between social groups. And his
simple definition of a group as people sharing an
"interdependence of fate" is still the most profound one I have seen, and when one reflects that
it was written in 1939, it is chillingly prophetic.
What I have found least enlightening in the
literature were surveys of this or that set of
characteristics of Jews in the United States.[2-7]
Without a point of view or an organizing structure,
it is difficult to know what to make of much of
these data. I do not know that much insight is
given into Jewish life by research data which
reveals, for example, that Jews are relatively high

in verbal scales and low in performance scales[8] or
that we show less alcoholism and more diabetes[9] or
that we have a relatively low rate of admission to
state mental hospitals or low suicide, but tend to
be high in diagnoses of psychoneurosis and manic-
depressive disorders.[10,11] I, for one, could not
get very excited by such research information, nor
could I reflexively accept the self-evident validity of the calls for more research on the social-
psychological characteristics of Jews.[12] Without
clear purpose and contexts, such research, in my
view, is not particularly enlightening.

In any case, in approaching the writing of
this chapter, it became clear to me that if I could
make a contribution, it would come from applying
the frame-work with which I am most conversant, the
psychoanalytic one, to the topic of Jewish life in
the United States.

Further, a psychoanalytic viewpoint may provide some insights into the critical psychological
role played by tradition and values and it is
around this issue that I would like to organize my
remarks.

My main thesis, following Erikson, will be
that cultural, ethnic, religious, and even political tradition contribute importantly to the formation of ego identity and integrity. This is as
true for other traditions as it is for Jewish
life. My second thesis, also not an original one,
is that a particular crisis of modern life is the
relative absence of sustaining traditions.

In the early days of psychoanalytic theory, it
used to be thought that instinctual gratification,
defined mainly in terms of sexual, and, to a lesser
extent, aggressive, needs were the primary imperative and that the vicissitudes of such gratification were the primary determinants of personality
development. The early infant-mother relationship
was characterized as "anaclitic," which meant that
the mother's importance to the infant leaned on the
former's role as supplier and gratifier of the primary instinctual needs. The claim was that the
infant's attachment to mother was a secondary derivative of the mother's role in gratifying the
traditional primary needs of hunger, thirst,
shelter, among others. A clear implication of this
view is that the baby would not form an attachment
to its mother were it not for this role. A defini-
tive experiment by Harlow and Zimmerman,[13] however,
showed that infant monkeys consistently fed by a
bare artificial wire mother will nevertheless
develop an intense attachment to an artificial

terrycloth mother that provides what Harlow called
"contact comfort." Further, Harlow reported that
if one raises infant monkeys in a bare cage, without any mothers at all, the infant mortality rate
will drop if one includes in that cage an ordinary
piece of cheesecloth. Now these findings power-
fully demonstrate that independent of the so-called
primary needs, such as hunger and thirst, primates
have a need for objects from which they can satisfy
their "contact comfort" needs.

A good deal of research during the last number
of years, with animals and humans, provides evidence for the existence of an instinctual attachment system that is relatively independent of the
universally recognized biological needs. It has
been shown that even when these needs are met, that
is, even when an infant is well fed, kept warm and
clean, he will not develop favorably without a constant relationship with a caretaker, without what
is referred to in psychoanalytic theory, an object-
relation.[14-17] Thus, right from the start, man (as
well as other primates) does not live by bread
alone. Right from the start, man is a being who
cannot survive without ties to objects in the
world. In this fact lies the biological roots of
community and culture.

That an infant cannot physically survive
without the physical care of an adult is evident.
And this is, of course, a most important biological
function of mothering and attachment. But, less
obviously, an infant cannot psychologically survive
without constant object relations. What does it
mean to say that an infant cannot psychologically
survive without object relations? It means, among
other things, that functions which comprise our
humanness will be impaired--functions such as mediating reality, remembering, thinking, conscience,
and the development of sense of self and identity,
of individual personhood. To state it in a somewhat different way, from the very start, our
physical and psychological survival requires some
minimum degree of community.

Let me elaborate a bit more on the development
of object relations. To the young infant, who has
not yet developed a stable sense of self or even
separation between self and other, the mother is a
sort of auxiliary self, and the world is not yet
the world of stable objects that we, as adults
experience. Long periods of absence from its
mother cannot be well tolerated during a period
when the infant cannot yet conceive of an object
which can be present at one time and absent at

another time. One of the hallmark developmental
achievements is the new capacity of the infant to
look for something, maintain an interest in an
object when it is absent. This achievement, called
"object permanence" by Piaget, means that the
infant has, on his level, grasped that an object
continues to exist even when it is not perceptually
present. The world has become more stable, more
constant. This wonderful new cognitive achievement
enables the infant to tolerate mother's absence
better (for reasonable periods of time) because now
she continues to exist psychologically even while
absent. One can say that memory has been achieved
and, as an integral part of memory, the capacity to
form a rudimentary symbol that is, a memory image.

The cognitive development of the child continues and another hallmark is the formation of
what Winnicott called "transitional objects."[18] We
are all familiar with the remains of the favorite
blanket or teddy bear which is taken to bed, on
trips, and all places in which the child is likely
to be anxious. As Winnicott notes, the "transitional object" is transitional in at least two
senses: in the sense that the child is at a transitional stage in the move from complete dependence
to psychological separation and autonomy, and in
the sense that the "transitional object" represents
a transitional stage in the development of true
symbols. Like an abstract symbol, the "transitional object" represents mother, in its capacity
to comfort and soothe the child and yet, it is
responded to, in a somewhat magical way as if it
itself had direct soothing and comforting properties. According to Winnicott, in transitional
phenomena such as the "transitional object" lie the
individual beginnings of culture.

As development proceeds, we give up specific
"transitional objects," but the psychological
process represented by this and other transitional
phenomena continues. As Winnicott puts it, we
introject environmental supports. What was once
carried by somewhat magical external objects is now
internalized. What helps make us feel at home in
the world and not entirely alone, even when
physically alone, continues to be ties to objects
in the world, but now includes objects as internally represented. That is to say, what now ties
us to the world are our beliefs, ideologies,
values, feelings, interests, and internalized
traditions. I am suggesting, following Winnicott,
that our hobbies, interests, attachments serve a
psychological function similar to the one served by

the child's "transitional objects." These enable
us to feel at home in the world. I am not saying
that cultural and intellectual interests are
nothing but transitional phenomena. Of course,
these pursuits have their own functional
autonomy. I am saying, however, that their
developmental history as well as one of the important psychological functions they serve can be seen
in the context of transitional phenomena.

The most important psychological function
served by ties to objects in the world, by feeling
at home in the world has to do with the maintenance
and growth of integrity of self, of personhood.
Both developmentally and in adult functioning, an
intact sense of self cannot be maintained without
affective and cognitive ties to the world. We have
already referred to this in relation to the infant. Failure to establish stable ties with objects successfully results in failure to develop an
intact sense of self.

There is a good deal of evidence from a
variety of sources that the same thing, although
more complex and subtle, is true of adult functioning. For example, a frequent report from the
horrors of the concentration camp experience is
that the prisoners most likely to survive, both
physically and psychologically, were the ones who
had some kind of attachment, cognitive or affective, to another person, to an ideal, to a profound
interest, to religious teachings, to a future
plan -- that is, people who had strong ties to
objects (represented internally) in the
world.[19,20] One also finds in reports of ordinary
prisoners that psychological integrity and even
personality growth are made possible during
imprisonment by the development of interests and
acquisition of an ideology.[21,22] In artificially
induced conditions of isolation, as in sensory
deprivation where subjects are kept in a state of
social isolation with as little as possible sensory
input, people with rich inner lives are less
subject to anxiety, distress, and partial breakdown
of functioning. Finally, in clinical work, one
finds that some patients who seem quite disturbed,
by the usual diagnostic criteria, are able to
maintain reasonably adequate functioning and
intactness, often on a higher level than less
severly disturbed patients through the sustaining
power of an abiding interest or commitment. What
all this evidence suggests is that in conditions of
stress and isolation, the capacity for internalized

ties to the world helps maintain personality,
integrity, and intactness of self.

At this point, I would hope that the connection between the material I have presented and
the idea of tradition is clear. The experience and
appreciation of tradition is one important expression of internalized ties to the world. The acquisition and internalization of any set of values
partakes of the process of tradition. Through
these values one expresses a tie, a connection to
at least one earlier generation and to the historical process of the society in which one lives. As
Erikson puts it, one develops ties of fidelity to
certain objects in the world.[23] What I am
suggesting, in the present context, is that the
sense of tradition is both an expression of and a
contribution to a sense of one's place (one's ties
to internalized objects) in the world and in a part
of its history. Like the child's transitional
object, the sense of tradition permits one to recall one's home (and its self-sustaining functions)
while away from home. Of course, while the attachment to the transitional object is, in fact, an
attachment to an external object, one's sense of
tradition involves an attachment to a whole range
of internalized historical aspects and objects of
the world.

Also like the child's transitional object, a
sense of tradition involves responding, not simply
to mere objects and events in the world, but to the
meanings of these objects and events. After all,
the raggedy blanket is not, in itself, comforting
and soothing. It derives its soothing and comforting potential from the meaning it is given, its
representation of home and mother. Similarly, a
sense of tradition involves the response not simply
to events and objects in the world but to the meanings given to these events and objects. That we
respond to meanings of events is not, of course, a
startling statement. The point I am trying to make
here, however, is that having ties to the world
necessarily involves experiencing meanings. To
experience the world as meaningless is to have no
ties to it and, conversely, to experience no
cognitive or affective ties to the world is to
experience it as meaningless. As the phenomenon of
the "transitional object" shows, we create the
meanings of objects (the blanket, in a certain
sense, means mother, home) and then employ these
meanings (as if they resided in the object) to
sustain the self (when I have my blanket, I am
safe). Similarly with tradition, we create the

meanings of our history and then look at these
meanings to sustain us.

Fingarette has argued that the essesce of
anxiety is the experience of meaninglessness.[24]
Others, object relations theorists for example,
have argued that the essence of anxiety is separation and isolation from others, and therefore they
have proposed that the basic form of anxiety is
separation anxiety. It seems to me that similar
phenomena are being described for, as I have argued
above, meaning is created through ties to objects
and meaninglessness accompanies the absence of such
ties. The connection of all this to the idea of
tradition lies in the fact that a sense of tradition, insofar as it imbues past and present
events with meaning, enables one to establish ties
to objects in the world and hence, is a force which
serves to sustain personality integrity and ego
identity.

A good deal of epidemiological research has
recently been reported which deals with effects of
social environment upon physical and mental
health. Much of the reported evidence can be
interpreted in terms of the critical importance of
the stability of object ties for physical and mental integrity. Let me offer some examples. Adults
living alone, with few or no attachments to family,
kin, neighbors or any other group are more suscep-
tible to tuberculosis,[25] multiple accidents,[26-28]
alcoholism, schizophrenia and suicide. A
dramatic finding is that widowers in the year
following their bereavement showed a mortality rate
of 40 percent above that of married men of the same
age.[29] Other findings suggest the importance of
ethnic group supports. Rabkin and Struening conclude that "as a given ethnic group constitutes a
smaller proportion of the total population in a
particular area, diagnosed rates of mental illness
increase both in comparison to the rates for other
ethnic groups in that area and to members of the
same ethnic group in neighborhoods where they constitute a significiant proportion or majority."[30]
This finding has been observed with Chinese in
Canada,[31] French and English in Quebec,[32] and black
and white residents of various census tracts in
Baltimore.[33]

The importance of group supports has been
shown in recent studies on the psychological fate
of holocaust survivors. Eidinger attributes the
fact that Norwegian Jewish concentration camp
survivors have managed better than non-Jewish
Norwegian survivors to the "close-knit milieu and

the active acceptance and support of the small
Jewish community in Norway."[34]   Klein also im-
plicates group support and "group identity" in the
readaptation and reintegration of holocaust survivors on kibbutzim in allowing the survivors to
"reinterpret their holocaust experiences in a
context of meaningfulness" and in permitting a
"historic continuity with the past."[35]   Thus, not
only, as noted earlier (in referring to the work of
Bettelheim and Frankl) do object ties make for survival in the extreme conditions of the concentration camps, but also increase the likelihood of
personal and social integration following survival.
    There is also a vast literature relating
changes in social environment and personal life
changes to the incidence of physical and mental
illness.[36]   There is evidence that the magnitude of
life changes, whether positive or negative, is
positively correlated with subsequent physical and
mental illness. Other studies have suggested that
whether life changes will lead to illness is a
function of their interaction with other variables,
a particularly important one being degree of social
support available.[37]   The findings described above
reflect clearly the powerful importance of ties to
others in the world. I would interpret the more
general findings on effects of change in a similar
fashion. Radical change makes more difficult the
establishment and maintenance of ties to objects in
the world and thereby threatens personality (and
physical) integrity. I would also suggest that the
presence of internal structures, such as systems of
values and traditions, modulates the stressful
effects of change. In other words, as in the more
extreme conditions of concentration camps and imprisonment discussed earlier, the internalization
of object ties enables one to maintain personality
integrity in the face of external vicissitudes.
    My delineation of, so to speak, the virtues of
values and traditions can be understood, or rather,
misunderstood as a kind of inspirational suggestion
to "go develop values and traditions; they're good
for you." Such advice would be similar to the advice given people who experience meaninglessness
and apathy to "go develop interests." One of the
sobering facts of life is that things such as
values, traditions, and interests are organic
phenomena, they grow out of the conditions of one's
life and cannot directly be pursued, at least not
in any meaningful way. It is one of the ironies of
the human condition that ends devoutly to be desired, such as happiness, meaning, serenity, and, I

add, having interests, values, and a sense of
tradition, are by products of a way of life rather
than goals to be pursued directly. Direct pursuit
only renders these states and goals more elusive
and chimerical. Another way to put it is to say
that these goals are developmental, that is, are
historical phenomena, and emerge as a product of a
way of life. One is reminded of the situation in
which someone who, in the wake of a recent retirement (or divorce or widowhood or whose children
have all grown up), develops a depression and is
given the advice to develop interests. What this
advice overlooks is that the development of true
interests emerges out of a way of life. What often
occurs in these cases, when the advice appears to
work, is that earlier abandoned or even nascent
interests are rediscovered. For example, in
someone very close to me, the synagogue and its
community life begin to play a central role in
social life, and an earlier interest, abandoned for
many years, is rediscovered and pursued again. But
this person, rather than developing new interests,
is drawing on the earlier interests and meanings of
his life.

The search for immediate interests to fill up
a life that has been rather abruptly emptied of the
usual activities is not unlike the search for instant religious and value affiliations which characterizes many of the current religious sects and
fads. Many young people seek objects of fidelity
and, not finding it in their personal histories and
in their families and community, find these immediate objects of fidelity and devotion in this or
that new religious movement. The tenacity of such
movements only attests to the power of the need for
ties to objects in the world. And the shallowness,
exploitation, and simple hype that characterizes
such movements only attest to the futility and
mindlessness of attempts to create instant fidelity, devotion, and tradition. Keniston notes both
that "an increasing number of young people are
disaffected from the historical institutions of our
society" and that "they wish there were values,
goals, or institutions to which they could be
genuinely committed; they continue to search for
them...."[38] And, as one student replied in a
recent survey of Jewish students' religious and
secular attitudes, "Nothing is permanent anymore.
We're looking for a rock that remains unchanged and
we can't find it."[39] It is such longings and needs
that are exploited by the religious cults and fads.

What about attempts not to create fidelity,
and tradition, but to maintain or revitalize traditions that are already part of our history? That
is, what about the maintenance and revitalization
of Jewish life, tradition, and fidelity in the
United States? And here one would have to say that
the problem of maintenance and revitalization is
not that different from the problem of creation of
tradition. For each generation's psychologically
significant tradition and heritage are experienced
in its lifetime. The psychological question is not
simply one of how rich and ancient the tradition
but to what extent one's life experiences take
place in a ground and context which assimilate and
reflect the heritage. Or, to put it another way,
the question is whether one's current context and
one's historical tradition, as a people, can be
meaningfully related to each other.

In an informal study of American Jewish
teenagers done some years ago, Boroff concluded
that "viewed in historical terms, the image that
Jewish teenagers have of their milieu represents a
decisive break with the past. The sense of
uniqueness--as special destiny--seems to be fad-
ing. Jewish life is conceived of as middle class,
nonideological, and entirely consonant with the
dominant modes of American life."[40] He also
observed that while most of these teenagers believe
in maintaining a Jewish identity, they lack
sufficient reasons for justifying their position.

My own answers to this question--and I have no
evidence, but only informal observation and sense
of the matter--are consistent with Boroff's conclusions and entail strong doubts as to whether
Jewish life in the United States provides a meaningful ground for the maintenance of Jewish
history, values, or traditions. That is, to put
the matter simply, I find it difficult to see
distinctive aspects or qualities of current Jewish
life in the United States that would provide objects of fidelity and devotion, that would enrich
ego identity, and that serve the need to find meaningful ties to objects in the world. I do not believe that is solely or even largely the fault of
Jewish institutions but simply a question of the
ground not being sufficiently organic or fertile
for the nourishment and growth of Judaism and
Yiddishkeit. I can see other things growing in
this ground, but not Yiddishkeit. Furthermore, I
view some reactions and efforts of many spokesmen
for Jewish institutions--and I do not mean this to
be insulting--as not that different in form from

the efforts made by spokesmen for the new cults.
It is simply that the latter are generally more
successful. What both have in common are such
things as self-conscious attempts to win support,
to count numbers, to launch campaigns. Neither, so
to speak, grows from the earth. Judaism and other
established religions have hundreds and thousands
of years of history and tradition, but, as noted
earlier, it is the congruence between that history
and current life that matters. Indeed, the
advantage held by the cults and sects is that they
are free to invent and tailor history (as well as
philosophy, creeds, and values) in order to create
an apparent relevance.

I am familiar with the stance, as I'm sure you
are, that concerns with traditions, -- ethnic and
religious, -- for example, are misguided and
inappropriately parochial in a period of instant
communication, universalism, and a concept of the
world as a McLuhanesque global village. I can
recall never being able to appreciate Pasternak's
Dr. Zhivago fully because of my smoldering
resentment at his brotherly suggestion that Jews
solve the "Jewish question" by giving up their
irrationally stubborn insistence on preserving
Judaism and express a true universal spirit by
adopting Christianity. I can also recall a
symposium published in Commentary in 1961 in which
a number of young Jewish intellectuals were asked
to write about the influences and experinces that
shaped their thought. Almost to a man, the
respondents seemed to go out of their way to deny
the importance of parochial experiences and
stressed instead the universality of their
spirit. It may be difficult to imagine such
responses during the present new respectability and
desirability of ethnicity, which, after all, is by
definition, parochial. But such, indeed, were
their responses. I felt then as I do now that
these intellectuals both confused ends with means
and also misrepresented the ends. They failed to
see that the end or goal or universalism can only
be achieved through parochial means. That is, universal ideals that are not simply empty intellectual abstractions are achieved through concrete,
that is, parochial, experiences and meanings.
Whatever flesh and blood universalism may have is
given by concrete and experiences and struggles.

I want to link this point to what is really
the main theme of this chapter. Insofar as objects
are concrete, and insofar as we achieve ego identity and meaning through ties to objects in the

world, a universalism that is not simply an ab-
straction must necessarily have emerged through
concreteness. The point can be made another way by
returning to mother and child. The adult who has
become capable of a true universal spirit was once
an infant embedded in a biological-affective libid-
inal matrix of a quality unique to him, parochial
in its very essence. If his universalism is truly
human, it will have emerged organically from this
early matrix and will, in very subtle ways, reflect
its early roots and early ties. The relationship
between mother and child is always concrete, parochial, and so is, I believe, any human relationship between man and man. Any universalism which
overlooks this fact has permitted ideology to
dominate flesh and blood. It usually leads to an
objectification of man and permits what to Kant was
the cardinal ethical violation, namely, the treatment of man as an object and his subjection as a
means to an end.

Emperor Hadrian is supposed to have said of
the Jews that they are a strange people, up to
their eyes in a cloaca, with their brows touching
heaven. I have always found that description extremely moving and have felt that it captures an
essential differences between Judaism and
Christianity. Judaism is more embedded and embodied, less free of the cloaca, less abstractedly
spiritual--that is, more parochial. And herein
lies a major crisis for Judaism; it is a parochial
way of life in an increasingly nonparochial
world. I hope it is clear by now that by "parochial" I do not mean narrow. For I believe that
the crisis I refer to is a particularly modern one
that affects us all, Jew and non-Jew. If I am
correct in believing that our ties to objects in
the world are always mediated through parochial
means, then the inhospitability of our social
ground to parochialism affects us all. And these
effects can be seen in a variety of expressions
ranging from greater susceptibility to physical and
mental illness, to problems in defining one's ego
identity and selfhood, to a vague sense of root-
lessness and lack of community. The crisis, then,
of Jewish life is but one expression of the general
crisis of how we relate to the world, a world that
is complex, ever-changing, technological, unstable,
abstract.

Ethologists use the term "environment of
evolutionary adaptiveness" to refer to the environment to which early man's naturally selected
evolutionary characteristics were suited. This

environment, according to the ethologists, was
pretechnological, pre-agricultural, that is, in a
certain sense, "precultural." It was one in which
man's survival mode was as hunter-gatherer. This
formulation is certainly consistent with Ernst
Cassirer's description of early man as being part
of nature.[41] That is, society had not yet been
fully created to stand opposite nature. But, of
course, society was created and its creation immediately presented the problem of how to relate to
the world. For now the relation could no longer be
one of unreflective embeddedness in nature but
required a self-conscious apposition of man to
nature as well as man to man. Of course, this
story that philosophers and ethologists tell is, in
essence, remarkably like the biblical one: from
the unreflective embeddedness in nature, the Garden
of Eden, via the Tree of Knowledge, to disembeddedness and self-relectiveness, that is, to the possibility of culture.
      With self-reflectiveness and the creation of
culture, one must solve the related problems of
identity, meaning, relatedness, and ties to the
world. For, it turns out, we are peculiar creatures. We are born with the biological imperative
of attachment; that is, we cannot survive nor can
we define ourselves without ties to objects in the
world. And we are also born with the biological
capacity and imperative to disembed ourselves from
early attachment and from nature. We create culture which then confronts us with the problem of
finding new ways to connect with the world. The
early Jews found a remarkable means of finding rich
meanings and of relating to the world. They were,
not people of the land, but people of the book and
their God was abstract and ubiquitous, not con-
cretized or represented, not limited to time or
place. In this sense, the history of the Jews
reflects most clearly the disembeddedness from
nature and the successful creation of culture. I
say successful because profound meanings, ties, and
traditions were created which enabled one to live
with a sense of identity and community in an environment that was no longer one of evolutionary
adaptiveness. Expulsion from the Garden of Eden
(that is, from nature) could only mean physical and
psychic annihilation unless community and identity
could be created. And, indeed, community and
identity were created. The modern crisis that
faces us is that we are still in our environment of
evolutionary non-adaptiveness, and I hope it is
clear that I am using this phrase borrowed from the

ethologists almost as a symbolic abbreviation of
the stresses, complexity, and demands of our social
environments--and our traditional vehicles and
means for providing community and identity no
longer serve us.

If I may return for a moment to the domain
with which I am most conversant, psychoanalysis, it
is interesting that Freud was little concerned in
his theory with issues of ego identity and meaning. With regard to the latter, Freud remarked
that promptings to ask questions regarding the
meaning of life were pathological expressions.
With regard to the former, it was not until Erik
Erikson's work in the United States and the work of
the so-called object relations theorists in England
that issues of ego identity and intactness of self
became prominent issues in psychoanalytic formu-
lations. For Freud, man's major life issues were
how to achieve instinctual gratification in the
face of the complex and often conflicting demands
of reality considerations, social prohibitions and
rules, and the internalized rules of conscience.
When one reads Freud, it seems clear that, as with
the question of meaning, the question of identity
is taken for granted. Surely, the greater social
stability of Freud's era had something to do with
the tacit assumption that questions of identity and
meaning were non-problematic. By contrast, current
psychoanalytic writings are virtually preoccupied
with problems of identity and self. As any therapist knows, a large proportion of today's patients
present, as their major concern, not so much
specific, circumscribed distressing symptoms, but
vague complaints of a sense of meaninglessness and
emptiness. When the more traditional neurotic
symptons do appear, and they are frequently part of
the problem, they are generally accompanied by the
feelings of aimlessness I have mentioned.

As Erkison notes, ". . . the patient of today
suffers most under the problem of what he should
believe in and who he should--or, indeed, might--be
or become; while the patient of early psychoanalysis suffered most under inhibitions which
prevented him from being what and who he thought he
knew he was."[42]

In the past five to six years, there have been
a number of books (I have counted eleven) and many
articles in psychoanalytic journals on so-called
borderline conditions and narcissistic personality
disorders. I bring this up here because these
conditions are characterized particularly by disturbances in self-cohesiveness and by difficulties

in developing stable value and interest systems and
in forming meaningful ties to objects in the
world. These difficulties and disturbances are
often related in the literature to faults in early
mothering and it is highly likely that early de-
privations play a central role. It seems to me,
however, that the prevalence of these conditions
also reflects the unavailability of stable social
structures and values systems. Confusions and
radical discontinuities in these areas affect us
all, but I would imagine that they would affect
with particular force individuals whose early
experiences have left them with relatively unstable
inner structures. They, particularly, require
external nutriment and structure. But, and this is
often the case with clinical phenomena, the patho-
logy presents clearly and in extreme form issues
which confront us all, but which in most of us have
not led to responses of clinical proportions. And
the issues, to repeat, have to do with the avail-
ability of a social-cultural context which will
permit the formation of internalized meanings, of
ties to objects in the world, and an intact self.
Jewish life once represented such a context, but, I
believe, there are strong doubts whether it continues to do so.
     Whether we can find new meanings and a
revitalization of social and cultural context is an
open question. What disturbs me is that the new
meanings, new cults, new quasi-ideologies that have
emerged during the last number of years are sin-
gularly unimpressive in their intellectual and
spiritual content.
     The gobbledygook of McLuhanism, the analysis
of society offered by counterculture critics, the
antiscientific stance of the new humanisms, the
jargon and antirationality of this or that so-
called spiritual or religious cult are all remarkably shallow and glib. What counts as evidence
sometimes boggles the mind. I remember in one
class lecture trying to provide an example of
specious reasoning to Chariot of the Gods. Much to
my amazement and sorrow, a large number of students, even after much discussion, simply could not
understand that anything was wrong with the evidence and reasoning contained in the book. In my
experience as a professor teaching young under-
graduates and graduates I see evidence that our
intellectual heritage is in jeopardy. As should be
no surprise, Jewish students are no less likely
than other to be impressed with Chariot of the
Gods, to engage in specious reasoning, to show a

shallow grasp and engagement with a subject
matter. Freud once mentioned two traits which he
felt he owed to his Jewish ancestry: a broad
intellectual outlook and the readiness to live in
opposition.[43] I do not see impressive evidence
that Jewish students are especially aware of this
heritage.

I know I have sounded quite pessimistic and
Jeremiah-like, but as far as I am aware, I have not
done so for dramatic effect or any other peripheral
reason. What I have described is what I believe is
the case with regard to the possibilities of developing and maintaining traditional ties in contemporary America. It may be that I am too old and too
rigid to appreciate the virtues of the newer
values, beliefs, and rituals that have emerged in
our time. Perhaps from these confusions will
emerge new and richer meanings and new ways of
relating to the world. Only time will tell.

Some take comfort in the fact that
contemporary alarms at the state of culture echo
past disaffections. My own view is that at least
some past concerns were merely prescient regarding
the direction of our culture. Thus, the conclusion
of The Protestant Ethic and the Spirit of
Capitalism". In describing the "iron cage" of
material goods, Weber writes "No one knows who will
live in this cage, in the future, or whether at the
end of this tremendous development entirely new
prophets will arise, or there will be a great
rebirth of old ideas and ideals, or, if neither,
mechanized petrifaction, embellished with a sort of
convulsive self-importance. For of the last stage
of this cultural development, it might truly be
said: 'Specialist without spirit, sensualists
without heart; this nullity imagines that it has
attained a level of civilization never before
achieved.'"[44]

NOTES

1. K. Lewin, in K. Lewin and G. W. Allport, eds.,
   Resolving Social Conflicts: Selected Papers on
   Group Dynamics (New York: Harper and Row,
   1948).
2. J. A. Fishman, "Social Science Research
   Relevant to American Jewish Education" (First
   Annual Bibliographic Review)," Jewish
   Education, vol. 28 (1957), pp. 49-60.

3. _____ "Social Science Research Relevant to American Jewish Education" (Second Annual Bibliographic Review), Jewish Education, vol. 29 (1959), pp. 64-71.

4. _____ "Social Science Research Relevant to American Jewish Education" (Third Annual Bibliographic Review), Jewish Education, vol. 30 (1960), pp. 35-45.

5. V. D. Sanua, "Social Science Research Relevant to American Jewish Education" (Fourth Annual Bibliographic Review), Jewish Education, vol. 32 (1962), pp. 99-114.

6. _____ "Social Science Research Relevant to American Jewish Education," (Fifth Bibliographic Review), Jewish Education, vol. 33 (1963), pp. 163-175.

7. _____ "Social Science Research Relevant to American Jewish Education," (Sixth Bibliographic Review), Jewish Education, vol. 34 (1964), pp. 187-202.

8. B. M. Levinson, "Some Research Findings with Jewish Subjects of Traditional Backgrounds," Mental Hygiene, vol. 47 (1963), pp. 129-134.

9. K. Gorwitz, "Jewish Mortality in St. Louis and St. Louis County, 1955-1957," Jewish Social Studies, vol. 24 (1962), pp. 248-254.

10. E. R. Ellis and G. N. Allen, Traitor Within: Our Suicide Problem (New York: Doubleday and Co., 1961).

11. L. Srole and T. Langner, "Religious Origins," in L. Srole, T. Langner, S. T. Michael, M. K. Opler, and T. A. C. Rennip, Mental Health in The Metropolis: Midtown Manhattan Study, vol. 1, (New York: McGraw-Hill, 1962), pp. 300-324.

12. V. D. Sanua, "A Review of Social Science: Studies on Jews and Jewish Life in the United States," Journal for the Scientific Study of Religion, vol. 4 (1964), pp. 71-83.

13. H. G. Harlow and R. R. Zimmerman, "Affectional Responses in the Infant Monkey," Science, vol. 130 (1959), pp. 421-432.

14. R. A. Spitz, "Anxiety in Infancy," International Journal of Psychoanalysis, vol. 31 (1950), pp. 138-143.

15. _____ The First Year of Life (New York: International Universities Press, 1965).

16. J. Bowlby, Attachment and Loss: Attachment, vol. 1 (New York: Basic Books, 1969).

17. _____ Attachment and Loss: Separation, vol. 2 (New York: Basic Books, 1973).

18. D. W. Winnicott, "Transitional Objects and Transitional Phenomena," in D. W. Winnicott,

Through Pediatrics to Psychoanalysis (New York: Basic Books 1975), pp. 229-242.

19. B. Bettelheim, *The Informed Heart: Autonomy in a Mass Age* (New York: Free Press, 1960).

20. V. Frankl, *Man's Search for Meaning: An Introduction to Logotherapy* (Boston: Beacon Press, 1962).

21. Malcolm X, *The Autobiography of Malcolm X* (New York: Grove Press, 1964).

22. G. Jackson, *Soledad Brothers: The Prison Letters of George Jackson* (New York: Coward-McCann, 1970).

23. E. Erikson, "Youth: Fidelity and Diversity," in E. Erikson, ed., *The Challenge of Youth* (New York: Anchor Books, 1965), pp. 1-23.

24. H. Fingarette, *The Self in Transformation* (New York: Harper and Row, 1973).

25. T. H. Holmes, "Multidiscipline Studies of Tuberculosis," in P. J. Sparer, ed., *Personality Stress and Tuberculosis* (New York: International Universities Press, 1956), pp. 65-152.

26. J. Cassel and A. Leighton, "Epidemiology and Mental Health," in S. F. Goldston, ed., *Mental Health Considerations Public Health* (Washington, D.C.: Public Health Services, 1969).

27. A. Linsky, "Who Shall Be Excluded? The Influence of Personal Attributes in Community Reaction to the Mentally Ill," Social Psychiatry, vol. 5 (1970), pp. 166-171.

28. L. Levy and L. Rowitz, *The Ecology of Mental Disorder* (New York: Behavioral Publications, 1973).

29. C. Parkes, B. Benjamin and R. Fitzgerald, "Broken Heart: A Statistical Study of Increased Mortality Among Widowers," British Medical Journal (1969), vol. 1, pp. 740-743.

30. J. G. Rabkin and E. L. Struening, "Social Change, Stress, and Illness: Selective Literature Review," in T. Shapiro, ed., *Psychoanalysis and Contemporary Science*, vol. 5 (New York: International Universities Press, 1976) pp. 573-624.

31. H. B. M. Murphy, "Social Change and Mental Health," in *Milbank Memorial Fund Conference, Causes of Mental Disorders: A Review of Epidemiological Knowledge* (New York: Milbank Memorial Fund, 1961).

32. D. Sydiaha and I. Rootman, "Ethnic Groups Within Communities: A Comparative Study of the Expression and Definition of Mental Illness,"

Psychiatric Quarterly, vol. 43 (1969), pp. 131-146.

33. G. Klee, E. Spiro, A. Bahn and K. Gorwitz, "An Ecological Analysis of Diagnosed Mental Illness in Baltimore," in R. Monroe, G. Klee, and E. Brody, eds., Psychiatric Epidemiology and Mental Health Planning, Psychiatric Research Report 22 (American Psychiatric Association, 1967), pp. 107-148.

34. L. Eidinger, "Jewish Concentration Camp Survivors in Norway," Israel Annuals of Psychiatry and Related Disciplines, vol. 13 (1975), pp. 321-334.

35. H. Klein, "Holocaust Survivors in Kibbutzim; Readaptation and Reintegration," Israel Annuals of Psychiatry and Related Disciplines, vol. 10 (1972), pp. 78-91.

36. J. G. Rabkin and E. L. Struening, op. cit.

37. C. Nuckolls, J. Cassel, and B. Kaplan, "Psychosocial Assets, Life Crises, and the Prognosis of Pregnancy," American Journal of Epidemiology, vol. 95 (1972), pp. 431-441.

38. K. Keniston, "Social Change and Youth in America," in E. Erikson, ed., The Challenge of Youth (New York: Anchor Books, 1965), pp. 161-187.

39. J. N. Nusan, B. Rachovsky, and A. B. Agrillo, "The Jewish Student: A Comparative Analysis of Religious and Secular Attitudes," YIVO Annual of Jewish Social Science, vol. 15 (1974), pp. 297-338.

40. D. J. Boroff, "Jewish Teenager Culture," Annuals of the American Academy of Political and Social Science, vol. 338 (1961), pp. 79-90.

41. E. Cassirer, An Essay on Man (New Haven: Yale University Press, 1964).

42. E. Erikson, Childhood and Society, 2nd ed. (New York: W. W. Norton, 1963).

43. S. Freud, "Address to the Society of B'nai B'rith," in Standard Edition of the Complete Psychological Works, vol. 20. (London: Hogarth Press, 1959), pp. 272-274.

44. M. Weber, The Protestant Ethic and the Spirit of Capitalism, Trans. by T. Parsons (New York: Charles Scribner's Sons, 1958), p. 182.

Chapter IV

JEWISH LIFE IN THE UNITED STATES: SOCIAL AND POLITICAL VALUES

EVERETT CARLL LADD, JR.

Probably no topic involving the political position and commitments of Jews in the United states has received as much discussion as their political liberalism. I intend in this chapter to comment further on Jewish liberalism, but I have no intention of reviewing once again in detail what already has been firmly established. Among the latter, I would include the following: Jews are more liberal than any other white ethnocultural group. Jewish voters are typically more Democratic than any other white ethnocultural group. The liberalism of blacks and their high support for Democratic candidates represent a response consistent with their life situation in the sense that as a group they are notably deprived in social and economic terms. Jews throughout the entire post-World War II period have been responding politically in a manner which contradicts their life situation, as they are usually highly attaining socioeconomically while unusually supportive of liberal and change-oriented policies. Despite all of the speculation in the 1970's about a realignment of the Jewish vote in the face of new political-ideological alignments, the current "rank-ordering" of Democratic support finds Jewish voters during this period occupying about the same position nationally as they did three decades earlier; their relatively greater backing for Democratic presidential nominees, compared to other groups of whites, has not been diminished.[1]

THE FRACTURING OF LIBERALISM AND THE
RESPONSE OF JEWISH LIBERALS

It is very hard indeed to explore possible changes in the political stance of Jews in the United States without first being quite clear and specific as to what ideological changes are occurring within the public at large. Consider this basic if somewhat simplistic question: Are Jews becoming more conservative? Given one general usage of conservative and liberal, this query is not very helpful. Liberalism came into wide usage in the United States in the 1930s to refer to the programs and policies developed by the administration of Franklin D. Roosevelt. Central to New Deal liberalism was a greater reliance on the state as a primary instrument for national integration and national development, replacing the older business "nationalism." Also, the state was to be relied upon to assure that basic standards of living were met for the entire population, as, for example, through the provision of a minimum wage, unemployment insurance, social security, and welfare programs.[2]

As a number of people, including myself, have shown, there has been in the past, very broad acceptance among Americans of the general policy approach of the New Deal.[3] If the basic commitments of New Deal liberalism have won this widespread support, it would be quite inconceivable to find Jews turning away from the New Deal, toward conservatism in the New Deal sense. (One might, to be sure, find the relative distance between Jews and non-Jews decreasing, in terms of support for New Deal-type liberal programs, as backing for such policies has become generalized).

The question of whether or not Jews are becoming more conservative, becomes a serious one only when the contemporary ideological fracturings -- and the new meanings of liberalism and conservatism -- are carefully considered. Here, I will have to beg the reader's indulgence. I will try to set forth fairly briefly the central characteristics of the new ideological division and its sources. It will not be possible to explore systematically all of the points being made. So I offer these observations as working hypotheses, which must be considered if this inquiry into the state of Jewish liberalism is to be fruitful.

THE NEW LIBERALISM AND THE NEW CONSERVATISM

Liberalism and conservatism in the New Deal setting were reasonably coherent ideological stands. There has been a fracturing of both positions over the last 15 years, but the fight among the heirs of New Deal liberalism is probably the more important to the future of American public policy. Surely, it is the more important in the context of this chapter because the preponderance of the American Jewish population was located in the New Deal liberal camp.

Let me, for a moment, jump ahead of my story. The appropriate question is not, Are Jews becoming conservative? Rather, it is, Are Jews moving toward the new conservative end of the ideological continuum which is emerging out of the fracturing of the New Deal liberalism?

CLASS CONFLICT AND IDEOLOGICAL CONFLICT

The division between the new liberalism and the new conservatism has arisen as the United States has entered upon a period with a structure of class conflict very different from the sort which became familiar during the New Deal era. In the Roosevelt years, indeed up through the 1950s, a middle class confronted a working class. The conflict was muted, as it always has been in the history of the United States, but it was real enough. It made its impact felt in formulation of public policy. It helped organize the partisan split. The middle class was more inclined to conservatism--in the New Deal usage of that term-- and the working class more to liberalism. The former group regularly gave more backing to the Republican party, the latter to the Democrats.

Today, the primary emergent form of class conflict pits a lower-middle class against an upper-middle class. This is profoundly confusing. It is not made much less so by this terminological improvement. The emergent conflict pits an "embourgeoised" working class against an "intelligentsia." Neither of these groups is conservative in the New Deal sense; both start out from the liberalism of Franklin Roosevelt. But they occupy markedly different places in contemporary American society, and thereby display contrasting needs, goals, values, and the like. The intelligentsia and its articulating interest groups are today inclined to a political stance which, given the

long-standing American preference for terminological confusion, is called liberalism. But
clearly the positions emphasized differ from those
of the New Deal era; ergo, it is the "new liberalism." The "new bourgeois" opponents dissent from
this new liberalism; they must, therefore, be mani-
festing a new conservatism. Were all this not confusing enough, the ascendant form of class conflict
and its ideological expression is not organized on
interparty lines, as was the conflict of the New
Deal years. It is concentrated, rather, within the
Democratic party.

Two key developments in social structure have
set the stage for the forms of conflict just suggested. First, the upper-middle class in the
United States has become increasingly an intelligentsia in contrast to (as was the case in times
past) a business class.[4]

Entrepreneurial business has found its position significantly weakened. Managerial business
remains an important stratum. But it experiences
peculiar fracturings which could not have been contemplated in earlier periods. Increasingly, large
segments of the broad, new upper-middle classes, of
the professional and managerial community--
primarily those at once the most affluent, secure,
and most closely associated with advanced technol-
ogy--cease to function as defenders of business
values. More to the point, they cease to think of
themselves as "business" in the historic sense.
They become incorporated into our rising "new
class," the intelligentsia, responding to intellectual values and orientations rather than those
traditionally associated with business.[5]

The extraordinary expansion of higher education in the post-World War II period is a key
factor defining the intelligentsia and its emergence as a new class. The number of students enrolled in degree-credit programs in the country's
colleges and universities--now about ten million--
is seven times greater than what it was on the eve
of World War II. College students are now nearly 5
percent of the total population of the country,
compared to just over 1 percent in 1940. Roughly
40 million Americans age 21 and older have received
college training at some level--30 percent of the
total population over 20 years of age. Some 16
percent of all Americans 21 years and older--about
21 million people--have completed at least four
years of formal college training.

This huge college population, as noted, seems
increasingly unlike a business class. About 60

percent of all college graduates hold professional
positions; only 17 percent occupy managerial and
administrative jobs.[6] These people share contact
with intellectual activity (which does not mean, of
course, that its members participate in high culture or advanced intellectual pursuits) through the
2,900 colleges and universities with some 600,000
faculty members. The size of this college population has made it the decisive, controlling audience
for an elaborate national communication structure.

As the American upper-middle class, through
the expansion and centralization or higher education and the emergence of the university as the
institution that disseminates ideas to the contemporary society, has been transformed into an intelligentsia from a business class, a new bourgeoisie
has appeared on the scene. The working class of
the Depression decade included people who were,
disproportionately, "have nots," and it behaved
accordingly. Today that working class has become
the new bourgeoisie. Surely, the skilled manual
workers and those in related blue-collar occupations have moved decisively into a "have," rather
than a "have not," economic position. Producing a
wonderfully American semantic contradiction, a
large segment of the working class has become
(lower) middle class.

A complex set of events brought this about,
but one stands out. In the quarter-century after
1947, the median income for all American families
almost doubled, junping from $5665 to $11,120
(these figures are adjusted for inflation based on
the 1972 purchasing power of the dollar). More
purchasing power was added at the level of individual families in this brief span than in all pre-
ceeding periods of American history combined. When
it is remembered, too, that at the close of World
War II the United States was an exceptionally
wealthy country by any historical or national comparative standard, the extent of this "abundance
revolution" is more sharply etched. A lot of people have moved a long way in their basic economic
position--needs, interests, tangible possessions,
and the like--through this momentous change.

The long-time patriarch of the American labor
movement, George Meany, once commented on the
transfiguration of labor's place as a result of the
economic advances wince World War II. In a 1969
interview with the New York Times, Meany was willing to accept both "middle class" and
"conservative" as descriptions of the membership of
the labor movement:

> Labor, to some extent, has become
> middle class. When you have no property,
> you don't have anything. You have nothing
> to lose by these radical actions. But you
> become a person who has a home and has
> property, to some extent you become con-
> servative. And I would say to that
> extent, labor has become conservative.[7]

A working class that is middle class and conserva-
tive--yes, that is a distinctive feature of the
contemporary social structure.

If This is so, What Then?

Some elements in the above argument can be
firmly established. Colleges and universities have
become vastly more central institutions in the
contemporary society. The size of the college-
trained population has increased enormously. Large
segments of the working class were economically
deprived in the 1930s and have acquired the kind of
economic status in our own day which we think of as
middle class. But other facets of the argument remain highly speculative. First and foremost here,
does much of the old working class now occupy a
position in social structure and hence in social
and political values which requires that one see it
as the new bourgeoisie? Is a large segment of the
upper-middle class so positioned in social structure that it manifests social and political values
of an intelligentsia? And as a result are these
two strata in persisting opposition on a wide range
of salient policy and value questions?

Survey data sustain one sort of empirical
inquiry that can be aimed at establishing--or,
conversely, rejecting--these more speculative
aspects of the argument. I first inquired as to
how the two strata should position themselves ideologically if the basic premises underlying the
argument are sound. And then I looked at survey
data to see whether the strata are in fact so
responding.

If the theory is generally well-founded, what
kind of ideological cleavage should have opened
up? Has it? If it has, the theoretical perspectives are not thereby established with the certi-
tude of the Pythagorean theorem, but they can be
offered with much the same assurance as the properties of the atom are explained by physicists.

Support System

These two broad strata should manifest significant differences in the way they feel about
American society and how critical they are of it.
There is no need to suggest massive alienation on
the one hand or overwhelming system support on the
other. But an upper-middle-class-as-intelligen-
tsia, sharing in the critical orientations vis-a-
vis the society and the culture long associated
with secular intellectuals, should be more system
challenging. The new bourgeoisie, like its counterparts of earlier eras, should defend the system. This should hold both on domestic as well as
foreign affairs.

Social Values

The college-educated, upper-middle class
should reduce its support for a range of traditional bourgeois values including commitments to
work, thrift, the importance of material acquisi-
tions, and the like, whereas the working class
should defend these old bourgeois values. The
higher strata should be more change oriented, more
inclined to reject traditional cultural norms and
lifestyles together with older codes of ethical behavior. Employing the terms in fairly casual
fashion, the new morality should receive its
strongest backing from college-educated professionals, and the old morality, its greatest backing
from the working class as the new bourgeoisie.

Economic Life

The two groups should differ in their attitudes toward economic growth and the relative importance of material as opposed to nonmaterial
values. Both because it has more in its economic
standing, and because as an intelligentsia it
should be increasingly disdainful of business values, the upper stratum, variously defined, would be
expected to give less emphasis to the importance of
continued high economic growth than the less affluent, aspiring new bourgeoisie. Specifically, the
former group should give more backing to the
environmentalist movement. It should be more
inclined to emphasize such values as "clean air"
when the pursuit of environmental cleanup collides
with the production requirements of industry. It

should place more emphasis on measures to curtail
energy use.

Views of the State

In the New Deal context, the working class
provided the main support for the growth of the
state. It should not be expected to have backed
off from a generally high level of support for the
kinds of governmental intervention pioneered during
the New Deal. But like other bourgeoisies, it can
be expected to worry increasingly about its pocket-
book, about inflation, about the impact of new
public spending programs on its economic position.
By way of contrast, the intelligentsia should
be notably in favor of the state--indeed, the pro-
state class of the contemporary United States.
This is so because large segments of the college-
educated, professional stratum--people in research
and development, in education, in public bureau-
cracies, and the like--are directly dependent upon
the state for their personal sustenance and for the
sustenance of the endeavors with which they are
associated. The upper-middle strata should thereby
give a higher level of backing to new governmental
programs and indeed to the whole range of public
spending than the old working class.

Interest Group Connections

The two strata should manifest distinctive
differences in their allegiance to various interest
groups. The most notable development involves attitudes toward unions. Labor was the font of American liberalism during the New Deal. Today the
upper-middle classes should be associated disproportionately with the new liberalism. At the same
time, in an interesting twist from the historic
experience, the new bourgeoisie, committed to the
"new conservatism" should operate as the pro-union
class. Hence the historically anomalous situation
of an upper-middle class which is more "liberal"
but is suspicious of unions, not from a traditional
business aversion to the union movement but on the
grounds unions are too "conservative."

A Scrambling of Categories

In times past, the people with a college education who hold professional, managerial, and related positions were associated with support for conservatism, while people with a grade school and high school education who have manual labor jobs support liberalism. The argument presented here suggests that a scrambling of these relationships has occurred.

The college educated now hold a place in an intelligentsia, while the high school educated, the blue-collar workers, have become a new bourgeoisie. The census categories, thus, remain the same, but the social-structural positions of the two groups are different. So, then, are the ideological commitments. Neither the new class (the intelligentsia) nor the working class (what is now a new bourgeoisie) should manifest much support for conservatism in its New Deal sense. The two strata should divide along the lines identified by the "new liberalism" and the "new conservatism."

Is this in fact the case?

The Findings In Capsule Form

I found that the college educated and the upper occupational groups of the New Deal era responded in substantial measure as a business class and thereby were inclined to conservatism, while the high school and grade school educated, and those in lower-status occupations, were a (relatively) change-oriented working class. In our era, by way of contrast, the opinions and attitudes of these groups has been strikingly reversed.

The distributions which I located on a broad range of issues makes sense only granted the assumption that the college and upper-professional people now favor change while the grade school- and high school-educated, and the blue-collar work force, probably to an increasing degree, favor stability.[8]

What is especially striking in the survey data is the consistency of the inversion of the old New Deal relationship of class and ideology, and the range of this inversion. Thus, those who are college trained are more "new liberal" than their high school- and grade school-trained counterparts not only on the social, cultural, and lifestyle issues that are so often discussed, but on a broad assortment of public-policy matters from economic

growth and environmentalism to foreign affairs and
national defense. And behind the specific issues
and the new relationships of the upper and lower
social strata lie more diffuse differences in views
of the society and of the state, in orientations
towards social change, in constituting social
values.

I employed literally scores of alternate con-
structions and ways of conceptualizing the basis
for the new class as I probed divisions over the
various policies and values associated with the new
liberalism. And consistently I found education
displaying the clearest and most unambiguous relationship to the new ideological divide. The "New
Liberalism Index" is introduced here not so much to
prove this point as to summarize it and to illustrate it.[9]

Table 1 shows the unusually strong relationship between higher education and support for the
new liberalism. Thus, 31 percent of those with
five years of college or more are recorded in the
"most supportive" quintile, compared to 23 percent
of those with one to three years of college, 13
percent of high school graudates, and just 11 percent of respondents with less than high school
training. No other variable discriminates so
strikingly. (All tables appear at end of chapter).

There are clear variations by occupation, and
these correspond roughly to the pattern prescribed
by various theoretical efforts dealing with the
occupational base of the new class and by other
studies of the sociopolitical perspectives of
groups within the intellectual stratum. Thus, professionals are clearly more liberal than managers
and (lower) white-collar workers. Among professionals, the social scientists, journalists, and
the literary group, give much more backing to the
new liberalism than do the engineers, natural
scientists, and those in applied professions like
medicine. These latter distributions parallel
almost exactly what Martin Lipset and I have repeatedly found among the American professors whereby social scientists and those in the humanities
are markedly more liberal than biological and physical scientists, and professors of engineering.[10]
And there presumably are common factors at work
accounting for these distributions, especially the
tendency of the various fields to attract people
quite disparate in political orientations, and the
capacity of the subject matter of a discipline to
define different subcultures which reach far beyond
the political dimension but which are linked to

proclivities toward sharply contrasting political
stances.

On the whole, though, the data tend to indicate that the differences separating the basic
occupational categories--professional, managerial,
white-collar, blue-collar--are more modest than
those which education alone produces. The most
applicable and narrowly defined occupational categories, such as "word workers," indicate that people are inclined to support the new liberalism, as
are those with a postgraduate education.

The distinction between profit and nonprofit
yields almost nothing. In fact, and contrary to
the usual expectations, professional men and women
employed by profit-making firms are consistently a
bit more liberal than are their counterparts in the
non-profit organizations.

What is even more telling is that when education is held constant, the occupation-related differences disappear completely. College-graduate
professionals, managers, and clerical workers and
sales and blue-collar people show almost identical
distributions on the New Liberalism Index and on
the entire range of specific issues we have been
discussing. By way of contrast, education-linked
variations are sharp within each occupational
category. Employing education and occupation together does not discriminate more sharply as to
support for or opposition to the new liberalism.
For example, 29 percent of those who are college
educated and in professional and managerial jobs
(new class) are in the most supportive quintile on
the new liberalism support index, compared to 11
percent of the grade school and high school educated who hold manual positions (the old class category). This is less of a differentiation than
education alone yields. It is important to stress
that the relationships I am describing hold all
across the spectrum of new liberal--new conservative policy questions--defense, foreign affairs,
views of the state, and social and cultural
issues. The liberalism measure employed faithfully
represents the degree and direction of differences
evident on a host of individual issues.

It would be overstating things to claim that
the analysis which I have performed "proves" the
emergence of a form of class conflict with tensions
between an intelligentsia and a new bourgeoisie.
However it has demonstrated the presence of some
consistent and persisting differences among the
social strata on a broad range of policy and value
questions which are exactly the sort one would

expect to find if the intelligentsia/new bourgeoisie conflict were emerging as postulated.

JEWS AND THE NEW LIBERALISM:
THE INVERSION IS VERY MUCH EVIDENT

Although the Jewish commitment to liberalism
has cut across all segments of the community, we
know that during the New Deal era it was more pronounced among those of lower socioeconomic stand-
ing--paralleling the relationship of class and
ideology in the American population at large. The
high-status Jewish voters most likely would break
with the Democrats and vote for more conservative
Republican nominees. Thus, Levy and Kramer found
that "in state after state, there was an urban-
suburban split in the 1960 Jewish presidential
vote. John Kennedy had no trouble at all with city
Jews, but with their suburban cousins his vote fell
substantially."[11] And Schneider, Berman, and
Schultz observe that "traditionally, lower-status
Jews have been more solidly Democratic in their
partisanship than higher-status Jews...."[12]
In the late 1960s and now in the 1970s, however, there have been clear signs of an electoral
inversion within the Jewish community, paralleling
once again that for the general populace.
Himmelfarb found that upper-middle class Jewish
communities in the greater New York area supported
McGovern in 1972 more heavily than did the poorer
Jewish neighborhoods.[13] Schneider and Schoen offer
the general conclusion that "since the late 1960s,
it is the poorest Jews who have shown signs of de-
fecting from the Democratic party,..."[14] Various
local races show essentially the same inversion--
although often with party labels absent or
scrambled. In the 1969 New York mayoralty race,
for example, Mario Procaccino was the Democratic
nominee but John Lindsay was clearly the liberal
candidate; and Lindsay did far better among upper-
status Jews than among those of lower status.[15]
It is important to note that one can find many
exceptions in recent elections to this inversion of
the traditional New Deal relationship of class and
voting--within the Jewish community as within the
general public. For example, the 1976 Democratic
presidential nominee over his long campaign attempted quite successfully to muffle the various
social and cultural issues which have been trans-
forming the meaning of liberalism. He did not seek
to mobilize -- indeed, he sought to avoid

mobilizing -- a distinctly McGovern-like, new
liberal coalition. And the 1976 balloting showed
some clear backing away from the inversions of
1972, among Jews and non-Jews alike.

But there has been no backing away from the
primary dimension of the inversion as I have been
describing it in this paper. A new division between the liberal and conservative ideologies has
opened up in the contemporary period; the contend-
ing stands have clear class bases; support for the
new liberalism is greatest within a class which I
identify conceptually as an intelligentsia and
which, with survey research data, is most effici-
ently defined as having attained a college degree;
the college-trained take positions that differ
sharply from those who have not graduated from college on the entire range of issues defining the new
liberal, new conservative split. As Tables 2
through 8 show, the new class division applies as
sharply in the case of Jews as it does for non-
Jews.

According to the 1972 through 1977 General
Social Surveys conducted by the National Opinion
Research Center, 61 percent of college-trained Jews
describe themselves as liberals, compared to just
43 percent of Jews who have not attended college.
Only 3 percent of Jews who are not college graduates dissent from the proposition that "the American way of life is superior to that of any other
country," as against 22 percent of the college educated. Fifty-four percent of the former, in comparison to only 24 percent of the latter, described
communism as "the worst kind [of government] of
all." Thirty-four percent of those who are college
graduates say they have "hardly any confidence" in
the leadership of the American military establishment, the position taken by only 18 percent Jews
who are not college graduates. There is virtual
unanimity among the college-trained (97 percent
taking this position) that it should be possible
for a pregnant woman to obtain a legal abortion
simply because she does not want to have the child;
but more than a quarter (27 percent) of non-college
Jews who did not graduate dissent from this
position. Thirty-eight percent of those who have
not attended college, compared to just 4 percent of
those who have, hold to the view that "there should
be laws against the distribution of pornography
whatever the age [of the recipient]."

In the New Deal era, higher status groups were
dependably more resistant to public spending. This
is no longer the case. The National Opinion

Research Center has examined public attitudes on a
range of spending programs, -- improving the conditions of black Americans, welfare, space explo-
ration, environmental matters, health, urban problems, education, crime, drug addiction, defense,
and the like. On most of these, college-educated
Americans -- Jews and non-Jews alike -- are more
supportive of increased public expenditures than
are their high school and grade school counterparts. In only three of the ten areas of public
spending examined were the middle-to-lower strata
more supportive of public spending than the college-trained groups, -- funds to halt the rising
crime rate, to respond to increasing drug
addiction, and to provide for the national
defense. In all of the other areas, for both Jews
and Christians, the familiar New Deal relationship
of class and support for public spending has been
turned on its head. Table 6 summarizes these data.

Discussions of Jewish voting in a contest like
that between Procaccino and Lindsay in 1969 often
suggest that the new pattern--with lower-status
Jews supporting the more conservative candidate--
emerges from experiences rather specific and peculiar to the community. The less affluent occupy
"embattled" neighborhoods, for example, are more
vulnerable to crime and cannot afford the liberalism of their more affluent counterparts. Undoubtedly, there is a large element of truth in
these explanations. But it is important to note
that the inversion of the familiar New Deal relationship of social class and political ideology is
going on among all Americans in all kinds of community settings. The less affluent non-college
Jewish population is clearly and consistently less
supportive of all stands taken by the new liberalism, in exactly the same fashion and degree as
its Gentile counterpart.

                THE CASE OF THE INTELLECTUALS

Writing in the National Review, Jeffrey Hart
argued that a major shift has occurred in the relative political stance of Catholic and Jewish intellectuals:

        In a development that could have far-
    reaching consequences for American culture
    and politics, Catholic intellectuals have
    been moving leftward, while their Jewish
    counterparts, in a kind of reverse

migration, have been moving to the right.
. . . Ludicrously enough, these culturally freaked-out Catholic academics and
intellectuals are now wearing, with mod
stylistic alterations, the hand-me-down
radical clothes discarded by the Jewish
intellectuals during the 1960s. . . . The
shift rightward among Jewish intellectuals
has been just as spectacular as the
Catholic leftward lurch. During the early
1960s. . .the influential magazine
Commentary took New-Leftish,
Aldermastonmarch positions and sponsored
C. P. Snow as a culture hero. Today
Commentary publishes pro-U.S. essays by
Daniel Patrick Moynihan, muses about
invading Saudi Arabia, denounces Jimmy
Carter for allowing the Sovietization of
Africa, and takes a very hard line on both
the Soviets and the Third World.[16]

No observer of the scene Hart is looking at
could deny that something has happened. Magazines,
such as Commentary and The Public Interest, which
serve as a primary outlet for the arguments of the
"new conservative" brand of New Deal liberalism,
are sustained in very substantial measure by the
contribution of Jewish intellectuals. On the other
side, there is surely plenty of evidence for what
Hart calls a "leftward lurch" among some Catholic
intellectuals.
But is there any overall shift in the position
of these two intellectual communities? Is Hart
describing the (admittedly important) exceptions or
the rule?
It happens that Martin Lipset and I have been
examining the social and political views of one
large segment of the American intellectual com-
munity--college and university professors--for the
last decade. We have an abundance of survey research materials from large national samples of
faculty, data admirably suited to a testing of
whether the Hart description applies to the whole
intellectual community. I believe that what Hart
is describing does not seem to be a generalized
phenomenon. Jewish and Catholic academics are not
changing places ideologically. Indeed, the relative distance separating them has not diminished
over the past decade.
Martin Lipset and I published in the American
Jewish Yearbook an article comparing the political
views of Jewish, Catholic, and Protestant

academics.[17] The piece was based upon rather
extensive analysis of data from the 1969 Carnegie
Commission survey of the professoriate. We found
very large differences between Jewish academics on
the one hand, and Protestant and Catholic faculty
on the other--but only modest differences between
the latter groups. Catholics were a bit more
liberal than Protestants for the faculty as a
whole, but holding constant discipline and type of
school removed what little there was of a
consistent difference between them. Analysis of a
national faculty survey which Lipset and I
conducted in 1977 yields this same finding. There
were no consistent differences in sociopolitical
views between persons of Catholic background and
those of Protestant parentage within the academic
community. This being the case, I have chosen once
again to merge the two groups in the following data
presentation.

Tables 10 through 12 compare the political responses of faculty raised as Jews, and those raised
in the Protestant and Catholic denominations holding constant university setting and discipline.
The variations in the political outlook of the
faculty by type of school and by field are enor-
mous, and Jews are located disproportionately at
the major colleges and universities and in certain
fields especially the social sciences, law, medicine, and other of the life sciences. To eliminate
spurious relationships, those which might appear to
involve religion but in point of fact flow from the
intellectual subculture defined by institutional
setting and disciplinary experience, I have confined the present analysis to professors in the
liberal arts and sciences at research universities
and the "elite" four-year colleges.

On every issue which we examined in the 1977
survey (only a small subset of which have been
presented in Tables 10 though 12) the Jewish academics are more liberal than their Christian counterparts. Thus, 41 percent of the Jews describe
themselves as "very liberal," the response of only
17 percent of the non-Jews. While there has been
extensive discussion of Jewish concern over quotas
and the commitment to "equality of results" rather
than to "equality of opportunity," our survey shows
Jewish faculty significantly more supportive of
equality of results than their non-Jewish colleagues in the same fields and at the same institutions. The Jewish professors are more committed to
the goal of income equality, and they are more critical of private business in the United States. On

the latter, 62 percent of the Jews, as against just
37 percent of their non-Jewish colleagues, describe
the structure of the private business system in the
United States as "fundamentally deficient" or as
"requiring major amendment."

Fifty-nine percent of Jewish faculty in the
arts and sciences at the major universities maintain that there should be a large constant dollar
reduction in defense spending, the position of 40
percent of their Christian colleagues. The Jewish
professors are less supportive of the military
intervention of the United States in various hypothetical situations--with one exception, as we put
it in the survey, "if Israel were attacked by Arab
countries and threatened with defeat."

It is not possible to achieve a precise comparison of the relative standing of Christian and
Jewish faculty in 1969 with what we find now in the
1977 survey. Many of the same substantive areas
are covered in the two studies, but the specific
questions are different. I have carefully compared, however, the opinion distributions among
Jews and non-Jews in 1969, and I have done the same
with the 1977 data. That there has been no significant shift in the relative standing of the two
groups over the past decade, is very clear.

A large proportion of American academics (31
percent) describe their present religious affiliation as "none." In Tables 10 through 12, I
compare the political orientations of professors
who were raised as Jews or Christians and now pro-
fess no religious preference to those of faculty
who claim at least nominal adherence to the religious tradition in which they were reared. Those
moving from Jewish to "none" are consistently more
liberal than their "Jewish born--Jewish now" colleagues. The magnitude of the differences varies
from one question to the next, but the direction is
unchanged across the entire array of social and
political issues. Non-Jewish faculty show this
same differentiation by present religious commitment. The overall difference in opinion between
faculty raised as Jews who describe their current
religious preference as "none," and Christian-
reared academics who claim continuing attachment to
one of the Christian denominations is really quite
extraordinary, especially since we are dealing with
people who otherwise have a lot in common; they are
all professors, in a related set of disciplines, at
schools of a similar type. Fifty-four percent of
the former describe themselves as "very liberal,"
the response of only 10 percent of the latter.

Other measures of religious commitment show
the same thing. There is a strong association
between religiousness and political opinions for
Jewish and Christian faculty alike. Those more
deeply committed to, and involved in, religious
practice are politically much more conservative.

THE GENERAL PUBLIC - THE MAGNITUDE OF THE DIFFERENCE BETWEEN JEWS AND NON-JEWS

We would like to determine if issues involving
the new division between liberals and conservatives
has widened over the past decade and a half, and if
the "opinion distance" between Jews and non-Jews
has tended to widen, decrease, or remain essentially unchanged.
The problem is not an easy one to resolve,
especially in view of the unavailability of adequate data from the New Deal era. The conventional
Gallup survey from the 1940s, for example, was
based on about 30 to 35 Jewish respondents, and, as
a result, it may be quite impossible to make reliable assessments of the opinions of Jews. Analysis
involving the Jewish population, except in the case
of a few variables such as party identification and
vote intention which are asked in a number of studies conducted at about the same point in time and
which, as a result, can be combined so as to increase the number of cases--is typically fore-
closed. There are, I should note, some possible
remedies, but they are both time-consuming and
expensive, and they were beyond the reach of the
present inquiry.
Even in the contemporary period, there are
many studies with questions that would permit a
more extensive comparison of the political orientations of Jews and Christians that cannot be used
because they contain so few Jewish respondents.
What we can do is look closely at the social
and political commitments of Jews and Gentiles, and
of subgroups within each of these populations, on a
wide range of current issues. And from this examination some answers pertinent to the question with
which I began this section do emerge.[18] However,
before turning to these data, I should note that
shifts in the relative political stands of Jews and
non-Jews are likely to appear first and most clearly on the policy issues themselves rather than in
voting behavior. Voting tends to reflect ideological change imperfectly, in part because of the
persistence of traditional partisan attachments,

and partly because candidates often try to blur
emerging ideological divisions. With rare exceptions, the new class alignments described earlier
in this paper have been far more sharply etched in
direct responses to the social and political issues
themselves than in voting behavior. Looking at the
large collection of survey data presented in Tables
2-9, one can draw a number of conclusions fairly
securely. In the first place, Jews are indeed more
liberal than non-Jews on the entire range of issues
that dominate contemporary American social and
political life.

The Jewish population is located disproportionately in the Northeastern and Pacific states
where roughly two-thirds of the total national
population resides. Only about one-third of
Protestants and Catholics reside in these areas.
Region makes no difference in terms of the general
political responses of Jews, a minority which is
responding to stimuli and experiences that apply
rather uniformly across the country. On the other
hand, region makes a very large difference in the
political orientations of the Christian majority.
Non-Jews in the New England, Middle Atlantic, and
Pacific states (especially among the college educated) are more liberal than their counterparts in
the South and Midwest. Thus, when one compares the
political orientations of Jews to Protestants and
Catholics residing in the Northeast and Pacific
sections, one consistently finds somewhat smaller
differences than appear when Jews and non-Jews are
compared nationally.

The proportion of adult Jews with college
training--about 60 percent--is much higher than
that of non-Jews--about 30 percent of whom have
attended college. Exposure to formal higher education is, we have seen, especially important in
defining the new class divisions and hence in shap-
ing responses to a range of social and political
issues. When college-educated Jews are compared to
college-trained Protestants and Catholics located
in the Northeastern and Pacific areas, the differences are notably smaller than those found between
Jews and non-Jews generally. But the shrinkage of
"opinion distance" is hardly massive. College-
trained Protestants and Catholics living in the
most liberal sections of the United States are
clearly and consistently more conservative than
their Jewish counterparts.

The sociopolitical differences separating Jews
and non-Jews surely are not less on the various
sociocultural, "feeling for the system" and foreign

policy issues which are so prominent in the new
liberal-new conservative divide, than they are on
"older" policy disputes closer to the argument of
New Deal liberalism and conservatism. Overall, the
magnitude of differences seems to be roughly the
same in these two areas, as the summary data in
Tables 2 and 6 suggest.

Eight of the National Opinion Research Center
questions on whether "too much money, too little
money or about the right amount" is being expended
for public needs involve programs directly in the
domestic arena. To summarize the overall responses
of Christians and Jews, I constructed an "Index of
Public Spending." Class interests in spending have
shifted, as noted earlier, but these questions are
direct extensions of those which arose in the New
Deal. All eight domestic expenditure areas, equally weighted, were included. And all respondents
were located in one of five quintiles defined by
the index, -- that (roughly) 20 percent most
supportive of public spending, on to the 20 percent
least in favor of these expenditures.[19]

The "New Liberalism Index" shown in Table 2
was constructed from six highly intercorrelated
questions that are distinctly part of the post-New
Deal political agenda -- questions involving
spending on environmental problems, spending for
defense, busing, the death penalty, and public
policy as to whether divorce should be easier or
more difficult to obtain.[20] A comparison of the
distributions for Jews and non-Jews shows the two
groups divided by about the same order of magnitude
on these two indices. The differences in mean
scores between all Jews and all Christians, and
between the college-educated segments of these two
populations, are almost exactly the same on the
public spending and new liberalism measures.

There are some specific issues where differences between Christians and Jews are fairly
sharp. Two are notable matters of public policy
with regard to personal morality and lifestyles and
foreign policy and defense. On the former, such
questions as homosexuality, policy on abortions,
and legislation dealing with pornography reveal
large differences between Jews and non-Jews, even,
between the college-educated populations. College-
educated Jews, much more than their Christian
counterparts, take the stand that the state should
not intrude.

Interestingly enough, despite their concern
over the security of Israel, Jews appear less
confident than non-Jews that a forceful resistance

to the Soviet Union and her sister communist states
is necessary and desirable; that an ascendant
leadership role for the United States, especially
in the military-technological area, is essential;
that the extension of communism is a threat to the
United States; and that a pax Americana offers more
promise of a satisfactory world order than any
foreseeable alternative. To cite one example,
according to both national data collected by
National Opinion Research Center and New York State
data gathered by Dresner and Associates, college-
educated Jews are much more of the opinion than
their non-Jewish counterparts that the United
States is spending too much at the present time on
the military and defense.

CIVIL LIBERTIES: A COMPARISON OF THE STOUFFER AND NATIONAL OPINION RESEARCH CENTER DATA

In the summer of 1954, a major study of
American attitudes involving civil liberties was
conducted under the direction of Samuel
Stouffer.[21] A number of the questions employed in
Stouffer's national survey have been used without
any alteration by the National Opinion Research
Center in their General Social Surveys between 1972
and 1977. It is possible, then, to compare directly the attitudes of Jews and non-Jews and their
changes, over the last two decades towards civil
liberties.
The two groups have begun to agree increasingly with regard, for example, to the rights of
atheists and socialists to speak in public forums,
to have their books in public libraries, and to
hold jobs in education. But as Table 13 makes
clear, this agreement has come about almost exclusively through Jews "standing still," not surprising since they held such strong pro-civil liberties
positions in 1954 while Protestants and Catholics
have moved in the direction of "catching up" with
Jews.

ENVOI

Probably the most striking finding to emerge
from this survey is the extent to which an inversion involving class and ideology, already demonstrated for the public at large, has occurred
within the Jewish community. College-trained and
Jews who have not attended college are sharply

differentiated in social and political perspectives
across a broad range of issues, with the latter now
decisively the most (new) conservative.

Overall, Christians and Jews remain rather
sharply differentiated ideologically. Many of the
issues of the new liberalism have generated considerable resistance among lower-status Jews, as among
non-college, manual-worker Protestants and Catholics. But so heavy has been the higher education
of Jews and their entry into the professional
occupations that, as a group, they seem as notably
inclined to the new liberalism of the 1970s as they
were, three and four decades ago, supportive of the
old liberalism of the New Deal.

Some Jewish intellectuals are articulate
spokesmen today for positions associated with the
new conservativism. But if our faculty data adequately capture currents in the larger intellectual
community, Jewish intellectuals on the whole remain
as distinctively liberal in comparison to their
Protestant and Catholic colleagues as they were a
decade ago.

A NOTE ON THE JEWS AND THE "NONES"

When interviewers ask their respondents to
specify their religious preference or identity,
only one group identified, rivals the Jews in overall support for liberal programs and policies.
This group is not the Catholics or any of the Protestant denominations but rather those Americans
who say "none." As Table 14 indicates, the "nones"
rival the Jews in their commitment to many of the
issues of the new liberalism. Ten percent of the
"nones," as compared to only 3 percent of Jews, now
choose to call themselves "extremely liberal."
These two groups are about equally of the opinion
that the United States is spending too much in the
military-defense area and in this view they differ
sharply from Protestants and Catholics. On our
composite New Liberalism Index, the Jews and the
"nones" show very similar distributions.

It is only when one moves into areas with a
strong connection to traditional New Deal liberalism -- such as, spending for basic social
programs -- that the Jews and the "nones" part
company. On the public spending issues, the
"nones" more closely resemble protestants and
Catholics -- in whose denominations most of them
were raised -- than they do the Jews. This
interesting split in the political orientations of

Americans who describe their present religion as
"none" (very "new liberal," not nearly so "old
liberal") probably originates in the special type
of cultural protest that the rejection of all
regular denominational ties implies. The "nones"
are drawn disproportionately from among the upper
status, college-trained professional segments of
the population, groups in any case most supportive
of the new liberalism. But they have in addition
taken the step of putting extra distance between
themselves and the prevailing culture. Only 7
percent of all Americans identify religiously as
"nones." One would expect a relationship between
this type of cultural differentiation and the commitment to social and cultural change associated
with the new liberalism. One would not expect much
of a correlation between a rejection of the conventional religious denominations and support for
public spending for basic social programs. The
"nones" are a distinctively new liberal group; they
are not committed to the programmatic thrusts of
the old liberalism in any special fashion.

In the various tables presented in this chapter, I have compared the responses of Jews and non-
Jews, putting Protestants and Catholics together in
the latter category. It is worth noting here,
where we have given the "nones" a line by themselves, that this "merging" of Protestants and
Catholics is fully justified, and not only because
the chapter has been concerned primarily with comparing Jews and non-Jews. As Table 14 suggests,
there simply are not major differences in general
social and political orientations between Protestants and Catholics at the present time although a
few issues do produce substantial divisions.
Northern white Protestants and Catholics, in particular, display fundamental similarities in sociopolitical ideology.

NOTES

1. Among the many studies that sustain and docu-
   ment these conclusions, the following are
   especially valuable: Lawrence H. Fuchs, The
   Political Behavior of American Jews (Glencoe,
   Ill.: The Free Press, 1956); Stephen D.
   Isaacs, Jews and American Politics (Garden
   City: Doubleday and Co., 1971); Beverly
   Allinsmith and Wesley Allinsmith, "Religious
   Affiliation and Politico-Economic Attitude,"

Public Opinion Quarterly vol. 12 (Fall, 1948),
pp. 377-389; William Schneider, Michael D.
Berman, and Mark Schultz, "Bloc Voting
Reconsidered: Is there a Jewish Vote?'"
Ethnicity (1974), pp. 345-392; William
Schneider and Douglas E. Schoen, "The Centrist
Phenomenon: The Jewish Vote and the Changing
Structure of Coalition Politics in America"
(Center for International Affairs, Harvard
University, not dated), p. 91; Allan M. Fisher,
"Continuity and Erosion of Jewish Liberalism,"
American Jewish Historical Quarterly vol. 66
(December, 1976), pp. 322-348; and Allan M.
Fisher, "Realignment of the Jewish Vote? Some
Empirical Evidence," Political Science
Quarterly (forthcoming).
2. I have discussed this at length elsewhere.
See, in particular, American Political
Parties: Social Change and Political Response
(New York: W. W. Norton, 1970), especially
Chapter 5; and Transformations of the American
Party System: Political Coalitions from the
New Deal to the 1970s, 2nd ed. (New York:
W. W. Norton, 1978), pp. 36-41.
3. For example, see Everett C. Ladd, "The
Democrats Have Their Own Two-Party System,"
Fortune (October, 1977), pp. 213-214; Ibid.,
Where Have All the Voters Gone?: The
Fracturing of America's Political Parties (New
York: W. W. Norton, 1978), especially Chapter
2.
4. I use intelligentsia to include those persons
whose background and vocation associates them
directly in the application of trained intel-
ligence. It includes, that is, not only
intellectuals--people involved in the creation
of new ideas, new knowledge, new cultural
forms--but also that larger community whose
training gives them some facility in handling
abstract ideas, or whose work requires them to
manipulate ideas rather than things. College
training, an experience shared by some 40
million Americans, defines the outer boundaries
of the intelligentsia.
5. Louis Harris, the public opinion analyst, has
found confirmation of one aspect of this
argument in his survey data. Noting that in
the contemporary United States, "at the key
executive level, more people [are] employed in
professional than in line executive capaci-
ties," he puts special emphasis on the survey
finding that "the one quality that divided most

professionals from line executives in business
organizations was that the professionals felt
much more beholden to their outside disci
pline -- whether it be systems engineering,
teaching, scientific research, or other
professional ties -- than to the particular
company or institution they worked for." Louis
Harris, The Anguish of Change (New York: W. W.
Norton, 1973) p. 45.

In my own analyses of survey data, I
located a consistent set of distributions which
tie into the Harris argument. Professionals
working for firms in the profit sector display
social and political orientations very similar
to those of their professional counterparts who
are employed by nonprofit organizations.

6. These percentages are derived from six large
surveys of the American population conducted
between 1972 and 1977 by the National Opinion
Research Center of the University of Chicago.
The total number of cases in this composite
file of National Opinion Research Center,
General Social Surveys is 9,120.

7. "Excerpts from Interview with Meany on Status
of Labor Movement," The New York Times (August
31, 1969).

8. Everett C. Ladd, "Pursuing the New Class:
Social Theory and Survey Data," manuscript in
press; "Liberalism Upside Down: The Inversion
of the New Deal Order," Political Science
Quarterly (Winter, 1976-1977), pp. 577-600.

9. The index has been constructed from six variables which possess these properties. Each
involves opinions or values subsumed by the new
liberalism as described in this paper; the six
variables are highly intercorrelated; and they
were selected so as to represent several dimensions, rather than a single dimension of the
new liberalism.

The data set with which I worked in this
index construction is the composite 1972-1977
National Opinion Research Center, General
Social Survey. This data set is especially
useful because of the large number of cases
(9120 respondents) and the rich assortment of
policy and value questions which it contains.

The following are the six questions as
posed by the National Opinion Research Center
interviewers:

Q.1 and   We are faced with many problems in
  2   this country, none of which can be

solved easily or inexpensively. I'm going to name some of these problems, and for each one I'd like you to tell me whether you think we're spending too much money on it, too little money, or about the right amount.

Q.1 Are we spending too much, too little, or about the right amount on improving and protecting the environment?

Q.2 Are we spending too much, too little, or about the right amount on military, armaments and defense?

Q.3 Should divorce in this country be easier or more difficult to obtain than it is now? (Easier/more difficult/stay as is).

Q.4 We hear a lot of talk these days about liberals and conservatives. I'm going to show you a seven-point scale on which the political views that people might hold are arranged from extremely liberal -- point 1, to extremely conservative -- point 7. Where would you place yourself on this scale? (Extremely liberal; liberal; slightly liberal; moderate, middle of the road; slightly conservative; conservative; extremely conservative).

Q.5 In general, do you favor or oppose the busing of (Negro/Black) and white school children from one school district to another?

Q.6 Do you favor or oppose the death penalty for persons convicted of murder?

This index was computed much like the spending measure described in note 19. Responses were assigned scores according to the following formula (with some variation made necessary by variations in the structure of possible responses): The "new liberal" position was given a value of three, the opposed response received a value of zero; while intermediate stands -- those reflecting some support but some opposition to the "pure" new liberal view -- were assigned a value of one. Each respondent's "scores" on the six

variables were then added together. The
totals, ranging from 0 to 20, were divided by
the number of items which the respondent
answered; and all respondents were located in
one of five quintiles, -- that of the sample
with the highest new liberal scores, on down to
the fifth of all respondents with the lowest
scores on this additive measure.

10. See in particular, by Everett C. Ladd and
    Seymour M. Lipset, The Divided Academy:
    Professors and Politics (New York: W. W.
    Norton, 1976), pp. 55-92.
11. Mark R. Levy and Michael S. Kramer, The Ethnic
    Factor (New York: Simon and Schuster, 1073) p.
    104.
12. Schneider, Berman, and Schultz, op. cit., p.
    359.
13. Milton Himmelfarb, "The Jewish Vote (Again),"
    Commentary (June, 1973), pp. 81-85.
14. Schneider and Schoen, op. cit., pp. 54-55.
15. New York precinct voting data, kindly made
    available to me by William Schneider.
16. Jeffrey Hart, "New Directions: Catholics and
    Jews," National Review (April 28, 1978), pp.
    517-519.
17. Everett C. Ladd and S. M. Lipset, "Jewish
    Academics in the United States: Their
    Achievements, Culture and Politics," American
    Jewish Year Book, 1971, vol. 72, pp. 89-128.
18. It might be noted that this chapter draws upon
    survey data -- not because I believe that all
    truth flows therefrom, but more modestly be-
    cause I think some useful information bearing
    on the social and political position of Jews in
    the United States can thus be gained. Once the
    commitment to the use of survey data was made,
    a number of things followed. In particular,
    Jews became all those and only those who when
    asked--"what is your religious preference? Is
    it Protestant, Catholic, Jewish, some other re-
    ligion, or no religion?"--answered "Jewish."
    The same sort of construction applies, obvi-
    ously, to the Christians.
        At various times in this chapter, I speak
    of "Christians," "non-Jews," and "Gentiles."
    The terms refer to exactly the same people --
    to all survey respondents who answer
    "Protestant" or "Catholic" -- and excluding
    those who say "none" -- when asked to indicate
    their religious preference.
19. The index has been constructed from eight
    domestic spending variables: to improve and

protect the environment; for health services;
to solve urban problems; for education; to
improve the condition of blacks; for welfare;
to deal with the rising crime rate; and to cope
with drug addiction. The response that the
United States is spending "too little" was
given a value of three; "too much," zero; while
"about the right amount" was assigned the value
of one. Each respondent's "scores" on the
eight variables were then added together. The
totals, ranging from 0 to 24, were divided by
the number of items which the respondent answered. All respondents were located in one of
five quintiles -- ranging from the 20 percent
most inclined to high public spending, to the
20 percent least supportive.
20. For information on the construction of this
    index, see note 9.
21. Samuel A. Stouffer, Communism, Conformity, and
    Civil Liberties (Gloucester: Peter Smith,
    1963).

TABLE 1

DISTRIBUTIONS ON THE NEW LIBERALISM INDEX,
BY SELECTED DEMOGRAPHIC CHARACTERISTICS OF RESPONDENTS

	Quintile Most Supportive of the New Liberalism 1	2	3	4	Quintile Least Supportive of the New Liberalism 5
Everyone	17	24	20	18	22
College					
All graduates	31	23	16	13	17
Some college	23	25	17	16	19
High school or less	12	23	21	20	23
College					
5 years or more	31	23	15	14	17
4 years	31	23	16	12	18
1-3 years	23	25	17	16	19
High school graduates	13	22	22	20	23
Less than high school	11	24	21	20	24
Whites	8	21	21	22	27
Blacks	21	35	17	15	11
"NEW CLASS"					
Young	36	27	13	12	12
ALL	29	23	16	14	18
Old	20	19	20	16	25
WORKING CLASS					
Young	18	24	23	18	17
ALL	11	21	22	21	26
Old	6	17	22	23	32

(TABLE 1 CONTINUED)

Respondent's occupation	Quintile Most Supportive of the New Liberalism 1	2	3	4	Quintile Least Supportive of the New Liberalism 5
Professional	28	23	16	15	18
"word workers"[1]	43	24	13	8	12
"the liberal professions"[2]	36	23	14	9	17
Teachers	25	23	16	16	20
"number workers"[3]	17	22	23	20	18
non-profit sector	26	25	17	16	17
profit sector	29	23	15	15	19
Managerial	13	23	18	19	27
White collar[4]	22	20	18	21	18
Blue collar	14	23	21	19	22

NOTES:
[1]"Word workers" include the clergy, social scientists, actors, editors and re-porters, public relations specialists, radio and television announcers, among others.
[2]"The liberal professions" are comprised of architects, lawyers, physicians, among others.
[3]"number workers" include engineers, mathematicians, biologists and physical scientists.
[4]"White collar workers" are those employed in clerical and sales positions, as technicians, and in the semi-professions.
Source:

TABLE 2

DISTRIBUTIONS ON THE NEW LIBERALISM INDEX, BY RELIGION

	Quintile Most Supportive of the New Liberalism 1	2	3	4	Quintile Least Supportive of the New Liberalism 5
ALL					
Jewish	31	29	18	12	9
Christian:					
Whites	14	24	20	19	23
Blacks	12	22	21	20	26
NORTHEAST AND PACIFIC STATE RESIDENTS					
Jewish	32	39	14	8	6
Christian	31	26	20	15	8
	17	25	21	17	21
COLLEGE GRADUATES					
Jewish	40	32	12	12	4
Christian:					
Northeast and Pacific States	31	21	20	11	17
Other Sections	22	26	15	16	22
NON-COLLEGE					
Jewish	22	23	28	12	15
Christian:					
Northeast and Pacific States	13	25	22	19	22
Other Sections	11	22	21	21	26

Source: These data are from the 1972-1977 General Social Surveys, National Opinion Research Center.

TABLE 3

POLITICAL SELF-DESCRIPTION, BY RELIGION

	Liberal	Moderate	Conservative
ALL			
Jewish	52	35	13
Christian:	27	41	32
Whites	25	42	33
Blacks	43	34	23
NORTHEAST AND PACIFIC STATE RESIDENTS			
Jewish	49	37	14
Christian	30	40	30
COLLEGE GRADUATES			
Jewish	61	33	7
Christian:			
Northeast and Pacific States	37	28	35
Other Sections	33	23	44
NON-COLLEGE			
Jewish	43	40	17
Christian:			
Northeast and Pacific States	27	45	28
Other Sections	23	46	31

Source:
    These data are from the 1972-1977 General Social Surveys, National Opinion Research Center.

TABLE 4

VIEWS ON RACIAL ISSUES, BY RELIGION

| | PERCENTAGE AGREEING OR FAVORING: | | |
	Homeowner Could Not Refuse to Sell Because of Race or Color[a]	There Should Be NO Laws Against Black-White Marriages[b]	Busing for Integration[c]
ALL			
Jewish	51	86	19
Christian:	33	62	18
Whites	– –	62	13
Blacks	– –	– –	53
NORTHEAST AND PACIFIC STATE RESIDENTS			
Jewish	47	86	16
Christian	40	73	20
COLLEGE GRADUATES			
Jewish	52	96	25
Christian:			
Northeast and Pacific States	48	91	19
Other Sections	39	85	19
NON-COLLEGE			
Jewish	44	73	12
Christian:			
Northeast and Pacific States	37	66	21
Other Sections	28	49	18

[a] "Suppose there is a community-wide vote on the general housing issue. There are two possible laws to vote on. Which law would you vote for? (1) Homeowner decide for himself, even if he decides to not sell to blacks; (2) Homeowner can't refuse to sell because of race or color."

[b] "Do you think there should be laws against marriages between (Negroes/blacks) and whites?"

[c] "In general, do you favor or oppose the busing of (Negro/black) and white children from one school district to another?"

Source: These data are from the 1972-1977 General Social Surveys, National Opinion Research Center.

TABLE 5

VIEWS ON SOCIAL ISSUES, BY RELIGION

	Favor Legal Abortion on Demand by Married Women[a]	Homo-sexuality Always Wrong[b]	Should Be No Laws Against Pornography Distribution[c]	Women Should Leave Running the Country to Men[d]
ALL				
Jewish	85	37	20	13
Christian:	42	76	8	39
Whites	43	75	7	38
Blacks	37	79	16	45
NORTHEAST AND PACIFIC STATE RESIDENTS				
Jewish	83	33	16	12
Christian	50	67	8	35
COLLEGE GRADUATES				
Jewish	97	13	26	2
Christian:				
Northeast and Pacific States	66	42	9	14
Other Sections	55	60	7	14
NON-COLLEGE				
Jewish	73	57	12	24
Christian:				
Northeast and Pacific States	45	74	9	43
Other Sections	33	85	8	47

Notes on following page.

Notes for Table 5

[a]"Please tell me whether or not <u>you</u> think it should be possible for a pregnant woman to obtain a <u>legal</u> abortion if she is married and does not want any children?"

[b]"What about sexual relations between two <u>adults</u> of the <u>same</u> sex -- do you think it is <u>always</u> wrong, almost <u>always</u> wrong, wrong only sometimes, or not wrong at all?"

[c]"Which of these statements comes closest to your feelings about pornography laws? (1) There should be laws against the distribution of pornography whatever the age; (2) There should be laws against the distribution of pornography to persons under 18; (3) There should be no laws forbidding the distribution of pornography."

[d]"Do you agree or disagree with this statement: Women should take care of running their homes and leave running the country up to men?"

<u>Source:</u>

These data are from the 1972-1977 General Social Surveys, National Opinion Research Center.

TABLE 6

DISTRIBUTIONS ON THE INDEX OF PUBLIC SPENDING, BY RELIGION

	Quintile Most Supportive of High Public Spending 1	2	3	4	Quintile Least Supportive of Public Spending 5
ALL					
Jewish	32	28	22	10	9
Christian:	18	20	24	19	20
Whites	14	19	25	20	22
Blacks	48	23	14	9	7
NORTHEAST AND PACIFIC STATE RESIDENTS					
Jewish	29	27	24	11	9
Christian	20	20	23	18	19
COLLEGE GRADUATES					
Jewish	38	27	16	11	7
Christian:					
Northeast and Pacific States	24	18	24	18	17
Other Sections	19	20	22	19	20
NON-COLLEGE					
Jewish	29	27	26	8	10
Christian:					
Northeast and Pacific States	19	21	23	18	20
Other Sections	15	19	25	20	21

Source: These data are from the 1972-1977 General Social Surveys, National Opinion Research Center.

TABLE 7

VIEWS ON FEDERAL SOCIAL PROGRAMS, BY RELIGION

	Favor a Strong National Health Insurance Program[a]	Oppose Presidential Vetoes of Social Spending Bills[b]
ALL		
Jewish	88	79
Christian:	79	64
Whites	77	61
Non-whites	87	76
COLLEGE GRADUATES		
Jewish	87	92
Christian	86	70
NON-COLLEGE		
Jewish	92	56
Christian:	79	62
Whites	76	60
Non-Whites	87	72

[a] "I favor a strong National Health Insurance program for all Americans even if we have to raise taxes to do this."

[b] "President Ford is right to veto social spending bills."

Source:
These data are from a survey of voter attitudes in the State of New York, prepared for Daniel Patrick Moynihan by Dresner and Associates, Inc., 1976.

TABLE 8

VIEWS ON FOREIGN AND DEFENSE POLICY, BY RELIGION

	Communism Worst Kind of Government	Hardly Any Confidence in Military	U.S. Spending Too Much on Defense
ALL			
Jewish	40	30	56
Christian:			
Whites	53	12	30
Blacks	54	12	29
	39	15	35
NORTHEAST AND PACIFIC STATE RESIDENTS			
Jewish	38	34	57
Christian	46	15	36
COLLEGE GRADUATES			
Jewish	24	37	67
Christian:			
Northeast and Pacific States	27	23	53
Other Sections	35	14	42
NON-COLLEGE			
Jewish	54	18	43
Christian:			
Northeast and Pacific States	51	12	30
Other Sections	61	9	22

Notes on following page.

Notes for Table 8

[a]"Thinking about all the different kinds of
governments in the world today, which of these
statements comes closest to how you feel about
Communism as a form of government? (1) It's the
worst kind of all; (2) It's bad, but no worse than
some others; (3) It's all right for some countries;
(4) It's a good form of government."

[b]"I am going to name some institutions in
this country. As far as the people running these
institutions are concerned, would you say you have
a great deal of confidence, only some confidence,
or hardly any confidence at all in them -
military?"

[c]"We are faced with many problems in this
country, none of which can be solved easily or
inexpensively . . . . [Do you think] we're spending
too much money, too little money, or about the
right amount on. . . ."

Source:
        These data are from the 1972-1977 General
        Social Surveys, National Opinion
Research Center.

TABLE 9

VIEWS ON FOREIGN POLICY AND DEFENSE, BY RELIGION

	JEWS	CHRISTIANS
CIA should not work inside foreign countries to strengthen pro-American elements[a]	58	33
Favor full diplomatic relations with Cuba[b]	87	59
Would be a threat to United States if...became communist[c]		
Western European countries	62	82
Italy	40	61
Japan	53	78
African countries	48	62
Latin American countries	51	80
Favor United States military intervention if North Korea attacks South Korea[d]	8	20

Notes on following page.

Notes for Table 9

[a]"In general, do you feel that the CIA should
or should not work inside other countries to try to
strengthen those elements that serve the interests
of the United States and to weaken those forces
that work against the interests of the United
States?"

[b]"All in all, do you favor or oppose the
United States establishing full diplomatic
relations with Cuba?"

[c]"If [named country] were to become communist,
do you think this would be a threat to the United
States, or not?"

[d]"There has been a lot of discussion about
what circumstances might justify United States
military involvement, including the use of United
States troops. Do you feel if North Korea attacked
South Korea, you would favor or oppose United
States military involvement?"

Source:
            These data are from the Harris 1974
       Chicago Council on Foreign Relations.

TABLE 10

POLITICAL SELF-DESCRIPTION OF COLLEGE PROFESSORS, BY RELIGION

Faculty in the Liberal Arts and Sciences at Research Universities and Major Colleges:	Very Liberal	Somewhat Liberal	Moderate	Conservative
Faculty raised Jewish	41	37	14	9
Faculty raised Christian	17	37	21	24
Raised Jewish/Now None[a]	54	35	7	4
Raised Jewish/Now Jewish[a]	35	38	17	11
Raised Christian/Now None[a]	23	42	20	15
Raised Christian/Now Christian[a]	10	33	23	34
Non-religious Jews[b]	42	41	10	7
Religious Jews[b]	34	28	25	14
Non-religious Christians[b]	21	41	19	19
Religious Christians[b]	14	33	24	29

Notes on following page.

Notes for Table 10

[a]Faculty were asked: "In what religion were you raised? What is your present religious preference?" In this table, a professor who said he was raised in one of the Protestant denominations or as a Catholic but is now "none" in religious preference, is located in the "raised Christian/now none" category. A comparable construction is employed for the other groups.

[b]Faculty were asked: "From the standpoint of personal belief, do you consider yourself: deeply religious; moderately religious; largely indifferent to religion; basically opposed to religion?" In this table, faculty are classified as "religious" if they chose either the deeply religious or the moderately religious response. Professors are described as "non-religious" if they chose either the "largely indifferent" or the "basically opposed" category.

Source:
These data are from the 1977 Ladd-Lipset Faculty Survey

TABLE 11

VIEWS OF COLLEGE PROFESSORS ON EQUALITY, BY RELIGION[a]

Faculty in the Liberal Arts and Sciences at Research Universities and Major Colleges:	Strongly Committed to Equality of Opportunity	3	In-between	5	Strongly Committed to equality of Results
Faculty raised Jewish	49	21	13	8	10
Faculty raised Christian	61	22	8	5	4
Raised Jewish/Now None	38	19	18	7	17
Raised Jewish/Now Jewish	52	25	12	6	5
Raised Christian/Now None	61	21	8	6	5
Raised Christian/Now Christian	65	23	6	5	3
Non-religious Jews	47	21	13	9	11
Religious Jews	55	23	9	6	7
Non-religious Christians	62	21	8	5	4
Religious Christians	60	24	8	5	3

[a]"Here are two ways to deal with inequality. Which do you prefer?" (A seven point scale where (1) represents the response Equality of opportunity: giving each person an equal chance for a good education and to develop his or her ability, and (7) represents the response Equality of results: giving each person a relatively equal share of income and status regardless of education and ability.)

Source: These data are from the 1977 Ladd-Lipset Faculty Survey.

TABLE 12

PRESIDENTIAL VOTE OF COLLEGE PROFESSORS,
1972 and 1976

	1972 for McGovern	1976 for Carter
Faculty in the Liberal Arts and Sciences at Research Universities and Major Colleges		
Faculty raised Jewish	92	88
Faculty raised Christian	69	71
Raised Jewish/Now None	93	92
Raised Jewish/Now Jewish	91	86
Raised Christian/Now None	78	75
Raised Christian/Now Christian	57	62
Non-religious Jews	95	91
Religious Jews	84	77
Non-religious Christians	76	74
Religious Christians	63	67

Source:
These data are from the 1977 Ladd-Lipset Faculty Survey.

TABLE 13

VIEWS ON FREEDOM OF EXPRESSION, BY RELIGION; COMPARING THE 1954 STOUFFER CROSS-SECTION STUDY AND THE 1972-1977 NATIONAL OPINION RESEARCH CENTER GENERAL SOCIAL SURVEYS
(Percentages are those taking a Pro-Civil Liberties stand)

	Jews	White Christians	College Educated Jews	College-Educated White Christians
1. Allow anti-religion speaker[a]				
1954	75	38	91	60
1972-77	82	63	92	83
2. Keep anti-religion book in library[b]				
1954	81	36	92	60
1972-77	87	60	93	80
3. Allow socialist speaker[c]				
1954	89	65	97	80
1972-77	90	79	98	89
4. Permit socialist teacher to hold job[d]				
1954	69	36	69	45
1972-77	79	57	94	68
5. Keep socialist book in library[e]				
1954	85	59	93	74
1972-77	89	73	95	86

TEXT OF QUESTION on following page.

TEXT OF QUESTION (continued from Table 13):

[a]"There are always some people whose ideas are considered bad or dangerous by other people. For instance, somebody who is against all churches and religion. If such a person wanted to make a speech in your city (town, community) against churches and religion, should he be allowed to speak or not?"

[b]"If some people in your community suggested that a book he wrote against churches and religion should be taken out of your public library, would you favor removing the book or not?"

[c]"Consider a person who favored government ownership of all the railroads and all big industries. If such a person wanted to make a speech in your community favoring government ownership of all the railroads and big industries, should he be allowed to speak, or not?"

[d]"Should such a person be allowed to teach in a college or university, or not?"

[e]"If some people in your community suggested a book he wrote favoring government ownership should be taken our of your public library, would you favor removing this book, or not?"

TABLE 14

SOCIAL AND POLITICAL VIEWS, BY RELIGION:
THE CASE OF THE NEWS AND THE "NONE'S"

THE NEW LIBERALISM INDEX

Present Religious Identification	Quintile Most Supportive of High Public Spending 1	2	3	4	Quintile Least Supportive of Public Spending 5
Jewish	31	29	18	12	9
None	43	21	14	14	8
Protestant	14	23	19	19	25
Catholic	15	25	23	18	20

Present Religious Identification	Extremely Liberal	Liberal	Slightly Liberal	Moderate	Slightly Conservative	Conservative	Extremely Conservative
Jewish	3	33	17	35	7	6	0
None	10	26	19	26	10	6	3
Protestant	2	10	14	40	18	13	3
Catholic	2	15	13	43	15	11	2

Text of Question:
"We hear a lot of talk these days about Liberals and Conservatives. I'm going to show you a seven-point scale on which the political views that people hold are arranged from extremely liberal -- point 1, to extremely conservative -- point 7. Where would you place yourself on this scale?"

(Table 14 continued)

Present Religious Identification	Too much	About Right	Too Little
Jewish	56	36	8
None	54	32	15
Protestant	28	51	21
Catholic	34	47	19

Text of Question:

"We are faced with many problems in this country, none of which can be solved easily or inexpensively... [Do you think] we're spending too much money, too little money, or about the right amount on...the military, armaments and defense?"

Present Religious Identification	Quintile Most Supportive Of High Public Spending 1	2	3	4	Quintile Least Supportive Of Public Spending 5
Jewish	32	28	22	10	9
None	24	19	23	17	17
Protestant	17	19	24	19	21
Catholic	18	21	24	18	18

Source:

These data are from the 1972-1977 General Social Surveys, National Opinion Research Center.

Chapter V

FOUR SOCIOLOGIES OF AMERICAN JEWRY:
METHODOLOGICAL NOTES*

SAMUEL Z. KLAUSNER

CONCEPTS ARE RULES FOR SEEING

The sociology of Jewry is an applied sociology.[1] General sociological concepts and propositions, established to describe "any" human society,
are applied to the understanding of this particular
human society. Ideas about religious organization
and religious leadership, developed in the study of
other religions, or even other social institutions,
are used to characterize synagogue organization and
rabbinical roles.[2] A sociology of the Jews and of
Jewry uses these ideas to understand Jewish life.
As a result, the Jewish community is defined by the
social forms it shares with other communities.
Jewry is then implicitly contrasted with these
other groups.

Sociological concepts are intellectual tools
of Western civilization--more particularly, of
European rationalism. The study of Jewry in a
sociological frame of reference is a reconstruction, in a rationalistic scientific schema, of the
reality constructed by the Jews living it. The
selectivity inherent in these concepts obscures the
essentially Jewish. However, through these concepts, Jewish particularity may be understood and
intellectually evaluated by comparison with the
social life of other communities.

Because sociology is an empirical science, its
general concepts may be used to ask questions of
the Jewish experience. The Jewish experience may

protest the question or may provide a Jewish
answer. This problem is not as acute for humanistic students of Jewish culture. They interpret
the written repositories of Jewry and Judaism. The
ideas and values they discover are definitively
Jewish even while traceable to Akkadian or Islamic
sources. The sociologist rarely asks a Jewish
question, that is, one framed by ideas formed in
Jewish experience. Asking a Jewish sociological
question is rare because of the peculiar filiation
of ideas in that tradition. Yet, a Jewish sociological idea is not impossible. Further, an idea
developed in the Jewish experience, the idea of
convenanting, for example, might be applied in
understanding Puritanism.

The notion of Jewish ideas to think about
Jewry suggests the use of Jewish values to interpret what is found. Sociological knowledge, with
its rationalist and externalist perspective, is
existential or factual. By itself, that knowledge
is no moral judgment. Ethical assertions require
that theological and philosophical thought be
applied to the factual discourse. Jewish ethical
judgments require interpretive criteria drawn from
experience consensually agreed to belong to the
tradition.

The scholarly moral duty of the sociologist is
to struggle against the influence of his or her
social values in revealing someone else's social
reality. Some sociological work on Jewry, consistent with this norm, has been objective and analytic. The effort to comprehend the subject's meanings involves a seductive closeness to the subject
and ethical interpretations become near irresist-
ible. Some work, driven by a passion for certain
models of Jewish living, has been hortatory.

The scholarly corpus of the sociology of
American Jewry includes historical, ethnographic,
and demographic studies centered on the economic
role of Jews, intermarriage and other topics in the
sociology of the family, anti-Semitism, Jewish-
gentile relations, the Jewish community and Jewish
welfare organizations, Zionism, orthodoxy and other
Jewish ideologies, and much, much more.[3]

This chapter concentrates on some of the
concepts that have guided sociological thinking
about Jewry. It is limited to a methodological
critique of four studies: Samuel Heilman's
Synagogue Life and Solomon Poll's The Hasidic
Community of Williamsburg were initiated as doctor-
al dissertations; Marshall Sklare and Joseph
Greenblum's Jewish Identity on the Suburban

Frontier was a community agency sponsored study; and Nathan Glazer's American Judaism was accomplished on a scholarly grant. None of these is a complete study of the Jewish community. Each observes a small, but different, aspect of Jewish social life. Each represents a different social research tradition. Heilman studies a single congregation, as would an anthropological field worker, as a participant in that congregation. Poll relies heavily on personal observations and interviews, in the tradition of American community studies, to learn about the social and cultural life of a religious sect. Sklare and Greenblum follow the attitude research tradition, exploring Jewish identity with the aid of questionnaires and interviews. Glazer uses an historical method to study religion and ethnicity in the organized American Jewish community.

Research begins with a researcher's sense of a problem, a question. Observation of the Jewish community is designed to clarify the question and to discover the community's response. The social problems of Jews, as perceived by the researcher or by a sponsoring agency, comprise the theme of the study.[4] A discrepancy between an actual and a socially expected or socially desired state of affairs defines a social problem for community representatives. The sociologist transforms such social problem questions into sociological questions and then proposes a sociological methodology for exploring them.

The critiques of each of the authors listed above will deal with his style of concept formation and its influence on his observations and explanations. Explanations make findings meaningful. By demonstrating a coherence between the observed event and other events, an explanation may lead to a new hypothesis-a new question.

The topics for critique emerge from the author's frames of reference. A frame of reference is an implicit set of criteria for concept formation. Thus, Heilman's frame of reference is dramaturgical. In this frame of reference, the very collective is conceived of as being created through the unfolding dramatic plot. Explaining social change becomes a challenge. Poll's effort to use the concepts of stratification and economic organization to understand a religious society will be scrutinized. The impact of survey methodology on our understanding of the Jewish community will be central to the critique of Sklare and Greenblum's work. The manner in which Glazer's historical method reveals the interplay between society and culture will be the theme in the critique of his study. Neither the quality of these reports nor the professional competence of the respective authors will be judged. Rather, the intent is to ask how their methodology shaped their vision of the Jewish community.

SOCIAL EXPRESSION IS SOCIAL EXISTENCE: HEILMAN SEES THE INNER LIFE OF A SYNAGOGUE

The Dramaturgical Approach

The puzzle of the survival of religious orthodoxy is one of the implicit questions of Samual Heilman's work. What influences an individual Jew to keep the Commandments while participating in the secular occupational world, in the American polity and in a culture governed by Christian ethics and following a Christian calendar? The more generic sociological problem is set in terms of the relation between the individual and the group. How is a social group created? And, by what processes does that group constrain the behavior of its members? Heilman is not hostage to a static view of society which treats the creation of the group and its ability to control individuals as sequential events. Rather, the process of forming a group is the same as that which constrains individuals to continue to share in the group. A small orthodox synagogue, an expression of collective life, is Heilman's subject. He observes and he participates. He selects events from the flow of events and interprets them.

A collectivity, as Heilman conceives of it, is an emergent reality. It emerges in the course of interaction. The collectivity transcends that interaction as an enveloping context framing each act. The members, and the researcher, recognize the collectivity by its culture. That culture consists of rules and interpretive perspectives around which members enact the life of the collective. These acts define their positions in synagogue life and their relationships to one another. The culture is a symbolism of social interaction. The symbols communicating, expressing, and creating social and cultural meanings are manifest in gestures and conventionalized expressions. In this "symbolic interactionist" frame of reference, meanings are the core of social reality. The

communication of meaning among actors is the
principal social process.

The tradition is that of George H. Mead on
this side of the Atlantic and of Alfred Schutz on
the other. The thesis of organicity, the meaning
of the part depending on that of the whole, continues a Durkheimian tradition. The empirical method
is that of the ethnographic study of intimate
groups as practiced by Erving Goffman, Heilman's
teacher. Heilman calls his approach "dramaturgical." The social group is the cast of the play
and the conventionalized culture provides the theme
and the script.

Here, though, are the limits of the model.
The script is not entirely given by a playwright
for the actors' interpretation. It is being
written, or, at the very least, being objectified
in the playing. The Jewish community and its culture are in place before the organizing of the
synagogue. The cultural tradition, already in
place, presents an image of a synagogue to the actors as a potential reality. The character of the
synagogue, one manifestation of community, is increasingly specified as the action proceeds.

Newcomers to the congregation are at home in
Kehillat Kodesh, the synagogue, because they have
been members of other orthodox congregations. Yet,
they are also strangers who must learn the cultural
usages and identify the individuals who enact them
in this setting. Certain usages or customs, perhaps nuances in the expression of established meanings, characterize worship in this synagogue, differentiating it from its neighbors. The limits of
variation are defined by the network of synagogues
with which Kehillat Kodesh identifies.

Heilman learned about life in this small orthodox synagogue in a large city by attending meet-
ings, visiting with members in their homes and in
the synagogue, and, most importantly, by participating in worship and study. As an ethnographer,
he notes his encounter and ponders them in search
of their cultural meanings. He advises his readers
not to expect an analysis of religious culture,
but, rather, an examination of social behavior
among religious practitioners as it is subject to
the "imperatives of commingling."

The intrinsic Jewish content of the synagogue's norms is not analyzed. That could be the
subject of a separate, humanistic study of
Judaism. The demands of Orthodox Judaism are
conceived, in the perspective of this study, as

qualitatively indistinct from the social constraints and claims made upon all people by their
culture. Nevertheless, Heilman clarifies social
activities in the synagogue by relating them to
their Judaic content. Heilman's success rests on
his ability to interpret that content accurately.

The activity Heilman studied was limited to
the synagogue, essentially a territorial concept.
He considers other activities, however, if they
involve the congregation or the synagogue. The behavior of the members in other organizational and
institutional settings, such as the marketplace and
the polling booth, are excluded.[5]

Interpretation: Discovering Meanings

Heilman observes and interprets the flow of
action. Selecting a form of behavior for consideration is an interpretative act. Heilman calls his
interpretation a "deciphering," a way of discovering the intellectual coherence among activities.
The intellectual coherence sought is, in the first
place, in the minds of the participants. More
precisely, it is in the culture which they share.
No researcher, even during a first peek at the subjects is "theory-less." Heilman recognizes this
and resists imposing the coherence offered by theo-
retic sociological concepts. Ultimately, however,
interpretation is an intellectual reconstruction of
the meanings of the events. This reconstruction
sharpens and narrows meanings so that they become
more explicit for the researcher than they are for
the actors.[6]

The interpretation is of a situation. A situation includes activities, actors, and material
paraphernalia. The principal synagogue situations
are "worship," or "study," or "assembly," or all of
these at once. The meaning of a situation rests on
the intention of the actors. Heilman discovers
this intention, the principle of coherence, in
part, by introspecting, drawing upon his knowledge
of other situations which, he asserts, are similar. In this scientific framework, understanding,
the outcome of interpretation, is the reward of
typification, discovery of the class of situations,
to which the observed one belongs.[7] The participants, too, arrive at their definitions by generalizing from past situations they consider to have
been similar.

Heilman describes social processes in Kehillat
Kodesh in terms such as gossip, conventionalization,

and spatial clustering of subgroups. The synagogue
is not set apart from any other small orthodox
synagogues, or for that matter, such groups as a
sporting club, when grasped in these terms. The
processes are "typifications"--typical ways in
which groups solve problems of living, working, and
worshipping together. Gossip and the other
processes are adaptations to Heilman's exigencies
of "commingling." In this sense, the study is of
small groups. Heilman, with his knowledge of
orthodoxy, looks through the Jewish content of the
activities to describe a small voluntary group. In
this sense, it is also a study of Jewish orthodoxy. The two perspectives are intertwined. For
example, proceeding from orthodox norms, he observes that a particular sexual division of labor,
with women assigned a secondary status, is prescribed. Admission to group activities and allocation of prestige are also explained as linked to
orthodox knowledge and practice. Proceeding from
the perspective of sociology, any small collective
adopts criteria for allocating prestige among the
occupants of its several statuses, and those criteria may be related to the significance the group
assigns the activities. Heilman brings these two
perspectives together to elaborate on the synagogue's prestige heirarchy.

The meanings of interest are collective or
cultural meanings. Language, a social currency, is
an indicator par excellence of cultural meanings.
Using this indicator, Heilman observes, for instance, that Yiddish is used for expressing secular
and Hebrew for expressing religious realities.
These are the collective meanings of the use of
those languages.

Another way to determine collective meanings
is to observe the comportment of individuals acting
in concert. The shulhan, or reading table, becomes
sacred when it is the resting place of the Torah
scroll, that is, when worshippers perform a sacred
act around it. The Torah is always holy. This is
known because individuals are always enjoined to
act respectfully in relation to the Torah. The
Torah, or the bundle of meanings it evokes, sancti-
fies that with which it comes in contact. Thus,
the sanctity of the shulhan is realized most clearly during the ritual communal reading of the Torah.

The collective being of the synagogue is created in the enactment, the objectification, of the
meanings.[8] The collective is reified, in a non-
pejorative sense, as an object of orientation for
the actors. Heilman considers conscious and

intentional meanings, and considers the mind to be
self-conscious. Thus, the actors may not quite
formulate their activities and intentions, in
Heilman's language, nor might they articulate all
of the latent functions of these actions, for group
existence. Yet, in each case, they could give
their assent to Heilman's interpretations without
having to peel through layers of unconscious
resistances. In fact, their assent to his
interpretations would be accepted by Heilman as
evidence of the validity of those interpretations. The concentration on concrete meanings
leads to a methodological rejection of the "hypothetical construct"--whatever its referent might
be.[9]   In much scientific work, observables are
interpreted as indicators of unseen concept refer-
ents. Heilman's approach resists the separation of
indicators from concepts. Heilman looks for patterns among events. Indicator events are interpreted in the light of their context. As an example, Heilman conceives of sociability (the concept
of interest) in relation to clique formation (an
observation). Alliances, nonobservable events, are
inferred to exist among members of the congregation. These are inferred from observations of who
sits with whom. He also observes a common culture
among clique members, a tendency among them to observe and deviate along similar lines from Halakhic
doctrine. Finally he notes a similarity of occupations among those who sit together. He could,
but does not, conclude that occupational similarities cause attitudinal and socio-relational affiliation. Rather, occupational status and interests
are intrinsic expressions of the clique. Occupations do not enter as external and objective facts,
but as these are perceived within the religious
collective. The criteria for grouping individuals
by occupation is given in the culture of the syna-
gogue--not by the outside industrial system. Thus,
cliques are formed around religious occupations and
around secular intellectual pursuits. The decision
to sit with one group or another is, thus, expres-
sive of, not a cause of or caused by, the underlying sociability. It is an aspect of that sociability which is, thereby, directly apprehended.

Another example is his observation of the restriction of members of the congregation to different parts of the synagogue. On occasion, men may
legitimately invade the women's section, but women
rarely enter the men's foyer. Heilman interprets
this behavior, and the rules which it follows, as
indicating the dominance of men in the community.

The restriction is not a correlate of but is ex-
pressive of the more general social control exerted
by men, of the dominance of men in the community.
The demonstration of control of space affirms the
more general control. Spatial access is the enacting of a relation of dominance on a particular
occasion.

Heilman validated his interpretations with the
subjects. However, the scientific community imposes a further burden of validation, better termed
confidence. In work of this type, the information
on which the validation was based is not shared;
raw data are not available for independent interpretation by colleagues. In principle, a colleague
could request Heilman's journal but, if he behaves
like other ethnographers have, his notes would be
too cryptic, not clear enough for reanalysis. A
colleague could repeat this study or study other
organizations of the same type. Reviewers do this
implicitly when they ask whether his argument is
persuasive. Unfortunately, precise repetitions of
a study are not possible. The change in time and
of researcher assure that a revisit could not re-
discover the initial situation. This problem makes
the assessment of the validity of Heilman's functional interpretations difficult. The role he
assigns to some particular event in the life of the
collective could be re-examined for the conventionalized event. Yet, the lack of a procedure, interpretive criteria, hermeneutic rules, limits a critique of the interpretations. The critique would
examine alternative interpretations which could depend on observations which Heilman excluded.

The rhetoric, the persuasiveness of Heilman's
writing, goes far to create a sense of confidence
in the reader who, of course, could not share
Heilman's experience--or even examine Heilman's
notes. The reader who would apply usual scientific
criteria for testing validity must view Heilman's
work as tentative. It would not be fair, however,
for a self-righteous scientific community to fault
Heilman in this respect, for the scientific community, under the avalanche of prescribed reading,
often follows the professions in relying on expert
judgment without review of the bases of that judgment. Some humanistic ethnographers write unique
personal documents whose validity, like art, is
internal. This approach also spills into the scientific community, encouraging a desultory attitude
toward documentation.

Explanation: Placing the Event in Its Setting

How does Heilman, in the dramaturgical frame of reference, explain events? An explanation of "why" an event takes place may sometimes be given as a "how," a description of the mechanisms involved, or it may refer to the motives of individuals, or to a set of predisposing conditions, or to a genetically prior state.

Explanation may mean locating the observation in a configuration of events. Like interpretation it becomes a matter of coherence. This is Heilman's preferred approach.[10] The method of coherence, used to arrive at and to interpret findings, is used to explain them. Deepening explanation rests on increasingly precise description of the event and of its context.[11] The most elementary descriptive statement is the existence statement--the mere assertion that an event occurs. Existence and meaning, thus, melt into one another, not a surprising result in view of Heilman's implicit ontology (see footnote 8).

An explanation of events presumes they might have been otherwise. For most scientific research, alternative external conditions would explain a difference in the events. Explanation which invokes an environment must assume an independent status for the outside world. Yet, Heilman's method admits the outside through its reflection in the inner life of the synagogue. The environment appears as a symbolism. Its status is subjective. The influence of external political systems, for instance, on the synagogue remains indeterminant. Without such information, it is not possible to ask, for instance, how this small American orthodox congregation might differ from a congregation in Eastern Europe in the last century. The attitude of the larger society toward voluntary association must influence the fact that the synagogue is chartered as an independent, not-for-profit corporation. Further, the fact that the state charters voluntary groups and the synagogues are tax exempt accounts for some differences between Kehillat Kodesh and its European predecessors, a point not lost on Nathan Glazer, as we will see later. Heilman also does not consider the comparative political structure of religious institutions, for instance, the fact that the synagogue is organized as a unit within a congregational rather than an episcopal polity. The authority of the network of synagogues to which Kehillat Kodesh adheres, for

instance, to appoint rabbinical leadership or to
collect funds is not treated.

Social Boundaries: Defining the Limits
of the Group

The synagogue is Heilman's unit of analysis.
In one sense, the unit is bounded by the premises. Actions external to the synagogue are relevant if recognized as such by the members. The
minimum action settings required for a traditional
orthodox Jewish community are a synagogue, a mikva
(ritual bath), a school, and a kosher meat market. Heilman, however, deals almost entirely with
the synagogue. The other three settings, objec-
tively conceived, are essentially outside of the
study. A Jewish community also includes households, religious leadership, a rabbinical court,
and so forth. The centrality of the synagogue is
recognized because only the synagogue is used by
men, women, and children. The mikva and the meat
market are primarily used by women and the school
by children.
Why is the inclusiveness of the synagogue defined in terms of men, women, and children rather
than in terms of some other social categories? The
centrality of a government, in contrast, is known
by the power exercised by those in control. A
synagogue might be central to the community because
both the working-class and capitalist members of a
community can meet there. Life in the synagogue
reflects neither power nor class structure. The
synagogue rather adumbrates family organization.
The participation of men, women and children in the
synagogue parallels their positions in the patriar-
chal families of the community.
Heilman does not study family life as such but
studies the synagogue against its family back-
drop. The commingling of the synagogue is similar
to the relationships within the family. The synagogue is a "transformation," to use Levi-Strauss'
notion, of the family.
The treatment of the occupations of members
offers another example of the concentration on life
internal to the synagogue. This particular synagogue is distinguished from other orthodox synagogues by the fact that members of more traditional
orthodox synagogues support themselves by religious
and educational work within the Jewish community.
Members of Kehillat Kodesh seek secular education,
attend college, learn a profession and, then, hold

jobs in the general economy. Occupation does not enter the discussion in its own right but only as a way of delimiting the synagogue's boundary.

The synagogue is not only a unit of analysis, it is the unit of analysis. Heilman, thus, never considered the questions so central to the other three authors to be reviewed here--questions of assimilation, the relations between Jews and non-Jews, and the question of Jewish factionalism, the categories of orthodoxy, Jewries, other Jewish religious denominations, and secular Jewry.

The boundaries of this particular synagogue are tested in the definition of the stranger. Interaction with the stranger takes place at the boundaries. Strangers are classified into foreigners who come to pray but are not known by anyone, visitors who are someone's friends, and mendicants or beggars, who are ignored in silence. The stranger may be given an honorific role but this, too, acts to distinguish him from one regularly within the boundary.

Gossip establishes the boundaries of subgroups within the synagogue. Gossip is permitted only among members, and mostly about members. There is an obligation of exchange connected with gossip. Cliques are formed within the larger group. Gossip is shared with the other members of each clique. Thus, there is a fine-tuned differentiation at the heart of the group.

The synagogue is also subdivided into spatial regions. The spatial location of the synagogue as a whole and of the ark, where the Torah rests, have relatively constant contextual meanings. However, the meanings of certain other locations within the synagogue, such as the shulhan, mentioned above, vary over time. For example, the "possession" of space by members changes. On the Sabbath and on holy days, people usually stay in one place during their prayers; on weekdays changing seats during the service is not unusual. Men may even pray in the empty women's section. The bimah itself becomes an open space available to any and all men on weekdays. The Sabbath and holy day sanctuary allows only a minimum of movement.

The meaning of the synagogue changes from a place of prayer to a place of study or to a place of assembly as the activity varies. These meanings may flow one into another. Heilman's comparison of the congregation at prayer to a "jazz ensemble" portrays this dramatic flow within the worship itself. Each worshipper is engaged in his own separate activity. But all periodically return in

unison to a central or basic, collective involvement.

Social Change as Social Clarification

The description of social change is the heart
of Heilman's study. However, Heilman provides no
account of the "causes" of change. He does not
explore the influence of outside groups or even of
history as an objective force. The outside becomes
"faceless and nameless." The influence of other
movements in Judaism is neutralized. For instance,
Heilman tells how members of a nearby Reform Jewish
Temple do not appear as real persons but as an
alien viewpoint.

The change Heilman describes is due to the
exigencies of interaction of the members of the
congregation in disagreements, strains, or the
formation of coalitions. A discord is resolved by
ejecting the person who created the disturbance.
Change is, thus, a process of moving toward clari-
fying the self-definition of the collective.

If the direction of change is toward increasing conformity to internal exigencies, with no external pressure for change, the future of the collective will eventually come to a stable state.
The rules by which actors organize their behavior
with respect to one another come to settle in but
ultimately it will avoid more change.

The method concentrates on the group as it
exists when observed. Any prior experience appears
as myth or ideology. Members recall and recount
crucial events in group history. These are the
basis of the group's consciousness, account for its
origins, and rationalize its current boundaries.
Historical memories include, for example, the expulsion of a subgroup accused of monopolizing honors. The distribution of honors is a way of allocating prestige. Heilman interprets this memory of
an expulsion as the symbolic murder of a leader, a
contribution to group solidarity. This is one of
the few cases in which Heilman delves below the
conscious. As ideology, this memory rationalizes
maintenance of the status quo. Once outside, those
who were expelled, like the outside world, are deprived of potential for introducing change.

Social Control: Holding the Course

There are means to maintain social control and
to discourage change. In Weber's theories of religious organization, charismatic leadership offers
an innovative element. There are no charismatics
and no prophets in Kehillat Kodesh. The leaders
are agents of social control. The gabbai, for
instance, represents the collective in distributing
kibbudim, or honors, symbols of prestige. The distribution is a system of rewards and a mechanism
for maintaining interaction. Kibbudim promote interaction by establishing obligations. One who
receives a kibbud is obligated to reciprocate by
participating in the group. The obligation may be
to the collectivity, such as to appear at services. The obligation may be to an individual,
such as joining a yahrzeit minyan in order to permit him to say kaddish. Such mechanisms, by encouraging interaction, of course, encourages conformity. Though the kibbud may have a variety of
individual meanings, it remains a means by which
the congregation becomes conscious of its own
worth. As a presentation, it expresses collective
sentiments which link individual members to one
another and to the group.
    The group may control its leader. The presi-
dent and hazan have a reality only in so far as the
group has a reality. One can have a community
without a hazan, but no hazan without a community. Their enactments are collective acts.
Heilman describes "quasi-hazanic" activity. In
this an individual, acting for the group with explicit delegation, controls the hazanic style. One
individual in the congregation audibly makes the
hazan aware that the congregation has reached the
end of prayer.
    Gossip, mentioned before as a means to main-
tain boundaries, is also a mechanism of social control. Through it, deviant individuals are censur-
ed. Gossip manipulates information and so constructs the "public faces" of the participants.
Gossip also encourages everyone to show a "public
face" consistent with collective norms. The collective, in this way, dominates deviant tendencies.

The Permanent and the Variable

Theories of social action include both "permanent" and "variable" elements. The permanent elements are some fundamental reality. The variable

may be particular manifestations of that reality
which might change under various conditions. Here,
the role structure of the collective, though in a
process of becoming, is a relatively permanent
reality. The performance of roles in that structure is among the variable elements.

Role performance varies with the characteristics of the role incumbents. The president of the
synagogue, for example, is empowered by and expected to act for the group. The group acts
through him. The group allows a range of ways of
meeting the role requirements. The president at
the time of the study was the mediator of arguments
and the mitigator of tensions. He was a host to
outsiders. Guests were introduced to the president
by host members who, thereby, felt that they had
been presented to the whole synagogue. The president was also a bearer of group-related news, and,
in the last resort, an assembler of the minyan.
His role was that of delegate of the collective.

A subgroup may be delegated to act for the
collective. Heilman points to the regulars who attend the minyan every morning as representing the
collectivity. The action of the regulars as a
group, like that of individuals, is initially variable. However, this minyan becomes structure, a
part of the permanent reality. Heilman's approach
thus allows for the variable to become structure.

The classification of strangers reflects an
interplay between the variable and permanent elements. The individual visitor is a stranger until
he is accepted both by individuals and by the collective. The stranger is accepted when his relations to an individual, the variable, find a place
in the permanent structure of the community.

Social control mechanisms encourage the transformation of the variable into the permanent. Either the individual visitor is absorbed into the
collective or he leaves. The conventionalizing of
prayer reduces the variable elements in liturgy.
The social freedom of the individual lies within
these defined structures. Individuation is not
individualization. Individuation is discovering a
group-sanctioned role and enacting it in a variant
way. Individualization is a form of alienation
from the group.

The Survival of Orthodoxy in a
Secularizing Society

Heilman portrays orthodoxy as surviving by
retreating into a sacred space free of

environmental pressure. The collective, within
this space, transforms the secular world for the
purposes of the religious. The apparent solution
is a function of the method which denies independent, objective power to the outside world to shape
the world within. This peculiarity will become
apparent when we compare Heilman's frame of reference with that of the next three authors. All of
them work in frames of reference which grant determining power to the environment. As a result, they
see the issues of assimilation and the resistance
to assimilation as central.

SOCIAL ALIENATION WITH ECONOMIC PARTICIPATION:
POLL ON THE HASIDIM

A Pariah People and Its Delegates

Solomon Poll's initiating question is: How
can a group remain separate, socially and culturally, from an encompassing society and, at the same
time, participate in its economy and material culture? This is the puzzle for Poll in his study of
Hasidim. Heilman is concerned with the maintenance
of Judaism by those who choose a secular occupation. Poll is concerned with the problem of economic survival for those who have chosen to be
Hasidim. Both are concerned with life in two
worlds. Poll reintroduces Max Weber's concept of a
guest or a pariah people, a subgroup ritually separated and, ordinarily, occupationally specialized. The pariah people fill an economic niche in
the wider society.
The issue Poll raises is not whether an individual who participates in the American economy
must compromise Jewish religious obligations.
Rather, it is how a community can maintain its
integrity while sharing in national economic
life. Heilman's work grows out of an ethnographic
tradition, with significant phenomenological over-
tones. Poll models his work on American community
studies of subcollectivities. These studies pay
particular attention to hierarchies of power. Poll
does not concern himself directly with hierarchies
of power. From the traditional community studies,
he adopts the image of community as a network of
externally related associations. How may a social
unit join others in a network but prevent the members of the network from influencing its own internal life. He discovers an answer in a social

mechanism by which only a few members of the Hasidic community enter the external economy. The rest of the community might never, in any significant sense, meet a member of the larger society in an economic role.

The Hasidim of Williamsburg, Poll notes, migrated to the United States after World War II, most of them after release from concentration camps. They have rigorously and, so far, successfully resisted acculturation to American societal patterns--a matter that calls for an historical comment. Which prior communities are the antecedents of the Williamsburg group? Are the communities which emerged during the eighteenth century in several European countries, vaguely joined by the term Hasidism, the actual or ideologically perceived predecessors? Alternatively, are the biological ancestors of current residents of Brooklyn the appropriate historical line? Some biological ancestors were Hasidim and some were not. Some came from Hungarian villages, and some did not. Poll decides, probably on the basis of the country of birth of a good number of the members of the community, that the Hasdim of Hungary will be taken as a group of origin. Social autonomy in the Hungarian village, Poll implies, was the condition that permitted the Hasidic society to form. Transferred to the United States, this form of autonomy becomes a model of segregated living. Yet, other Hungarian Jews enjoyed the same autonomy but rejected it in Hungary in favor of assimilation. Still others were religiously orthodox in Hungary but did not follow segregated living in the United States. Further, Hasidim from Poland and from the Russian pale, without having had political autonomy, live in segregated communities in America.

The Transferability of Sociological Concepts

The Concept of Sect

Heilman is conservative in applying general sociological concepts, derived to classify events in other times and places, for defining the reality of Kehillat Kodesh. Poll, on the contrary, subsumes the behavior of the Hasidim of Williamsburg under general sociological concepts. Using such general concepts Poll compares Williamsburg Hasidim to small groups in other faiths.

But, with which other groups should Hasidim be classed? The social type to which Hasidim belong

is, Poll writes, the religious sect. Sociologists
have studied the Dukhobors and Mennonites, who,
like Hasidim, are distinguished by their insular-
ity. Self-sufficient agriculture permits the first
two groups to remain aloof from the material culture of the general society. Most other kinds of
industrial or commercial pursuits would draw them
into work relations, if not into more primary social relations, with outsiders. In contrast, Mor-
mons have retained religious distinctiveness while
participating in commercial and industrial life and
sharing the material culture. Perhaps this case
bears greater resemblance to that of the Hasidim.

Poll invokes Troeltsch's church-sect notion.
This idea relates the internal structure of religious groups to their participation, or refusal to
participate, in the secular world. The church-sect
hypothesis emerged as a model of Christian religious organizational history. The rules governing
sectarianism are not equally helpful for understanding the emergence of Sufism in Islam or Zen in
Buddhism, if only because of the different roles
played by these religions in society. The Hasidim
share with other sects, as described by Troeltsch,
their small size, intimate social relations, and
intense and consuming religious life. They differ
on other criteria. Sectarian religious communities
organize in opposition to an established church and
question the legitimacy of the polity supporting
that church establishment. Hasidim stand outside
of but not in opposition to the national polity.
The Christian sects tend to be charismatic and to
legitimate rules on the basis of the inspired dec-
larations of a prophetic leader. Such rules may
even contravene tradition. The Hasidim are devoted
followers of a rebbe, but the rebbe is no law-
maker. He is a law interpreter and judge of case
law. Torah, and its exegeses, the legal system,
stands as the ultimate authority.

Poll, sensing an ill fit between the
Troeltschean sect-church and his observations of
Hasidim, abandons the analogy after a few pages.
Poll becomes ambivalent about pursuing the compar-
ative material which, perhaps, had been introduced
as a bow to the sociological profession. For some
reason, he does not review historical materials on
Hasidim.

His conceptual frame is that of institutional
sociology, the explanatory bias functionalist and
the method participant observation. General sociological ideas about assimilation and social segregation are prominent in his work. He is

particularly interested in those organizational
arrangements which foster social segregation and
which, thus, dampen the force of assimilation.

In Hungary and in the United States, the
isolation of the Hasidim is preserved by maintaining Hasidic schools and religious organizations
separate from those of Jewish orthodoxy. Other
orthodox Jews adapt to aspects of the wider culture. They may speak the language of the country,
here English, and dress in clothing which, though
ritually distinctive (not containing both animal
and vegetable fibres), is not visibly distinctive
in apparent material or in style. Hasidim associate these and other accommodations with the beginning of extinction of the "entire Jewish existence." Hasidim discourage communication with
outsiders by their reading of their own community
newspapers and ignoring the general mass media.
They also wear special clothing and speak Yiddish
and Hungarian in daily life and Hebrew in prayer.[12]

The Hasidim can resist assimilation for three
reasons. First, objective contrasts between the
societies limit interaction and, thus, maintain
segregation. Second, an ideology of elitism, held
by the Hasidim, accounts for their maintaining isolation. Third, social control within the community
is strong, which also accounts for a high level of
family stability, taken by them as a sign of resistance to assimilation. Sociological literature
has, ordinarily, reported family instability following a disruptive, disintegrating period. Poll's
observations are of scattered survivors of concentration camps, less than two decades after their
release. Thus, family stability among Hasidim
contrasts sharply with that in other groups.
Poll's explanation for this phenomenon is the
strength of control mechanisms of the community.

This sets the stage for the conundrum. Poll
describes the integrality of the community. At the
same time, he shows that it derives material resources from the wider society, the very contacts
being feared, if not proscribed. To explain the
behavior of the community in the face of this
issue, Poll calls upon classic concepts of sociol-
ogy--concepts of stratification and of economic
behavior. Hasidic behavior, defined by the actors
as "Torah-true," is analyzed using conceptual categories imported from general sociology.

Social Class: An Ill-fitting Concept

Social stratification is an ordering of social
positions. Societies differ in the criteria they
apply to establish ranks. The criteria used by a
larger society are often adopted by a subgroup for
its internal ordering. That subgroup, by accepting
a cultural principle of the larger society, is assimilating itself to that society. Cultural and
social segregation is expressed by the subgroup
that holds to its own criteria. The Hasidim do not
rely on general American criteria.

Poll describes Hasidim using the language of
social class stratification while, in actuality, he
is observing a system of prestige, not class, ranking. The concept of class, borrowed from general
sociology, implies a hierarchical order, such as is
commonly associated with economic stratification.
Prestige, based on religion, may neither be correlated with political power nor material wealth.
The Hasidim are ordered in six distinct social
"classes" according to the frequency and intensity
of religious observances. The rebbes and a handful
of other individuals are at the top. Closely associated with them are the shtickel rebbes. The lowest rank consists of yiddin, all of those not
labelled as outstanding in terms of their religious
qualifications. The community is a hierocracy, a
system of religious statuses differing in scope and
area of authority.

Poll follows the methods used by sociologists
who have studied social class. Warner and his
associates, for example, using interviews, sorted
families and groups of families by prestige reflected in associational preferences. The personal
associational preferences extended to community
organizational participation, mate selection and
residential location. Families sorted in this way
were then found to differ in cultural interests, as
indicated, for example, by reading habits as well
as in education, occupation, and income level.
Here the American community concept becomes misleading when applied to Hasidim. Among Hasidim,
members of all prestige ranks probably read the
same newspapers, attend the same synagogues, have
similar incomes, belong to the same communal organizations, and reside in the same buildings--though
they may differ educationally.

Poll also demonstrates a coincidence between
prestige and occupation in the Williamsburg community. This seems to be presumptive evidence that
the prestige ranking is, indeed, an indicator of

class. The occupational ranking, however, is based
on a measure of the religious involvement permitted
or prescribed within the occupations. Prestige and
occupational position, as Poll measures them, are
two manifestations of position in the religious
order. The correlation is artifactual.

In Poll's presentation, the two Hasidic leadership categories, the rebbes and the shtickel
rebbes, seem to have a social control function.
Yet, closer examination reveals that this seemingly
political role is exercised through their judicial
capacity. The judicial will, unlike the political,
is implemented by members of the community through
gossip and ridicule, among other informal means,
rather than by threat of force.

Stratification appears in all social groups
large enough to divide labor on some social basis
beyond age and sex. Social functions divided among
the social segments are differentially rewarded.
Talcott Parsons views this differential distribution of social rewards as a mechanism to assure
role performance. Again the concept fails to match
the empirical situation of the Hasidim. Rewards
based on stratification are not relevant for the
Hasidic community. As a religious society, the
principal rewards are intrinsic to the observance
of mitzvot, the enactment of religious duties.
Aristotle distinguished the authority of a master
over a slave from that of a father over a son. The
authority relation between industrial classes follows Aristotle's first model. The subordinate is
compelled to serve the ends of the superordinate.
In a religious society the father-son model is more
apposite. The superordinate expects conformity to
religious norms on the part of the subordinate in
the interest of the subordinate's own welfare.
That is, higher ranks do not exert authority to
control resources but have the responsibility to
serve, guide, and teach the lower ranks.[13]

In the American studies, family is the unit of
analysis in the analysis of the hierarchical ordering of families in the community. Poll would have
found a model fitting the empirical data more
closely had he borrowed concepts used for the
internal analysis of kinship systems. The Satmar
and the Habad Hasidim are quasi-primary groups,
"quasi" in the sense that their solidarity depends
not on genetic ties but on the commitments of
faith.

Poll's use of the conceptual tools of sociology can enrich our understanding of the Hasidim by
comparing them with other societies but, that

method is less likely than Heilman's to allow a
society to speak for itself. Poll correctly seeks
a concept of social order. However, the specific
one he chose, stratification, distorts our view of
Hasidic society. The Hasidic "community" differs
from American communities in its structure of influence and power. Kinship concepts or those based
on Weber's notion of the religious congregation,
the gemeinde, would have been more suitable.

A Capitalist Economy in a Traditionalist Community?

The economic activities of the Hasidic community are the subject of the second part of Poll's
work. Principally, these are occupations involving
retail exchange and finishing manufactured material. Poll borrows from the analysis of capitalism
ideas of interest and profits to discuss the economic motivation of Hasidim.[14] Capitalism is associated with particular economic rules and practices. These include the tendency toward a free
market, free labor, and the rational organization
of the means of production by firms oriented toward
profit. The Hasidic economy does not operate
through a free market, nor would the Hasidim want
it that way. Commodities and services are not
traded solely for profit. Hasidic retail stores,
following Poll's description, are more like budgetary units in an economy of administered prices than
capitalist firms. Budgetary units are concerned
with price-efficient consumption rather than with
profit making. Prices in Hasidic shops are not set
by competition. They are established on the recom-
mendation of a community authority, based on a conception of an appropriate price.[15] The shops are
under the supervision of the rebbes.
The context makes the use of the term profits
equivocal. Poll refers to the "profits" of the
butcher shops, some of which are remitted for the
support of Hasidic schools. The followers of a
particular rebbe are captive buyers in the shops
for which he vouches. The "profits" are, thus,
guaranteed surpluses of near monopolies.
The products in the stores are specialized for
religious customers and, thus, they do not compete
with other stores selling similar products. These
products include Hasidic foodstuffs prepared in the
community and Hasidic clothing such as black stockings for women, referred to as Hasidic stockings.

In capitalist societies, earnings are tied to
productivity, hours on the job, and labor market
conditions in a particular occupation and industry. In Hasidic society, work and earnings are relatively dissociated, seeming to be set according
to a sense of equity and need. The incentive for a
woman to work in the shops is not financial, but,
says Poll, that she may thus contribute to her husband's peity. She thereby releases her husband to
spend more time in study and prayer.
     Hasidic schools are private and parochial.
They are supported by "taxes," really a tithing,
raised from both Hasidic and sympathetic non-
Hasidic orthodox Jews as well as a tuition
schedule. Collectors of these funds may receive a
commission. Collections are a transfer payment,
not an exchanging of goods or services. Wealth is
transferred on the basis of a communal relationship. By virtue of membership in this community,
parents must send their children to these schools
and pay tuition. Tuition is set according to
income and family size. Parents' commitment to a
particular rebbe carries the expectation that their
children will attend the school for which he
vouches.
     However, the Hasidic economy is not self-
sufficient. For it to survive, a flow of resources
must be available from outside. Poll does not
analyze economic relations with the wider economy
in any detailed fashion despite the significance of
the way this relationship is conducted for Hasidic
cultural integrity. This omission may derive from
his fascination with the mechanisms of social segregation which bar ties with the outside. Poll
does explain that no primary or secondary produc-
tive activities take place in Williamsburg. No
Hasid there, is a miner or farmer. The products of
some small-scale manufacturers, particularly of
religious articles and food, are sold to non-
Hasidic orthodox Jews.
     Poll hints at, but does not document, the em-
ployment of some members of the community by businesses outside the community. At the beginning of
his working life, a Hasidic Jew may earn initial
capital by working as an "operator" of a machine.
Presumably, this work is in a factory outside the
community. Income from such relatively menial
labor would hardly suffice to maintain the community. As a result of this gap in his analysis, Poll
does not answer the question about outside influence. The outside is simply not examined, although
there is nothing in Poll's field method or in the

community studies tradition to prevent him from
doing so. In fact, capitalist economic concepts
should have led him to look more at external
sources of income through a market analysis.
Heilman neglects a study of the objective social
environment because of the logic of the phenomenological frame of reference. Poll neglects the economic and political setting despite the logic of
the conceptual frame he imposes.

The limitation is influenced by the perspective of the other tradition he follows, -- the
study of small, separatist religious sects.
Students of those sects also do not, as a rule,
deal extensively with external relations. The
sociology of sects tends to consider only the
window through which those sects look at other
religious groups. Poll's academic heroes, Max
Weber and Ernst Troeltsch, did study the
institutional influences on religious culture.

A closing word about the use of capitalist
categories. Poll's own sociological analysis reveals the difficulty in using them. The capitalist
economy is characterized by the extent to which
economic transactions are free from control by the
polity, by the family, and by religion. Poll
emphasizes that economic institutions among the
Hasidim have not been separated from their other
institutions. Religion determines the items to be
produced and the items to be consumed and even the
items one may hold. His discussion of the
significance of "trusting" is revealing of the
affinity of economic and religious institutions.
The issue is not "trusting" regarding money, but
trusting that the foodstuffs are, for example,
ritually appropriate. As another example, taking
interest from a fellow Hasid, while forbidden, is
accomplished through a subterfuge which circumvents
religious strictures. A loan is treated as an investment for which the lender receives a share of
the "profit." The amount of "profit" is based on
the amount of money lent. The relationship resem-
bles that of partners in a business. Hasidim would
never resort to the civil courts in case of a de-
fault. The history of religious adaptations to
canons against usury demonstrates that capitalist
concepts of interest are unnecessary for Poll's
analysis and, probably, misleading.

The Sacred Community and Other Forms of Social Defense

Most sociological analysis begins with an image of order, or disorder, in social relationships. The conditions for achievement of social solidarity or social cohesion are analytically central. Poll breaks with this customary sociological concern, a matter which makes his work unique. He uses what might be termed a sociological "counter-concept."[16] Poll studies intentional and creative alienation. Alienation from the immediate social setting is the community's goal, and social and informational segregation are among the means to that goal. Poll studies socially ordered activities which prevent the formation of certain relationships.

As mentioned earlier, Max Weber's concept of a pariah people is reintroduced. the pariah or guest people are ritually separated from those around them. Generally, the image is of the dominant group excluding the pariah. In Williamsburg, in contrast, the Hasidim separate themselves from non-Jews, and from religiously Orthodox Jews.[17] The pariah status is enforced less by the society at large than by the segregated group through its own notions of ritual purity and special convenant. It is a notion familiar in the study of elites. Like many religiously "elect" groups, the Hasidim are elite in their own estimation. No one outside is asked to validate that judgment.

The most important concept by which traditional sociology designates creative alientation is that of the sacred. The sacred is set apart and a sacred people is a people set apart--a pariah people. From the perspective of the sacred, the profane is the alienated condition--symbolizing man's loss of relation to God. The world of the Hasidim is sacred and all others are profane. The Hasidim apply religious categories to all things. The concept of "purity and holiness," for instance, says Poll, distinguishes things according to whether they meet traditional Hasidic requirements.

Social control, through gossip and ridicule, as among many groups, is a way of censuring those who introduce ritual change and possibly open the way to outside relationships. The community's own specialized health and welfare organizations further limit opportunities for interaction with the larger society. The attitude of the Hasidim toward the group boundary is apocalyptic; even the smallest deviation presages Jewish extinction. To

understand this, usually sociological ideas are
inadequate. Religious imagery is more helpful.

The social boundaries are breached at two
points. Hasidim share the American society's technology and some enter occupations in non-Hasidic
settings. Technology tends to involve a particular
social organization for acquiring and using it. A
society that accepts a technology accepts a relationship with that organization and certain associated cultural constraints, a lesson familiar to the
Japanese after the mid-nineteenth century. Owning
an automobile, for instance, requires direct or
indirect contact with automobile manufacturers and
retailers, with gas station attendants and mechanics. Drivers become subject to rules, such as
those in the motor vehicle code and, then, are exposed to the law-making, law-enforcing, and judicial arms of the larger society. The Hasidim try to
neutralize these influences by viewing the automobile as a way of delivering children to the house
of study. They sacralize the secular act, says
Poll. This, though, is an argument from final
cause. Adaptations must be made in acquiring and
operating the automobile. These must leave their
mark, but only certain members of the community
need make this compromise.

Hasidim have no need for physical separation. They live cheek to jowl (that metaphor may
be appropriate in view of the political activism in
Brooklyn which Poll does not study) with non-Jews
and orthodox Jews. Their daily habits, clothing,
speech, and eating patterns are distinct enough to
set them apart.

Hasidim are especially attentive to the boundary between themselves and orthodox Jews. For
judgment on law, for instance, Hasidim will not go
to a non-Hasidic rabbi, who, it is asserted, would
not be a competent religious authority.[18] The line
is maintained by overconforming to the norm, per-
forming mitzvot in an excessive and minute manner. They accept the Torah-based norm but reject
the Jewish community's usual way of fulfilling
it. They pray in the synagogue, have an ark for
the Torah, and an Eastern orientation for prayer.
However, they reject the architectural appoint-
ments, such as the cupolas and fixed seating pattern of large institutional synagogues. They
criticize more liberal Jews whose synagogues are
decorated with stars and whose rabbis and cantors
wear academic robes.

Poll points out that non-Hasidic orthodox Jews
serve as agents when the Hasidic Jews must deal

with the outside world. These non-Hasidic Jews,
who are partially acculturated, provide a channel
through which some American cultural ways penetrate
the Hasidic community. Poll shows that this is the
case for Hasidim living in Israel. Hasidim find it
more difficult to remain separate in Israel where
they are one among many exotic groups appearing in
Jewish communities.

The acculturative influence is unidirectional,
a matter not explained by Poll. One reason is that
the relative power of the groups on either side of
a boundary controls the direction of flow of cultural influence. The Israeli situation is more
tenuous beause Israelis are less likely than Americans to exempt the Hasidim from civic participation
on groups of religious conscience.

In a sense, all scholarly work is unfinish-
ed. Generally, though, scholars try to bring a
sense of solution to the problem originally set,
that continuing the inquiry becomes only a matter
of increasing precision and depth or clarification
of unresolved issues. Poll's effort does not
achieve a sense of closure. A variety of issues
needed to resolve the problem are not mentioned.
Principally, the outside economic activity that
does occur is unanalyzed. The search for a sociological rubric in which to fit the data creates the
procrustean problem. He shortens the legs and
holds on to ill-fitting concepts. As an educated
Hasidic insider, Poll drew little from his own
cultural resources. Hasidic life is immersed in
the sacred text, yet, here is a study of Hasidim
with little Torah and no Talmud. And, even stranger, no Midrash, no prayer with kavanah and no song.

INDENTITY IN JEWISH SUBURBIA: THE PSYCHOLOGY OF
                    SOCIETY

Does Social Continuity Depend upon Cultural
                    Continuity?

Marshall Sklare and Joseph Greenblum's study
of Jewish Identity on the Suburban Frontier considers the commitment of Jews to Jewry as reflected in
their religious practice. May social continuity be
affirmed when culture changes? To what extent may
communal ties persist while the culture, previously
peculiar to that community, changes. This is an
old question. When did Christianity cease being a
Jewish sect and become a new religion? Is Judaism

organized around legal texts and rabbi-teachers
continuous with a faith, bearing the same name,
oriented to a priesthood and temple sacrifices?   If
Jews in American suburbia cease being Judaists,
will they still rally to Jewry?

Sklare organized the survey of a community at
the fringes of a major city. He arranged for the
American Jewish Committee to interview Jews and the
National Opinion Research Center to interview gentiles. Sklare supplemented the survey results by
studying records of synagogues in Lakeville, a
suburb of Lake City, the central metropolis.

Kehillat Kodesh and the Hasidic community were
of intrinsic interest to the researchers. They
were not studied as a way to understand other
Hasidim or other small orthodox synagogues.
Lakeville, in contrast, is a window for viewing the
wider American Jewish community. Heilman and Poll
study Jews who endeavor to limit change in their
way of life. Sklare and Greenblum and the work of
Glazer, to follow, study a rapidly changing sector
of Jewish society. They explain change as a response to an external press. Yet, the external
society is little analyzed, remaining a looming
presence.

For Heilman, individuals appear as enactors of
the collective script. Sklare and Greenblum assume
that individual identity existed prior to and is
the foundation of group identity. The strength of
the collective is the aggregated strength of its
individuals. The shift of individuals from a minority to a majority culture is self-annihila-
ting. Its aggregate result is a group nihilism.

The term frontier assumes a connotation of
cultural confrontation at a social boundary defined
territorially. The term clues us to the importance
of residential settlement for cultural change.
Jewish population densities, among other factors,
control the rate at which identities shift. Sklare
and Greenblum therefore chose to study Lakeville,
with a moderate concentration, but not a majority,
of Jews who are moving toward the social frontier,
because to study life in such a suburb is to look
into the future of American Jewry.[19]

The Dominance of Method

Data Gathering

Identity, A Measure of Intensity of Commitment.
Sklare and Greenblum used the term identity to

describe an attitude toward the self. It involves
perceiving one's location, as a group member, in
relation to members of other groups. Identity does
not emerge, here, as a psychological concept. It
is not a focus around which personality attributes
cohere. Identity, rather, draws the individual to
his religion and religious culture. The study
measures the strength, and the change in strength,
of identity. A Jewish ethnography might study the
content of this self attitude for its own sake.
These authors avoid the analysis of culture. They
use different positions on cultural items, whatever
those items may be, as indicators of the "salience"
or prominence of Jewishness in the individual's
life, and as measures of the "intensity" of the
individual's attachment to Jews. The study measures the attraction to or avoidance of the life
represented by the norms toward which an attitude
is assumed. Gentile society and culture, analyzed
in a companion work, is an attraction, for the most
part, away from Judaism. An identity, then, is
represented as a resultant of pushes and pulls, a
metaphor of physical force. Factors which influence identity include the length of the exposure of
the subject to acculturative activities of the
wider world. Exposure to the outside world is also
indicated by participation in political organizations, attendance at public high school, and participation in general local philanthropies. In the
face of these attractions, the authors measured the
strength of the respondents' attraction to Jewry by
their religious ritual observances. Respondents
were asked about holiday observances, home rituals,
and synagogue attendance. The extent of participation in secular affairs, Yiddishist or Zionist, was
not determined, probably reflecting the Jewish situation in Lakeville.

The method of taking traditional observances
as normative means that an individual's sense of
identity will be said to decrease with his ideological shift from Orthodoxy to Reform. The measures
would not tap the identity of a Reform Jew when it
rests solely on ritual adherence. The measure does
not assess the Judaic grounding of ethical commitment when that ground is not Halakhic.

Sklare and Greenblum also studied their subjects' attitudes toward Israel as an indicator of
identity. This relation is assessed in terms of
its meaning for American Jewish-gentile relations
rather than in terms of the meaning of Israel.

Generalization and the Independent Variables. As is wont in surveys, Sklare and Greenblum

rely on background variables to study Lakeville,
although these are not a part of the analysis of
identity. They provide a context for analysis and
indicate the extent to which the study can be
relied upon to understand other communities. The
average age of Jewish men in the sample is 43.1, of
women 37.6. They are in families with young and
adolescent children, a bit later in their family
life cycle than the average. Relatively high in
occupational prestige, they are, disproportionately, in professional, technical, and managerial
jobs. The authors are prepared to project their
findings onto populations with similar characteristics. The authors project the Lakeville social
profile as prospective for other Jewish communities. This line of reasoning is tenuous, but,
then, most social science propositions are "accidental universals"--true only under restricted
social conditions.

The suggestion that demographic similarity of
people in different communities means that a feeling of identity or assimilation would be the same
is a crude basis for making predictions. Age and
sex may be correlated with identity or assimilation, but they are not the relevant indicators by
themselves. The generalization of the findings to
other communities similar to Lakeville would have
to be made on the basis of the major independent
variables of the study, not simply on the basis of
demographic similarity. These facts include occupational opportunity and number of generations
since immigration. Other relevant independent variables could include the collective prestige of the
Jewish community and the religio-ethnic mix of the
surrounding non-Jewish community, among others.

The researchers hypothesize that identity is a
function of the number of generations since the respondents' ancestors' immigration into the United
States, and whether those immigrants were of German
or East European descent.

The exposure of a larger number of generations
to American society and culture implies greater
acculturation. Descent, whether from Germany or
Eastern Europe, is a proxy for the length of American cultural experience. Education, a common correlate of acculturation, is statistically eliminated from the analysis. It does not follow that
education has neither a theoretical nor a practical
influence on identity. This is rather an artifact
of the method the authors relied upon, multivariate
analysis, which strives to reduce the number of
variables rather than to weave all of them into a

pattern. If considering the number of generations
a family has lived in the United States as an indicator of acculturation can be used more successfully than education to predict institutional participation, then education may be eliminated from
the analysis. The number of generations of a family is a better predictor because of its association with other acculturative influences -- such as
area of residence, type of occupation, tradition-
alism in Jewish education, and degree of religious
mix among friends and relatives. However, education is a mediator in the acculturative process.
As a variable, it may not increase predictive power
but it is crucial to an explanation of how the result comes about.

The unit of analysis in this study is the
individual. Sklare and Greenblum discuss marital
and parent-child relations and hold that Jewish
friendship circles and Jewish organizational memberships are contemporary substitutes for traditional kinship ties. The community is thought of
as a collective of individuals who join organizations. Synagogues, in which membership is by
household, are organized on the basis of commonal-
ities among members such as their stage in the
family life cycle, secular education, and orientation to assimilation. The idea that individuals
join organizations as family delegates is not considered. Thus, it seems that no mediating group
exists between the individual and the community.
Of course, this may be a finding. If so, it would
reveal a change in the nature of Jewish identity.
Unfortunately, though, the reader cannot know
whether that is the case.

Unsociological Aspects of the Social Survey.
The survey method is a powerful sociological tool,
and yet it may be unsociological. Ordinarily, it
is characterized by a relatively standardized interview, guaranteeing that variability in responses
will not be attributed to variability in stimuli
related to the interview. A random sample of people is selected for questioning from the population. The responses are evaluated using quantita-
tive multivariate data analysis. The problem of
standardizing the stimulus implies isolating the
stimulus so as to isolate the response for treatment as a variable. However, most meaningful
social and personal characteristics may only be
revealed as patterns of social attributes, which
are finally revealed by using scaling and typological procedures. The method presumes that personal
characteristics, such as attitudes, can be treated

as if they are objects distributed in space. The
associations among the attributes are determined by
their relative positions in that space. Each location or attitude is considered to be independent of

all others; the search is for the occurrence of
objects at the same time.
        In sampling, unconnected social units are se-
lected, although the fabric of society consists of
relational patterns. The connections between individuals or households or norms are crucial. When
the unit of analysis is an individual, the tendency
is for the analysis to become psychological. Data
may be gathered from individuals in order to discuss cultural and social relations. Sklare and
Greenblum are, however, drawn to a psychological
analysis by the methodological characteristics of
surveys, the idea of the independence of the unit
of analysis.
        Procedures for multivariate analysis require
rather large data sets as well as a variety of assumptions about the scaling, level of measurement
and distribution of the data. The Lakeville sample
is small, from the perspective of the analytic procedures involved. Further, the data under consideration lack the precision and stability needed for
the proper application of small-sample statistics. In adapting to these constraints the ana-
lysts make decisions about quantification of data
which obscure the meaning of the data. We now turn
to an example of this.
        Identity Scores that Ignore Cultural Vari-
ability. Jewish identity is measured by the degree
of commitment to sacramental religion. Respondents
were asked about ritual observance: whether or not
ham is served in their homes, kosher meat bought,
candles lit, or kiddush said, among other practices. The intensity of identification is determined by the number of rituals observed in the
individuals' households. The mean for the entire
group is slightly over two observances with those
observing but one or two rituals being the largest
group. Those with a score of two, for instance,
could have observed any two of 11 rituals. Four or
five of the 11 rituals were disproportionately
selected.
        This decision to give a score based on the
number of rituals precipitates two problems--a
technical statistical problem in the data analysis
and a problem of interpretation of the meaning of
the data. The comparative analysis of the strength
of the feeling of Jewish identity among the several

groups in the study is technically encumbered. The authors compare mean levels of observance among those who differ in the number of generations the families have been in America and between those descended from German or East European forebears. A distribution of 11 items with mean and mode of two is highly skewed. The standard deviation, measures of dispersion, would be rather large relative to the differences between means of the groups. Consequently, the statistical significance of the differences between the observed means is often in doubt. The authors chose not to present the measures of dispersion and the tests of significance associated with the comparisons.

The work was written during a period of controversy over the use of tests of significance. It was argued that such tests were not appropriately applied when the distributions were seriously skewed, as is the case here, and when the cases do not constitute a random sample of the population of interest, as is also the case here. Under these conditions, presentation of a series of differences in means supporting a persuasive argument was recommended in place of the tests of statistical significance. Since the study examines only a small number of independent variables, principally generation and descent, such a series of tables is not possible. Further, because the sample consists of only a few hundred cases, when the population is classified by descent, for example, the compared means are, in one case, based on 13 and 26 cases. Given this paucity of cases, the differences in means are not likely to be found to be statistically significant.

The implication of this technical problem in the treatment of data is that the assertions about these differences in means between groups may not be true. A fortiori, any generalizations from these assertions about Jewish identity, or explanations of them, may be fatuous. This is not always the case. Some of the differences between the means appear, on their face, to be statistically significant. For instance, we learn that Jews living in Lakeville of the second generation, and of East European descent, averaged 3.3 while their parents averaged 7.5 observances based upon 140 cases. A difference so large is unlikely to have occurred by chance.

The problem of interpreting the meaning of the scores arises from the operation for obtaining them. Since, as mentioned above, the observances

which were combined to make up the scores may differ, the substantive meaning of the scores is elusive. The arithmetic summing of the number of
observances equates the contributions of each to
that score. The contribution of one ritual is sub-
stitutable for that of another. Were the several
practices alternate indicators of the same underlying dimension, called degree of observance, this
logic would be acceptable.[20] A factor analysis
might classify the 11 indicators into two or three
groups--each reflecting a meaningful, but different, aspect of sacramental religion. A score of
two, for instance, could be obtained by a person
who does not eat bread on Passover and who fasts on
Yom Kippur, but who smokes on the Sabbath and eats
ham the rest of the year. This individual might be
traditionally religious, or irreligious--but observes food taboos. Another person with the identical score might light candles on Hanukka and have
a Passover Seder but eat bread on Passover and not
fast on Yom Kippur. This individual might be a
secular nationalist, having participated in occasions which connote ethnic events. The overlapping
event, the Seder, would have divergent meanings for
each of them. Observing food taboos or lighting
candles or fasting on Yom Kippur defines diverse
kinds of Jewish religious expression.
     The authors are aware of alternative scoring
procedures. Is the difficulty simply a technical
problem of coping with a small sample?[21] The reasons for their decision are probably not simply
technical. These decisions are consistent with the
selection of the survey method for data gathering,
and its associated multivariate procedures for data
analysis. They all follow from their quantitative-
ly expressable lawlike statements.
     Their question is not about the type of ident-
ity but about the quantity of identity. The population is ordered on the basis of the extent (or
intensity) of identity characterizing each individual. The underlying variable of interest is the
strength of attachment to Jewry. They might have
chosen more direct measures of loyalty such as
willingness to declare oneself Jewish under varying
degrees of social penalty. Instead, they chose indicators of ritual behavior, assuming that cultural
conformity corresponds to social attachment. The
truth of this assumption is not obvious. Jews
bereft of Judaic culture may be fiercely loyal. On
the contrary, they may be deeply Judaic.
     Having decided for cultural indicators, why
did the authors treat culture as homogeneous. They

might have discriminated between rituals oriented,
for instance, to man and the cosmos, or to guilt in
the relations among men, or to fate and the contin-
gencies of human action, or to the discrepancies
between the actual state of the world and a utopian
condition--to mention a few. Each category of
rituals would correspond to a type of Jewish
identity.

Inattention to this issue is grounded in a
particular Jewish ideology of identity. This
ideology, in a sense, follows the academic psychology of ego involvement which often neglects the
nature of the object with which the ego is involved
in favor of a study of the degree of involvement.[22] The neglect of object analysis, treating
the 11 rituals as interchangeable, leaves a gap in
a study of Judaism or Jewry.

A colloquial Jewish saying has it that there
are many ways of expressing one's Jewishness. Some
express a secular national culture through commitment to the Hebrew or Yiddish language; others express loyalty to Jewry through political activity;
and others express a commitment to Judaism through
study of Torah, ritual observance of mitzvot or a
combination of these. Were Jewish identity a
single underlying characteristic having these
alternative manifestations, the measure need not
distinguish between its manifestations.

However, for most serious purposes, the arena
of expression has both intrinsic and extrinsic
importance. The intrinsic significance is, as
illustrated above, in distinguishing the cultural
meanings of the rituals. The extrinsic significance arises in relating identity to tendencies to
intermarry, to convert, to contribute to a hospital
run by Jews, or to build a synagogue, or, as occurs
in this study, to build a synagogue affiliated with
one or another Jewish denomination. Commitment in
each of these arenas is not equally predicted by
each of the rituals.

Data Analysis

Psychological Explanations for Social
Events. The meanings of rituals are not ignored
throughout the entire work. Sklare and Greenblum
point out that ritual observance is found to decline in later generations and some observances
decline more than others. The term generation is,
in this study, a proxy for exposure to accultur-
ating influences. Thus, the change in observance
from one generation to another is not explained as

a cohort effect but in terms of the way social and cultural factors impact on the observances. For example, Sklare and Greenblum explain that those rituals are retained which may be redefined in modern terms, which do not demand social isolation, which accord with the religious culture of the larger community, and which are centered on the child. Since the index score masks the identities of the specific retained rituals, these explanations could not come from correlates of those scores. Rather, the authors examine the "marginal" frequencies of observance for each of the rituals in the entire respondent population. This would reveal which rituals were most likely to be retained. The explanations are then hypothetical rather than tested explanations. This is neither unreasonable nor unusual in research practice.

One would expect the explanations to derive from the independent variables of the study, generation and descent. This is not the case. The authors observe the decline of food taboos and the increase in the frequency of the lighting of Hanukka candles. The explanations for these observations are plausible applications of a theory about the compatibility of cultural elements in an encounter between a minority and majority culture and about child-centeredness in contemporary religious community life. However, such explanations are shallow in view of the profundity of what is to be explained. Ignoring food taboos, for instance, implies a deep cultural shift. Religious conceptions of purity are being reevaluated.

Group behavior tends to be explained psychologically. This may be illustrated in the case of their measure of religious commitment. Some respondents score relatively low on the scale measuring commitment to sacramental religion but claim to be religious. The authors suggest that these individuals experience psychological dissonance. They try to reduce the dissonance by redefining religiosity in terms of moral or ethical rather than sacramental behavior. The analyst discovers this by identifying with the subject who is imagined to be suffering the dissonance, the traditional verstehende approach. The researcher and the subject presumably share psychological meanings. These individual attitudes are treated as a group attribute. Defining religiosity in ethical terms, the psychological response to dissonance is offered as a social characteristic.

The psychological interpretation of group behavior is pervasive in Sklare and Greenblum's

work. Another example is from the study of synagogues as organizations. The authors reviewed congregational records and conducted interviews with
leaders. The data consist of a combination of
individual acts and group decisions. The authors
might have examined, with these data, the functions
various synagogues fulfill in the overall life of
the Jewish community. Alternatively, they might
have explored the social roles enacted by individuals within the synagogue, the role of the rabbi,
of lay leaders, or of women's groups. The focus
might then have been on structural strains emerging
between internal factions.

Instead of pursuing such a societal analysis,
the authors propose that ideas and motives of individuals are the determining forces of organizational behavior. Some of the ideas reported are
those of only a few participants. Others seem to
be typifications which are said to reflect group
"motives." For example, the founders of the Wise
Temple were individuals, primarily of German-Jewish
background, who had previously attended a Reform
temple in Lake City. Hesitant to advertise their
presence in Lakeville, they first conducted a lecture series in which all the speakers were non-
Jews. Some of the leaders are said to have believed this would be perceived as a service to the
general community. This idea might have guided
some individuals. However, others may have wanted
to hear about a culture dominated by non-Jewish
thinkers.

In social functional terms, the attitudes of
service or of acculturation served to link the
synagogue and the national culture. Regardless of
what people learned, the lectures declared the concern of a Jewish community with cultural life in
Lakeville. The lectures provided occasions for
people of similar interests to mingle and affirm
the validity of that interest. The central factor
in explaining organizational or communal relations
is not the conscious motive, the psychological factor, but the social function of the lectures. The
organizational event served to rationalize contact
between the wider communities represented by the
speakers and the attendees. The synagogue, in this
instance, functioned less as a vehicle for facilitating the development of Jewish culture than for
relating Jewish society and the larger society.
Jewish culture, in this way, may develop an image
more harmonious with its environment. This gave
direction to community cultural development. The
social role of the lecture series may not be unlike

that of the Jewish-sponsored Educational Alliance
in Americanizing Lower East Side Jews around the
turn of the century.

Yet, another example. The congregation of
Wise Temple was reluctant to erect a building because, the record shows, they did not want to
proclaim that the Jews constitute a separate
group. The congregation was concerned with public
relations, but ultimately, a modest structure was
built which, Sklare and Greenblum also explain,
shows that the founders were not interested in encouraging more Jewish families to move into the
vicinity. The appeal to individual reasons to explain organizational decisions is, in itself, not
amiss since these could have been widely shared
opinions. This line of reasoning, however, calls
for information on the distribution of reasons and
specification of the role they played in the decision, and an assessment of the importance of these
reasons, among all relevant explanations.

Large buildings are not a major stimulus to
migration. The provision of worship facilities of
whatever size may influence those who are ready to
move nearby the new synagogue. The congregational
fathers must have known this. Selecting a building
involves more than interest in future membership.
Considerations include the expected use of the
building, the capability or willingness of the congregation to contribute, and the salience of the
synagogue in the lives of its members. These suburban Reform Jews doubtless were rejecting the then
popular idea of an institutional synagogue with
educational, catering, and meeting facilities in
addition to a worship and lecture hall. Their conception was that a synagogue would play a limited
role in the community, and they might well have
discouraged contributions to the building fund.
Such building funds do not rest on true mass participation. They require a significant commitment on
the part of a few wealthy persons. Perhaps, the
wealthy potential donors remained socially well located in Lake City, with little interest in a new,
not yet formed, community of younger families in
the suburbs. We learn later that some members re-
signed from the Wise Temple to establish the David
Einhorn Temple and that this group met under make-
shift circumstances.

Actions of members of the group tend to be
interpreted with reference to the identity concept,
the focal variable of the study. Sometimes concern
for identity leads to overinterpretation of the influence of that variable. Identity may be a minor

factor in certain community events, such as the decision to build a house of worship.

An observed increase in approval of intermarriage, a social event, is explained in terms of individual attitudes. Approval of intermarriage is
positively correlated with integration-
mindedness. Nevertheless, the authors report
general unease about intermarriage. Jews rationalize it with reference to romantic love. The authors conclude that romantic love has become a
higher value than traditional norms of endogamy.
But, this attitude cannot be isolated. Romantic
love can occur only where there is an opportunity
for courtship. The social conditions which expose
the candidates to the possibility of falling in
love are worthy of attention in the context of a
community study. Mate selection is socially controlled through the education system, for example,
or social segregation in a neighborhood. Intermarriage requires a decline of social segregation,
probably through common participation in the major
organizations of the society. Romantic love does
not explain the situation for the actors but it
does rationalize it.

The authors verstehende explanations reflect
their insights into the Jewish and non-Jewish cultures, as well as into personalities. The method
of verstehen is especially valuable in the "context
of discovery," the steps of research by which ideas
are proposed for study. The scientist is obligated
to take a further step into the "context of justification" to validate the explanations. From the
perspective of the positivist conception of science
to which Sklare and Greenblum are committed, this
requires verstehen and more. Settling upon an explanation for an observed association involves the
introduction of a third or control variable. With
so few cases, the authors are compelled to offer
tentative explanations in terms of presumed, but
untested, third variables. The control or explanatory variables are introduced discursively. Thus,
the retention of sacramental religious observance
by children is explained by the parental pattern of
observance. This explanation holds, the authors
say, irrespective of other Jewish influences, such
as Jewish education, percentage of Jews in the
neighborhood, character of the parents' friendship
ties, or the extent to which the parents choose
friends over relatives for social companions. It
is likely, however, that parental observance correlates with Jewish cultural and educational experiences. Observant parents are more likely to send

their children to religious schools and to have
Jewish friends. Thus, when paired with parental
observances, these factors do not contribute additional predictive precision.

Which of these notions is, however, the explanation: parental observance or education?
Parental observance survives the test. However,
had the authors not had such a measure, they might
well have concluded that education is the more significant factor. In truth, both are aspects of the
explanation. A pattern of observance in a home
cannot be considered as independent of the rest of
Jewish social relational patterns. These are mutu-
ally reinforcing experiences.

The major thrust of the work, however, is that
communal acculturation, rather than parental observance, is at the heart of the matter. Parental
behavior does not serve as a model which the child
duplicates but is rather a base line for change.
The change is due to outside variables such as the
social relations of the child. Such external factors are not explored within this study.

Limits of Correlational Analysis. The sociology of the Jewish community was termed, at the
beginning of this chapter, an applied sociology.
General sociological propositions are applied to
clarify the relationships observed in the case of
Jews. The general proposition may be modified as a
result. Sklare and Greenblum discover a case in
which an anomalous observation leads to a deeper
insight. In Lake City around 1900, the Jews became
more acculturated and less traditional as they rose
in social status. This is not the case with Lakeville Jews today. Lakeville Jews may be religiously liberal, belonging, say, to Einhorn Temple,
but have lower incomes than the more traditional
members of the Schechter Synagogue. The synagogues
in Lakeville are not organized around class nor
income nor degree of acculturation. They are extensions of social groups formed around wider
societal cultural interests. Thus, the Samuel
Hirsch Temple has its doctors and lawyers, and the
Max Lilienthal Temple its young families of East
European descent who have gone to less prestigious
universities. Income is less important as a criterion of social status than is occupation in an
increasingly bureaucratized society.

The alternative ways of being Jewish, discussed above, suggest, for example, that a commitment to the state of Israel may be functionally
equivalent to a commitment to traditional mizvot in
supporting a Jewish identity.[23] The argument for

functional equivalence does not require that the
two forms of commitment be negatively correlated.
Commitment to nationalism need not exclude commitment to religion--if either or both are ways of
expressing a Jewish identification. Zionism, itself, may take on religious rather than political
meaning, functioning as a messianic movement for
this population.

Sklare and Greenblum developed an index,
treated as a scale, to measure commitment to
Israel. Personal participation in the building of
Israel marks the higher end of the scale, a degree
and type of commitment which attracted one percent
of the Lakeville Jews interviewed. Approval of
fund-raising for Israel, at the other extreme,
attracted 91 percent. Measures of involvement in
synagogue life, frequency of synagogue attendance,
and extent of home observance correlate positively
with scores on this scale. The authors conclude
from these correlations that commitment to Israel
is not generally a substitute for Jewish observance. The two go together. Presumably, a negative correlation would have demonstrated that
commitment to Israel is a substitute for Jewish
observance.

The method of correlation is misleading as a
test for the functional equivalence of Zionism and
religiousness. This may be illustrated by dividing
the population into four types: those who are both
Zionist and religious (plus, plus); Zionist and not
religious (plus, minus); not Zionist but religious
(minus, plus); and neither Zionist nor religious
(minus, minus). The mean identity scores could be
obtained for individuals in each of these categories. If the (plus, minus) and the (minus, Plus)
individuals have equally high scores (that is,
either being Zionist or religious produces high
identity); while the (minus, minus) generates the
lowest, and the (plus, plus) the highest score, it
could be inferred that either religious or nationalist commitment by itself produces a high identity
while both together produce the highest identity.
That is, the functional equivalence argument is
that if $A \rightarrow C$, and $B \rightarrow C$, then A and B are interchangeable. The authors erred in merely testing
the argument that $A \neq B$, the test for joint occurrence or correlation.

The correlational method has yet another draw-
back. A coefficient of correlation expresses in
summary fashion the likelihood that two events will
occur at the same time. A positive coefficient
tells us that the likelihood of the population

being in the plus, plus (if Zionist, then
religious) and minus, minus (if not Zionist, then
not religious) categories is greater than that of
their being in the plus, minus and minus, plus
categories. The coefficient obscures the
independent social meanings of the four types.
Each of the four types exists and has a distinct
social meaning.[24] The social ideological
functional equivalence argument mutes the
examination of the variant implications for Jews
and Judaism of each of the types. The complexity
of the social fabric remains unrevealed.

    After this whole argument that Jews might be
religious and Zionist at the same time, it appears
empirically that in Lakeville being a member of a
synagogue and having pro-Israel sentiments are un-
related. A positive association between religion
and Zionism holds for those who belong to synagogues in which the cultural expectation is for
that duality. Religion and Zionism are two
expressions of the same religio-Zionist culture
complex.

    One final example of the misleading effect of
correlational methods occurs in a discussion of a
relation, purportedly negative, between family and
community organizational life. Seventy-one percent
of the respondents are members of a Jewish organization not sponsored by a synagogue. Further, the
current generation, compared with their parents,
spends relatively more time with friends than with
relatives. Organizations are then held to fill the
vacuum created by the erosion of the natural community, the neighborhood, and family. The cross-
tabulation showing that organizational members are
less likely to interact with relatives or with
friends is not provided.

    Conceivably, attention to relatives might be
positively correlated with attention to friends.
Each of these could, in turn, be positively correlated with organizational membership. The underlying variable might be sociability. Those who see
a great deal of their relatives may also see a
great deal of their friends and join organizations. Organizations, particularly religious or
ethnic organizations, may be extensions of, rather
than replacements for, family and neighborhood.
Organizations, like families, would then function
to promote Jewish identity.

    It is probably true that the emergence of or-
ganizations in the economy, firms and labor unions,
at the community level coincides with the with-
drawal of the household from participation in

at the community level coincides with the with-
drawal of the household from participation in
production.

Can Method Be Mastered?

The power of the survey is in its conquest of
myopia. Sampling exposes parts of society hidden
from the social location of the researcher. For
each problem raised about method, the sophisticated
practitioner has an answer. The sociological reality of isolated units may be overcome by constructing models of relationships--entering as a datum
the relation between a husband's and a wife's response. Synagogue committee members' responses may
be "coded" in the context of synagogue social cli-
mates. Samples may be drawn of social networks by
a "snowball" technique or by treating respondents
as informants about their networks. The limitation
of the correlational method may be overcome by
typological methods or by index construction. The
very externality of the method may be overcome by
entering information about internal meanings.

That this rarely occurs may be traced to two
contrasting situations. First, the survey method,
as a technique, may be applied by a technician
someone with little theoretical sophistication. At
the other extreme, the effort and methodological
sophistication needed to construct the valid and
reliable measures required for a sensitive survey
may overwhelm the research process. Assuring adequate sampling, monitoring field efforts and data
reduction efforts, constructing the best statistical models for analysis and, especially with com-
puter-aided analysis, poring over endless "output"
weigh heavily on the researcher's time.

The question of whether or not a society can
survive cultural change is answered in the affirmative. The answer is not discovered at the end of
a search, however, it is presumed in the method.
The measurement of identity by an index of cultural
commitment which then eliminates the cultural meanings has already answered the question for the purpose of the study. A specific culture is nearly
but not entirely irrelevent as a medium for
expressing and affirming the integrity of an historical society.

THE GRAND HISTORY OF AMERICAN JEWRY:
THE TRIUMPH OF SOCIETY OVER CULTURE

Theme: Religion, Ethnicity and Political Control

The Problem of Sociological History

Nathan Glazer's American Judaism is a history
of modern states in which religion and ethnicity
are becoming distinct as bases of loyalty. How can
a traditional society undergoing cultural change in
such a state resist separating its religious from
its ethnic character? For Glazer, as for the previous scholars, the possibility of social survival
amidst cultural change is the problem. Heilman and
Poll study groups for whom Jewish culture is essential for Jewish survival. Sklare and Glazer emphasize the centrality of Jewish social relations, the
cohesiveness of Jewish society, the numbers of Jews
and of Jewish communities, whatever their culture. Glazer's work is about Jewry, not Judaism,
the title notwithstanding.

The interdependence between religion and ethnicity, so important for Jewry, is not shared by
all peoples. Calvinism and Catholicism, not bound
to a specific set a social relationships, survived
the demise of ethnic ties. In fact, their pride is
in their transcendence of ethnicity. And, the
Teutons, Goths, Saxons, and Franks whose descen-
dents today adhere to Christian culture at one time
worshipped the gods of nature.

American Judaism differs from the previous
works treated in this chapter in its temporal and
social scope. Its subject is not a synagogue nor a
sect nor a suburb, but the whole of American Jewry
from 1654, the date of arrival in New Amsterdam of
a ship with Sephardic refugees, until the time of
writing, 1956.[25] Relatively speaking, this is
grand history and macrosociology. Its subject is
social mechanisms governing the cultural change of
American Jewry.

The study is based on secondary historical
materials. The sociologist using historical materials finds the data already relatively highly conceptualized. The great historico-cultural works of
Max Weber set a tradition and a standard for historical sociology based on secondary sources. That
tradition is one of plausible, sometimes brilliant
theory, and insufficiently critical acceptance of
the secondary sources. Glazer is cognizant of this
limitation. The sociologist using historical writ-

ings must also be critical regarding the validity
of the assertions found in them.

Validity, here, unlike that considered in reference to the previous authors, does not refer to
the truth of the proposition, hypothesis, or law.
It refers to empirical truth: Did the event occur
as described? His success in dealing with this
question of validity is difficult to assess. He
refers to almost no comparative primary sources, or
even very many comparative secondary sources. Not
all of Glazer's sources are works of professional
historians. Some are the perceptions of the
history of social movements by the ideological
leaders of those movements. Demographic and immigration data are offered; these constitute primary
data with face validity. Glazer's theory is social
interactionist. The theme is the social structur-
ing of opportunities for interaction among individuals, of differing groups, and the consequence of
this experience for Jewry.

Life Is At the Boundary

Glazer's analysis is contextual and relational. The strength of ethnic association, Glazer
implies, is influenced by events outside the ethnic
community. Members of ethnic groups attracted to
the wider society weaken their own group ties. The
opportunities offered by the wider society include
the opportunity to obtain education in the general
community and the opportunity for occupational
advance. The wider society, which controls these
opportunities, controls the fate of the ethnic
community.

Glazer studies the boundary between two
ethnic-religious societies--the Jewish and the
gentile. The relation of religion and ethnicity
within Jewry depends on the permeability of the
Jewish-gentile boundary. That permeability is a
function of two forms of social control. The
first, interpreting Glazer, is "locational control." Territorial rights involve social and cultural rights. For example, in discussing the Jews
in New Amsterdam, Glazer cites their interest in
residential permits as crucial to their ability to
act as a group. Their right to remain in New
Amsterdam was associated with the right to bear
arms, to trade, and to engage in the public practice of religion.

A second factor affecting the permeability of
boundaries is "political control." The degree of
centralization of political control is key in

maintaining the stability of ethnic groups within a
state. When control over community activities is
divided among several authorities, ethnic life
changes more rapidly. Authorities without and
within the group subtly struggle for control of religious activities. The outcome of this struggle
influences the degree to which ethnic identity is
preserved. Glazer compares European and American
Jewry in this respect. In Europe, the state controlled the appointment of clergy and was responsible for the maintenance of cemeteries, among
other activities. In America, the religious
community had, at the outset, a monopoly over religious rights. The Jewish community controlled its
clergy and its cemeteries, as well as ritual animal
slaughter.

In Germany, where the Jewish community was
organized centrally and rabbis were provided a government subsidy, religious "lobbies" to the government were recognized. The activity of these
"lobbyists" inhibited the Reform movement. Reform
in America could develop freely because members of
the Jewish community were not subject to pervasive
control by traditional religious authorities. The
general acceptance of pluralism and the congregational rather than the episcopal structure of many
American churches helped in this. The American
concept of corporate, voluntary groups permitted
the exercise of religion through congregations.
However, the control by congregations was, itself,
limited. In the New World, as illustrated by New
York's situation, a wide variety of synagogues
emerged. Synagogues eventually lost the function
of ritual slaughter to commercial butchers partly
because of their small size. This was a community
need cutting across specific congregations. Responsibility for charity, also originally a congregational responsibility, was assumed by independent
organizations. Public schools emerged, reducing
the need for congregational schools.

Contemporary historiographers complain that
traditional history has been a history of kings.
Why not? Until the recent emergence of "scientific
history," the primary social role of history was to
serve as the ideology of the polity. The demise of
theological history, such as that given in the
Bible, paralleled the control by the temporal pow-
ers of the definition of reality. Now, we have
economic history as well as histories of institutions such as church history, business history, or
the histories of the socialist internationals.
Jewish political history has been downplayed.

After all, Jews have been out of power. Thus, Salo
Baron wrote a Social and Religious History of the
Jews and Joseph Klausner a History of Hebrew Literature. Glazer's own interests in the confrontation
of American ethnic groups now revitalizes the political history of Jewry. Yet, the power struggles
that determine cultural outcomes, such as the
spread of the spirit of Reform, hang a bit free
when little is said about the economic bases of
power and less said about the content of the symbols around which the battle is waged.

The Individual Act In History

Those individuals who have high status both
within the ethnic group and within the larger community bring about cultural change. As such individuals become more numerous, the flow of ideas and
exchange of life styles between the groups increases. Religious as well as ethnic culture
changes. Thus, Glazer writes, in nineteenth century Germany, the higher status groups were more
likely to become Reform Jews. They introduced
Protestant type practices reflected, for instance,
in striving for decorous services. Through gradual
cultural diffusion, religious worship styles and
theological orientations are transmitted from the
majority to the minority group.
Interaction is not limited to high status
individuals, however. A specialized subgroup may
interact with the majority. The Reform movement in
Germany and the United States acted at the boundary
of Jewry, transmitting religious and ethnic ways
from the dominant society to the Jewish community. Glazer believes that the movement of Jewry
toward Reform and Reform-like religious culture is
the dominant trend. He does not deal seriously
with other movements in Judaism such as the Frank-
furt Orthodox reaction to this trend, Jewish secularism, or assimilationism as a silent movement.
The internal struggle within the Jewish community,
thus, eludes him.
The historical materials on which Glazer depends are not heavily weighted with data for sociological explanation. Generally, the sociologist
looks for the relationships between institutions in
order to arrive at propositions about their inter-
relations. In history, an event emerges from an
earlier event. For much historical writing, particularly that which is not written by professional
historians, the dynamic force is apt to be taken to
be individual decisions springing from individual

motives. Perhaps because he relies on this historical writing, Glazer tends to attribute collective
events to the motives of individuals, despite his
concentration on macrosociology. Thus, in tracing
the history of the rise of Reform Judaism in
Germany, he asserts, as was mentioned above, that
Reform Judaism began as the movement of Jews of
high social status who wished to make religious
services more decorous. This is not a psychological motive but a social attitude shared by high-
status Jews.

The superficiality of this explanation may be
the result of literal acceptance of the contentions
of the leaders of the movement. Their rationales
for sectarian development are taken as objective
social forces. Sectarians often select some minute
matters, such as a difference in liturgy or in a
Biblical interpretation, to rationalize the rise of
their sect. Discussions on liturgy are sometimes
the precipitants or historical antecedents of
schisms. The root of the schism is, nevertheless,
nearly always in a deeper value conflict or a more
serious theological controversy. The rationales
have an ideological and organizational function for
sectarian leaders to define the differences of
their new sect. Such rationales are also the ways
by which the leaders impose meanings on events.
The weakness of these rationales to explain the
past is revealed by their narrow and overly generalized character. The desire for decorousness,
culturally modelling the decorum and simplicity of
some Protestant churches, does not explain Reform
in Bavaria, where the dominant religious style is
Roman Catholic and liturgical.
Glazer might have related Reform to tensions
within the religious organizations of Jewish orthodoxy. He begins to do this in considering problems
of Jewish intellectuals. In Germany, he maintains,
the Jewish intellectuals were lost to the Jewish
community because of Rationalism and the Enlightenment. The argument then shifts to the political. Those who adopted nontraditional intellectual
orientations were less likely to gain a hearing
because of the corporate control of the Jewish
community. Traditional Jewish intellectual circles
excluded them, leaving them to pursue their intellectual life in other settings. Leading Jewish
intellectuals in Germany, such as Mendelsohn and
Geiger, introduced the thought of the Enlightenment
into Jewish learning and became leaders of German
Reform.

In America, in contrast, intellectuals also
introduced their thoughts into Judaism. Einhorn is
given as an example of an intellectual who developed a theoretical justification for Reform. Under
such leadership, religion was separated from ethnicity. Reform developed its own associational
structure of Reform congregations and the Central
Conference of American Rabbis. The crucial difference in the American situation was the lack of
corporate political force which could dampen the
rate of growth of the new movement.

This is a promising avenue of approach.
Glazer might have continued with an examination of
the Jewish response to the separation of church and
state in bourgeois societies and the general tendency, in these societies, for organizations concerned with the spiritual to relinquish their
ethnic bases. Perhaps, Reform might become the
belief of a new class of Jewish bourgeois who participated in capitalist markets and engaged in
international economic relations as Germans, protected by German polity, rather than as Jews.
Jewish merchants in earlier centuries acted as
Jews.

Culture as a Social Actor

Historians resist abstrations. In their
place, they established periods of time in which
concrete principles of thought and norms govern
people and events. Thus, Rationalism thematically
brings together technology and bureaucracy, among
other things. It refers to their "spirit" and
social organization. The Enlightenment brings together particular philosophical schools, secularism
and the ideology of science, among other things.
Glazer asserts that as the Bible became the subject
for critical study, questions are raised as to
whether it incorporates God's Commandments. As a
consequence of such questions, the foundations of
Jewish thought crumbled. Attributing the crumbling
of traditionalist thought to critical study is to
invoke Rationalism as the cause. Here, however,
the argument fails to explain how it was that some
critical students were atheists for whom tradition
had already crumbled. Others were religious funda-
mentalists who traditionalist thought did not
crumble. Heresy, atheism, and lack of faith were
not peculiar creatures of eighteenth-century central Europe. Jewish learning had weathered the
disputationists of other faiths for centuries.
Glazer waffles between explaining change in terms

of social relational, cultural and attitudinal factors. Rationalism may be examined from one or all of these perspectives. However, to understand its impact as a social force, it is necessary to specify the social structural arrangement through which the ideas are implemented. Were the rich Jews of Berlin more troubled by rationalist criticism than were the professional and bourgeois Jews of Munich? Glazer's analysis of the effect of rationalistic philosophy on Reform thinking in the United States illustrates an ambiguity that arises when the social relational elements are not introduced into the analysis. Thus, the practice of circumcision among American Reform Jews appears to be an anomaly. An enlightened, progressive view would have led to abandonment of the custom. Glazer explains the persistence of circumcision as the subconscious insistence that Jews be maintained as a people. This psycho-historical explanation suggests that Glazer considers subconscious ties as a basis of ethnicity when the manifest cultural behaviors have melted away. The puzzle of continued circumcism among Reform Jews remains unresolved. Glazer appreciates the fact that ritual behavior cannot be accounted for on the level of cognitive culture, relying on Rationalism. The anomaly might be evaluated against the rather rapid abandonment of circumcision among post-revolutionary Russian Jews. There the rite has been branded barbarian. Glazer is taken by the declared position of American Reform leaders. Reform has not abandoned circumcision but has, in some cases, abandoned ritual circumcision. A desacralized version of the ceremony persists in the United States. The services of the mohel are, increasingly, dispensed with.

An explanation for the persistence or for the abandonment of circumcision should combine social relational factors, such as the opening of the societies for Jews, along with the contrasting cultural assessments of circumcision by the wider societies in which they live. Doubtless, many other cultural and social organizational factors intervene -- including the practice of the medical profession, the frequency of circumcision among non-Jews.

Other reasons might be offered for the persistence of the rite. It is an explicitly Biblically enjoined act, a once-in-a-lifetime rite of passage, an alternative to a water ritual which is unacceptably close to the Christian form. A general explanation should encompass an historical description of the reasons why circumcision declined among the

Hellenizers prior to the Maccabbean revolt and
among Jews in the contemporary Soviet Union, but
has persisted elsewhere.

It is not clear whether Glazer is describing
the position of Reform authorities or a practice on
the part of individuals. The authorities would, it
seems, understand the ceremony in religious terms--
a matter of convenanting, certainly a popular idea
in America. If Glazer is explaining anomalous individual behavior, reasons might be sought within
the family, since circumcision is a family as well
as communal event. Something of the relation of
the family to the religious community might be at
issue.

In comparing the cultural consequences of Rationalism in Germany and eastern Europe on Judaism,
for instance, Glazer introduces cultural and social
explanations. The rationalistic force that led to
Reform in Germany, he observes, led to a revival of
Hebrew and secular nationalism in Eastern Europe.
To account for this he suggests differences in the
Jewish and non-Jewish environments, particularly
differences in the political control of the communities. The acceptance of ethnic heterogeneity in
Eastern Europe permitted Jewish communal structures
to persist. At the same time, the pressure of popular and official anti-Semtism transformed some
individuals into proletarians and others into
Zionists--depending on the strength of their commitment to Jewish tradition.

Ethnicity as the Constant

The Ethnic Basis for American Jewry

German and East European Jews in the United
States learned to cooperate as parts of a single
Jewish community. Glazer offers a tendentious explanation for this cooperation. He observes, quite
appropriately, that Jews identify with one another
across national boundaries. Common ancestry is
Glazer's explanation. He then observes that German
Jews in America reacted "almost instinctively" to
the oppression of East European Jews and pressed
for governmental intervention on their behalf,
although after East European Jews arrived in the
United States, they established institutions separate from those of the German Jews. However, other
Americans subjected them to common labelling, a
variant, perhaps, of "fate." Both were called

Jews, and this, Glazer argues, brought them together. For Glazer, an underlying explanation for the
emergence of a single Jewish community in the
United States is that the gentiles, by labelling,
and the Jews, by responding responsibly to the
needs of other Jews, were recognizing Jewish ethnicity. Jewish ethnicity engulfed even American
Reform Jews.

The fate and ancestry explanation takes the
reasons which the actor might articulate and offers
those as objective explanations. The rise in
status of German Jews separated them from gentile
Germans in the United States. This acted to crys-
tallize Jewish ethnicity further. The gentile
Germans were artisans and farmers and tended to
settle in restricted locales. The dispersion of
German Jews in the United States, through their involvement in commerce, exposed them more to the
wider English culture of America. This acculturation could well have led to the demise of Jewry.
That it did not is attributed to exclusions of Jews
from parts of American society, as evidenced by
their exclusion from clubs and hotels. The synagogue has been more important for American Jewish
life than has the immigrant aid organization.
Unification may well be traced to a common religious enterprise. Perhaps, Eastern Jewry overwhelmed
German Jewry numerically and in depth of passion
for Jewishness, whether religious or nationalist or
socialist; German Jews melted into the new Jewish
"mainstream." This would be an explanation in
terms of "cultural conquest." The cultural conquest explanation refers to an objective social
force which may not be comprehended at the actor's
level.

Glazer answers his question about cultural and
social survival by proposing that the group remains
an identifiable network of people loyal to one another. In his terms, neither Jewish religious association nor Jewish ethnic association requires a
particular commitment to traditional Jewish culture. The degree of change which can be tolerated
in that culture without threatening social association seems limited only by the extent of the affiliation with those non-Jews who are present in
the society. Thus, Jews would not declare for
Jesus in America or for the prophecy of Islam in
Syria. If, however, the Torah lesson is taught be-
side a lesson from Confucius in America, it might
be considered liberal, or radical, but not non-
Jewish.

In America, zionism is a political idea which
brought together East European and German Jews.
Zionism allowed for separation of religion and
ethnicity. The zionist could participate politically in the larger society, which expresses an
ethnicity compatible with American citizenship.
Religion, says Glazer, has become less and less a
form of social organization and more and more a
cultural expression. Ethnicity, joined to a political concept, is the basis of social ties which
integrate East European and German Jews. The cultural differences between them lessened as both
became more Americanized. The separate community
organizations of German and East European Jews have
declined. Social mixing and intermarriage between
these two types of Jews increased and Jews survive
as a single community.

The meaning of ethnicity is not sufficiently
clarified in this discussion. Traditionally, this
term has referred to common-culture groups, often
based on some common national origin. Here, there
is no longer an ethnic language, an ethnic theological orientation, nor ethnic rituals and observances. Only social relations remain, but the cultural content of these relations does not differ
from that of non-Jews. Western values filtered
through the American form of representative democracy and market capitalism. What then is Jewish
about the group so organized?

Glazer argues that the separation of religion
from ethnicity among Jews has never been completed. The loss of a Jewish religious cultural content in Jewish life is taken for a sign of the
emergence, paradoxically, of Jewish ethnicity.
Communal social ties appear rooted in a mystic bro-
therhood but not in traditional religion. Jewish
education, essentially religious education, has declined. Attendance at religious services is
down. Even in Schechter's seminary, nonreligious
materials are absorbed into the curriculum as
modern Hebrew and Zionism become more important.
The Conservative laity increasingly reject the
bindingness of law. Classic Reform Judaism,
insisting on religion separate from ethnicity, is
declining. Orthodoxy enters as a "saving remnant"
which supplies the fund of Jewish knowledge on
which the rest draw. But orthodoxy, the keeper of
the knowledge, does not imply leadership, for the
Orthodox do not legitimate the norms; they provide
only technical knowledge for carrying out religious
rituals.

Assimilation is Survival

New strength comes from a weakening of old
ties. This paradox is implicit in Glazer's arguments. He proposes indicators that have ordinarily
been measures of assimilation as signs of nonassim-
ilation. The demise of Judaism, as a specialized
culture, allows a reordering of Jewish social relationships around Jewish ethnicity. How does this
work? Jewish society, Glazer explains, has become
similar to non-Jewish society in a number of demographic characteristics. It experiences
suburbanization, a lower age at marriage, and a
decline in numbers of single adults; both right and
leftwing extremist political movements decline; and
individuals strive for middleclass respectability. All of these indices have, in the past,
been associated with assimilation, a process driven
by a need to adapt successfully. Successful
adaptation is necessary for survival and, therefore, assimilation is not the demise, but the survival, of Jews and Judaism.
Is this or is this not Orwellian? The answer
depends on the way one thinks of the relative roles
of association and of culture in social reality.
Assimilation is, of course, not an all-or-
nothing matter. Total cultural assimilation must
involve social assimilation. The serious problem
concerning a study of assimilation must concern its
extent, that is, the particular aspects of social
existence which change and those which do not.
Thus, medieval Jewry adapted by providing cultural
and commercial relations between the Christian and
Islamic civilizations. More recently, the synagogue, as an institution, has flourished in suburbia, because it met social needs, providing occasions for expressing social or ethnic ties. Now,
traditional religious culture seems not to survive
even in the synagogues. Yet, the ethnic group
continues.
The penultimate chapter, on the period between
1940 and 1956, illustrates some problems in formu-
lating the distory of the recent past. The two
cosmic events in modern Jewish history, the murder
of six million Jews and the creation of a Jewish
state, have had remarkably little effect, as far as
he can detect, on the inner life of American
Jewry. For him, synagogue membership is an indicator of the influence of these events on a feeling
of being Jewish. Twenty years later, he felt he
was mistaken and deleted this from his later edition. Why did Glazer miss the impact of these

events on Jewish life? Why did he not see the organized community efforts in fund-raising for overseas aid and the significant political involvement
of the community around Israel? Perhaps, his dependence on secondary writings, which had not yet
synthesized the contemporary period, is at fault.
He observes a "Jewish revival" which he relates to
migration to the suburbs and its associated child-
oriented religion, but not to these key events.

In the discussion of Heilman's work, above, a
distinction was made between those elements of a
theory which refer to "structure," the relatively
stable, and constant aspects of events, and those
concepts which refer to "variable" elements. For
Heilman, the emphasis was on the concrescence of
the collective as the variable components became
stabilized as structure. For Glazer, the
"structure" is the stable underlying reality of
Jewish association, the social relations which he
calls ethnic. The variable elements are its manifestation under changing conditions. The culture
may vary to such an extent that Judaism as a religion is not recognizable and yet, Glazer argues,
Jewry persists.

The closing chapter tells of a common refusal
to "throw off the yoke." "Jews refuse to become
non-Jews," says Glazer. But "non-Jews" is too complex a category to make the statement meaningful.
Jews join American civil society and participate in
a vaguely Protestant culture. However, as Glazer
is saying, they refuse to adopt Christianity in its
organized religious form. This was not the case
with German Jewry among whom religious conversions
had reached a significant level before the First
World War.

Glazer's interpretation of the refusal to
"throw off the yoke" grows from what he considers
the permanent structure (the social) and the variable (the cultural) elements. The underlying permanent structure is the net of social relations.
The traditional Jewish meaning of the "yoke" is the
"yoke of the commandments," the responsibility to
subject life to the rule of the Torah. Traditionally, culture, including the commandments, had been
considered structure. Glazer reverses the order.
The yoke is a psychic drive growing out of the social relations of the ethnic community. Glazer is
a child of his century, placing existence before
essence, the act before the idea. The idea emerges
to rationalize the act. Jews can survive and the
rationalizations they use to account for their actions my change.

The orientation is historical, genetic, temporal. A shifting balance is maintained among the manifestations of Judaism. Each generation relates itself meaningfully to some part of the Jewish past. The son of a Reform Jewish philanthropist becomes a Zionist. The son of a Yiddish-speaking socialist joins a Reform Temple. Glazer records various sectarian practices, including the Orthodox revival in Williamsburg and the Conservative movement's Hebrew summer camps. Here is a specialization in the types of Judaism. This is not a conflict among tendencies, such as between Yiddish and Hebrew or between Reform and Orthodox. A sense of organic interdependence reigns among those who live their Jewishness religiously and those who live it in a secular, Zionist way. In this sense, the total community becomes what George Mead would think of as an expression of the social act--the social act of relating Jewishly.

THE JEWS AND MODERN SOCIOLOGY

When, in 1911, Werner Sombart wrote of The Jews and Modern Capitalism, he identified an internal affinity of some characteristics of Jewish society for capitalist institutions. The Jewish geist was comfortable in exchange relations of the trades and, indeed, concepts of contract are discernible in Jewish religious institutions. The asceticism of the burgher allows a sublimation of sexual force into economic activity and, indeed, the Talmud espouses rational behavioral control. Much ink has been spilled in debating Sombart's thesis. Nevertheless, the underlying question remains. Do the sociological concepts which help us understand Western European society also apply meaningfully to Jewish life, or is the bed procrustean?

The four works reviewed are unanimous in affirming the frutfulness of an applied sociology of Jewry. They all assert that which is most explicit in Glazer. The essence of Jewry is not Judaism but a mystically based peoplehood. Sociology, however, cannot define reality. It is not an exercise in ontology. Sociology constructs a perspective on reality. History and ethnography provide another perspective, all supplementing the humanistic study of Jewish letters and laws.

Sociological concepts seek what is unique to Jews by providing a standard for comparing them with non-Jews. Thus, we learn of the different

occupational distributions of the Jewish and Protestant Americans or the different political commitments of American Jews and American Catholics.
Where, in the works reviewed, application of general sociological concepts was not helpful, the
problem lay more in the fit of particular conceptual tools than in the general character of the
method. In every instance, the conceptualization
of evidence and the explanation of findings was
dependent on the researcher's knowledge of Jewry
and Judaism, of Bible, of Talmud, of Medieval
mystical writings, of current responsa as well as
of current political movements and cultural
attitudes.
    The same may be said of the methodological
critique pursued in this chapter. It too is framed
by Western European and American philosophical categories. The Jewish content of those categories is
examined against other forms of knowledge, of ways
of studying, Jewish society and culture.
    The reader may be left with a sense that the
four studies reviewed are not of the same object.
Aside from the variety of Jewries examined by the
authors, each method generates its own statement
about its subjects. The dramaturgical approach de-
livers an inner Jewish reality protected from other
environing realities. The community study reveals
a collective effort at the self-segregation of the
sacred society. The survey monitors the changing
strength of attachment of Jews to the Jewish community and some psychological motives for Jewish
responses to the non-Jewish world. The macrosocio-
logical history traces the emergence of Jewish
ethnicity and the decline in significance of traditional Judaism. Taken together, these studies do
not offer a Baedeker to Jewry. For one seeking a
Baedeker, the task is not simply a matter of logically integrating the findings. It is a matter of
grasping the Jewish flesh and blood through, to use
Whitehead's word, the "ingressions" of these different perspectives. The final understanding then
awaits the more action-oriented, less contempla-
tive, perspective of policy and of Jewish living.

NOTES

* This work has been supported, in part, by the
Research Publication Fund of the Center for
Research on the Acts of Man and by a sabbati-
cal leave granted by the University of
Pennsylvania. An earlier draft was submitted
to the authors of the works reviewed here.
They do not agree with all of the interpre-
tations in the following pages. The paper has
benefitted from a critical reading by Harold
J. Bershady and Albert G. Crawford.

1. Some of the assertions of sociologists are
sociological. Others are historical narra-
tions or common sense interpretations of
everyday activities. Sociological assertions
interpret society by means of general concepts. These concepts tend to be constructed
in one of two ways. They may classify otherwise diverse events in terms of a common
attribute (the method of analytical abstrac-
tion) or they may place events under a common
rubric in virtue of a shared pattern of components (the typological method). The first
method leads to abstract analytical propositions and the second to the interpretation of
the event with reference to an encompassing
"historical individual." Of the authors to be
reviewed here, Sklare and Greenblum tend to
the former while Heilman, Poll and Glazer are
influenced by the latter method.

2. The idea of viewing the synagogue as a social
organization or the behavior of a rabbi as a
role highlights certain aspects of their
"reality" and ignores others. The sociology
of organizations has developed through studies
of western bureaucratic associations. Our
ideas of leadership roles are conditioned by
contemporary professions and politics. The
sociology of religion has grown out of ethnographic studies of tribal religions and organizational studies of European Christianity,
more than of any other religions. These
traditions determine what is highlighted when
these theories are applied.

3. An excellent survey and bibliography of the
sociology of contemporary American Jews may be
found in Marshall Sklare, The American Jewish
Community (New York: Behrman, 1976).

4. The study of Hebrew and of rabbinics by non-
Jews has a long history. Yet, few studies of

the Jewish community have been conducted by
non-Jewish sociologists.

5. Heilman is conscious of his role as both an
insider and an outsider; an inside member of
the community, with an understanding derived
through introspection of its inner life and of
the relevant questions to ask; an outsider
reflecting on that relationship with the
intellectual tools of the sociologist.

A "human subjects" issue haunts him. He
engages in social relationships which have an
element of pose in them. He visits other members as friends and they return visits to his
home. He is conscience-stricken for extrapo-
lating intellectual ideas from these relationships. Heilman elaborates on these problems
in "Jewish Sociologist: Native-as-Stranger,"
The American Sociologist, vol. 15 (May), 1980,
pp. 100-108.

6. To begin with an observation and then to
search for its meaning is a practice more
characteristic of psychologists than of
sociologists. The psychologist "factor-
analyzing" an array of test items is interpreting. The mathematical tool aids in the identification of the underlying meaning or common
factor. The sociologist, more confident in
the possession of relevent underlying meanings
or concepts, casts about for observations or
indicators which fit those meanings.

7. These meanings have the character of synthetic
or artistic knowledge. They are not arrived
at by analysis, by the isolation of attributes
found in numerous situations. They are realized through the patterns of acts, actors,
intentions, norms, evaluations, material objects, and so on, which cohere in a "type" of
situation. Max Weber's tradition refers to
such a cultural configuration as an "historical individual."

For centuries the bugaboo of science has
been the problem of solipsism -- the problem
of how can the scientist know that the world
has some reality beyond his or her personal
perceptions. Heilman's frame of reference
does not allow us to assert that the group has
an objective social reality. The collective
is the creature of the actors who construct
its meanings. The solipsistic problem is
avoided in its radical individualistic form
because of the presumption that these meanings

are shared. The possibility of social subjec-
tivism remains.

    Kehillat Kodesh could be a <u>folie à deau</u>
or <u>trois</u> or <u>quatre</u>--in two senses. The
observer does not take a position outside of
the group in order to evaluate the perceptions
of the group. His task is internal as an
interpreter and articulator of the action.
Secondly, events which occur outside the synagogue become relevant only through the perceptions of the members. There is no place for
extra-systemic factors which establish the
conditions of action in the group--objective
factors intervening from the world without.
This creates problems when we seek to account
for change. Heilman says, for instance, that
he cannot tell you why this group became Orthodox and, we might add, why it will continue
to be Orthodox.

8.   The implicit ontological assertion is that
    social expression is social reality. In the
    absence of expression, there is nothing. This
    position in its extreme leads to a skepticism
    about the reality of latent social events,
    except insofar as the possibility of such
    events is held in one's mind.

9.   This is a skepticism. "Hypothetical con-
    structs" are "entities" which may be inferred
    only indirectly. A firm grasp of common sense
    reality is held at the expense of forays into
    the types of abstraction needed for scientific
    theory-building. Thus, Heilman's work eschews
    what is commonly thought of as "causal analy-
    sis," a form of propositional thinking which
    requires abstractions.

10.   Perhaps the most prevalent model among social
    scientists involves subsuming an observed
    relation under some wider, general or covering
    law. The logic of this method rests on laws
    referring to analytically abstracted
    variables. These variables assume different
    values in the variety of circumstances and the
    laws have acausal form. For all of these
    reasons, Heilman, eschews the covering law.

11.   His refusal to abstract does not mean that
    Heilman, thereby, claims to look at the total
    society. He examines the synagogue only
    socially and culturally. This is a perspec-
    tival view but is not an analytic abstrac-
    tion. Such a perspectival view might be
    called componential abstraction. Talcott
    Parsons refers to this as a "type-part"

concept. Heilman examines a part of concrete
social reality, aware that other parts of that
reality are not being studied.

12. In an appendix, Poll describes the problem of
being accepted. He had attended a Hasidic
rabbinical school but did not live in the
community, nor wear the distinctive clothes.
He was resented as one who had left the community. His first contact was a non-Hasid who
was religious but tolerant of the study and
who introduced him, legitimating him, to a
Hasidic Jew. The second became a "reference"
individual and an informant and introduced him
to another Hasidic Jew. Poll did favors for
people in the community and contributed to its
organizations. Unstructured interviews were
conducted in Hungarian, Yiddish and sometimes
Hebrew all at once to demonstrate belonging-
ness.

13. The apologetics of industrial class theory
that have sometimes claimed that function
(Sumner, What Social Classes Owe to Each
Other) may exemplify the reverse error, that
of trying to conceptualize an industrial class
order in moral terms.

14. Some economic ideas are general. They apply
to any case of social adaptation to a resource
base and to the allocation of resources among
social units. Words such as resources, allocation, distribution or exchange could refer
to a feudal or a captalist economy or to the
economic relations in a business firm or in a
kinship group. Other terms are societally
specific. Serfdom is peculiar to a feudal
society, and the idea of a redeemer of land,
as in the Book of Ruth, belongs to a kinship
economy. Both of these concepts would distort
reality were they applied to data from a capitalist economy, in which employer and worker
are related by the labor contract and the
decision to sell land is responsive to the
real estate market.

15. Price administration reflects the intervention
of the polity in the economy and, in capitalist society, is considered as compromising
market processes. In socialist societies or
in regulated industries, such as public utili-
ties in the United States, prices are administered. Here the intervention is by religious
authorities.

16. All social states have their negations, though
we rarely study them. A creative theorist, in

a mental experiment, may examine conditions opposite to those conceptualized. This is not the same as comparing opposites in a dichotomy or the two values inherent in an ambivalence. In those cases, the comparison is between two extreme values of the same concept. An older tradition in sociology examines social degeneration, a topic that commands little attention today. Poll's problem is to understand how society remains separated without degenerating and, one might continue, without contributing to the degeneration of the larger system in which it exists.

17. Literally, the relationship of a host and a guest, as Weber conceived of it, is not a nonrelationship. In this case, however, social interactions between Hasidim and non-Jews are nil for most members of the community. The host and guest relationship in biological systems may be parasitic. Perhaps, because of this metaphorical suggestiveness, sociologists have been loath to follow Weber in his use of the term "guest." However, here the guest does not drain the host and, probably, offers an adequate exchange, though Poll does not explore that reciprocity.

18. Poll could, but does not choose to, use the deviance paradigm in order to account for the maintenance of segregation. He makes no reference to the literature on deviant subcultures (despite the fact that this paradigm was being used in his immediate academic environment to analyze the criminal subculture). He refers to this paradigm in discussing Hasidim in Israel, where most Jews identify with Judaism. There, he asserts, Hasidim, a deviant group, might not be tolerated.

19. Being at the frontier is not to be confused with cultural marginality though many at the frontier are Jewishly marginal. This analysis is based on the first edition of Sklare and Greenblum's work. A recent revised edition has been published.

20. The possibility of their being indicators of a single dimension is open to empirical test. For example, the observance scores may be used to predict some other Jewish behavior such as support of inter-religious marriage, or willingness to contribute financially to a synagogue, or advocacy of Zionist aliya. If all combinations have the same predictive value,

they may be considered equivalent for that purpose.

21. If these categories were viewed as dependent variables (in cross tabulations with two or three independent variable groups), they would have four to six cells, and with it the likelihood that one or more of those cells would be nearly empty. but using a single score, they obtain a mean for all the individuals in the independent variable category.

22. The study of cathexis in psychoanalysis, beyond the cathexis of primary objects and the counter-cathexis of the therapist, has little to say about differences among objects. Object-relations theory and the neo-Freudian approaches criticize orthodox analysis for its neglect of objects. In much academic psychology, the symbolic content of behavior is of less concern than motive strength. The same underlying personality characteristics, hostility, for instance, may be expressed in entrepreneurship or street mugging, for instance. The same underlying neural or physiological state may support a variety of contents. Much economic analysis follows this pattern by treating a variety of goods and services in terms of a single value, their price. Interest is restricted to relative positions in a matrix of exchange. Sociological, anthropological and political science analyses tend to be more attentive to the subjective meanings of action for the actors. One would expect an applied sociology or psychology of Jewry to deal with the content of Judaic culture.

23. In An Historian's Approach to Religion, Toynbee describes how the state may be taken as an object of veneration. Kings who rule by divine right or claim divine origin may be objects of religious veneration as an extension of religion. In more secular times, the veneration may be of a people or of a nation without explicitly rooting it in religion.

24. The relative proportions committed to each of the types may vary with the setting. Perhaps the nationalist, non-religious (plus, minus) category is the principal one among Jews in Israel. In an American Jewish population, the non-religious, non-nationalistic (minus, minus) is probably the numerically largest category, if being Zionist-nationalist implies a serious interest in migration.

25. A later edition is available. The critique is
     of the first edition.

Chapter VI

JEWISH LIFE IN THE UNITED STATES:
PERSPECTIVES FROM ECONOMICS[*]

ARCADIUS KAHAN

The contribution that economic analysis could
make toward a better understanding of the present
problems of the Jewish communities in the States is
necessarily limited by the tools and data at its
disposal. Data provide the economist with evidence
that either serves to prove his theoretical propositions or suggests that his interpretation is more
or less probable. Unfortunately, most of the data
on economic activities collected in the United
States, by either governmental or private agencies
do not distinguish among denominational or ethnic
groups, and therefore leave open the field of inquiry to conjectures or, at best, to sampling procedures with different degrees of probable
errors. Even the number of Jews in the United
States has to be derived by a painstaking process.[1]
Of the multitude of economic problems or economic aspects of social activities, the most pertinent for our purposes are those dealing with the
employment and incomes of the Jewish population in
the United States. The focus on trends in the
occupational structure of the Jewish population is
based upon the assumption that both the levels of
employment and the distribution of the Jewish labor
force by particular employment categories determine
to a large extent the income levels of the population in question. Data for cross-sectional analyses of the occupational structure of the Jewish
community in the United States exist or could be

reconstructed for different periods of the past
hundred years. It would, however, be simplistic to
view the changes in the structure as a continuous
undirectional process.

HISTORICAL BACKGROUND

The mass immigration of the East European Jews
during the period between 1890 and 1914 changed
drastically not only the numbers, but also the occupational structure, of the Jewish community.
Much has been written about the Eastern European
migrants and their economic adjustment in the
United States. The new migrants relied to a considerable extent upon the skills that they already
possessed and could utilize in their new home.[2]
Even those immigrants who arrived in the United
States without a definable trade, those described
in popular parlance as luftmenschen, who could not
find steady employment in the Pale of Settlement in
Russia or in the towns of Galicia, possessed discernible commercial skills which they could utilize
in a country with a high demand for labor of various categories. The skills embodied in the labor
force, the further investments in their human capital, and their consumption and savings patterns
enabled the wage earners among them to reach, within an approximate 15-year period after arrival in
this country, an income level and lifestyle equal
to that of the native born wage earners.[3] The
self-employed among them were also advancing rapidly in comparison with other ethnic groups among the
native or immigrant population. This was, in part,
owing to the greater vertical integration observed
in the areas of prevailing Jewish entrepreneurship
and labor.
Notwithstanding this gradual process in the
advancement of growing human capital and financial
assets, the economic life of the Jewish community
was neither uniform or continuous in its development. Although the discontinuities did not constitute a break with the evolutionary pattern of
economic adjustment and gradual change in the occupational structure of the community, they accel-
erated growth and qualitative change. Most of the
so called "discontinuities" resulted when the degree of discrimination was lowered either by the
business sector or by governmental authorities.
This change in social attitudes brought about a
considerable lowering of barriers to economic

mobility and provided additional opportunities for
economic activity in a variety of areas.

The first of the discontinuities can be
ascribed to the period of World War I, a period
during which the necessity of mobilization of resources for the war effort led to a lowering of
barriers in both the governmental and private sec-
tors. The net result, for the Jewish community,
was a sharper turn away from wage labor and into
self-employment and small-scale entrepreneurship.
The possession of skills and ability to organize
production of scarce goods, along with the relatively modest capital requirements and liberal
extension of credit converted many Jewish wage
earners into entrepreneurs and self-employed. The
accumulated profits served some of them as a means
of surviving the post-war period of contraction and
the transition to a civilian economy. The new positions and acquired status as well as attitudes
made it possible for their children to invest in
human capital on a larger scale than before.

While the Great Depression had a deleterious
effect upon the income of Jews and non-Jews alike,
it had a peculiar effect upon those who were in-
vesting in their education. The opportunity costs
of education declined because of widespread unemployment and thus encouraged the ones involved in
schools and colleges to continue perhaps beyond the
point of their initial intention or cost benefit
calculations based upon pre-Depression conditions. The full benefits from this protracted
decline of the costs of education became apparent
after World War II. After World War II the G.I.
Bill provided a massive subsidy for the acquisition
of skills and formal education to the many veterans
who constituted a broad stratum of the American
population.[4] Thus, a combination of the Depression
period and the G.I. Bill raised the educational
endowment and skill level of the American-born off-
spring of Jewish immigrants to the very top layer
in American society.

World War II, as did World War I, further
lowered discriminatory barriers in the United
States. Actually, in such areas as federal government employment, the New Deal already provided
greater opportunities for Jews and other minorities. World War II also prepared the ground for a
lowering of the discriminatory barriers in some
branches of American business. Whether the road to
the corporate structure led via science, and technology, or business administration depended upon a

number of factors peculiar to the several industries.

The Great Depression and World War II also
contributed to the spatial mobility of the Jewish
population. Although one could assume that immigrants are more mobile than the rest of the
population, mobility also depends upon the degree
of acculturation of the immigrants, their knowledge
of the language, mores, among other things, if
their employment depends upon the communication
with employers or customers outside their immigrant
milieu. Knowledge of the language and facility in
communication help to minimize both information
costs and transaction costs. The "second generation" was certainly better equipped than the immigrants in those respects. The accompanying
increase in spatial mobility, the movement away
from the metropolitan areas of the North-East to
other metropolitan areas, helped not only to
achieve a more advantageous regional distribution
of the Jewish labor force but also contributed
materially toward a more optimal utilization of the
skills in the various occupations followed by the
Jews.

OCCUPATIONAL DISTRIBUTION

While a number of Jewish community studies
provide data for an occupational distribution of
the Jewish population in the United States, they
are no substitute for national studies or reliable
national samples. At best, they are only suggestive of general trends. There are only a few
studies on a nationwide basis, and they can only be
conducted with a great effort. I shall here use
the two most recent studies, those of 1957 and
1970. Although those studies do not cover quite
the same age groups and hence might suggest a
somewhat misleading rate of change between the two
dates, the overall structure of employment is
reflected by the distribution of occupations in
Table 1. The direction of change, indicated by the
data in the table and supported by community
studies, suggests a growth of the professional
category, a slower growth rate or perhaps emerging
stability in the managerial and proprietor
category, and a gradual decline in the categories
of skilled, semiskilled, and unskilled workers
(sometimes referred to in the literature as
craftsmen, operatives, and laborers). The growth
in white-collar occupations and the simultaneous

decline in the blue-collar occupations is related
to the retirement of an older age cohort among whom
the latter were once conspicuously represented.
To what extent do those occupational trends
coincide with trends in the distribution of the
American labor force? The general impression that
one derives from the study of occupational trends

Table 1.

DISTRIBUTION OF JEWISH EMPLOYED MALES AND FEMALES
BY MAJOR OCCUPATION GROUPS, 1957 AND 1970.

	Males		Females	
	1957[a]	1970[b]	1957[a]	1970[b]
Professional	20.3	29.3	15.5	23.8
Managers, proprietors	35.1	40.7	8.9	15.5
Clerical workers	8.0	3.2	43.9	41.7
Sales workers	14.1	14.2	14.4	8.3
Skilled workers	8.9	5.6	.7	1.5
Semiskilled	10.1	3.9	11.2	2.3
Unskilled	.8	.3	-	.2
Agriculture	.1	-	.2	-
Unknown	-	1.7	-	3.1

[a]Employed persons 18 years old and over.

[b]Employed persons 25 years old and over.

Source: U.S. Bureau of the Census, "Tabulations of
Data on the Social and Economic Character-
istics of Major Religious Groups March
1957" (unpublished). Fred Massarik and
Alvin Chenkin, "United States National
Jewish Population Study: A First Report,"
American Jewish Year Book, vol. 74,
(1973), pp. 284-285.

in the American labor market, particularly for
labor with a high endowment of education, is of a
strong correlation between the shifts in the occupational distribution of the Jews and those of the
general population.[5] The growth of the tertiary
sector, of the role of services in the American
economy, particularly of the professional technical
group, coincides with the shift within employment
of the Jews.[6] The relative decline of blue-collar
workers, although not as precipitious as among the
Jews, is certainly typical for the white labor
force in the United States.[7]

In order to assess the impact of general
employment shifts upon the different areas of employment of the Jewish population, three areas were
selected for closer scrutiny: retail trade, wholesale trade, and some of the services.

Employment in retail trade in the United
States increased from about 8.2 million in 1950 to
about 12 million in 1975, while the volume of trade
was increasing in both nominal and real terms.[8]
But the data for sales suggest different growth
patterns for some of the branches of retail trade
resulting from changes in the spending preferences
of consumers. The relatively modest growth of such
branches as furniture, women's and men's apparel,
old strongholds of high participation by Jewish
businessmen, would probably cause some shift of
Jews from those into other branches of trade.

The much higher growth rates of the automotive, building materials, food, and general mer-
chandise branches, most probably attracted some of
the Jewish retail merchants. While the data show a
moderate growth of total employment in retail
trade, we lack any direct indication that the number of Jews employed in retail trade increased.
Thus, we might expect that Jewish retailers shifted
from branches that were not growing to the branches
that were expanding more rapidly.[9]

The situation in wholesale trade bears some
similiarity to that in retail trade. The business
censuses provide us with some insight into the number of wholesale merchant firms and the volume of
their sales. On the one hand, the slowest growing
branches in terms of employment were dry goods and
apparel, groceries, and tobacco. On the other
hand, the fastest growth was exhibited by the
branches of electricity and electronics, metals,
and automotive machinery and equipment.[10]

Circumstantial evidence supports the hypothesis that a parallel development also took place
within the Jewish group of wholesale merchants, in

addition to the long-term trend of movement from
the retail trade to wholesale trade.[11] In addition
to the problems of interpreting employment in such
areas as wholesale and retail trade for which at
least general information is available, there is
still another problem in detecting possible shifts
in Jews moving between ownership and the management
of industrial, trade, or service enterprises. Increased employment opportunities for Jews, as well
as for other minority groups, in the corporate sector of American business, provided the alternatives
of high earnings at a lower risk than the businesses proprietorship. It is therefore, possible
to conjecture that, within the employment structure
of the Jewish population, the category of managers
not only increased secularly, but perhaps also grew
at the expense of the number of owners of businesses. This presupposes confirmation of the view that
corporate managerial positions are somehow more
attractive than independent ownership of smaller
business establishments.

The most dynamic sector of employment of particular interest to us is that of professional and
technical workers. Definitional and computational
problems apart, this segment of employment grew
very rapidly, from about 3.9 million in 1940, 5.0
million in 1950, to 12.7 million in 1975. One of
the features of the growth of this segment of the
labor force is the growth of female employment
(from 2.7 million in 1960 to 5.3 million in 1975),
thus utilizing the education of females in jobs
requiring high levels of human capital.

While the totals of employment in this category are of considerable interest, representing the
general growth of services in the economy, they
cannot serve as a substitute for some more detailed
data pertaining to subgroups of this category. The
data in Table 2 include a number of such subgroups
chosen for illustrative purposes.[12] Among the
listed subgroups in Table 2, the group of business
services exhibits high growth. Circumstantial evidence suggests that the participation of Jews in
this category increased. The general pattern of
growth of the total professional technical category
suggests that the growing demand for specialized
services provided opportunities for Jewish employment, both for new entrants into the labor force as
well as for those who were transferring from other
occupations. In addition, a policy of discrimination against the Jewish element in this segment of
the labor market, even if attempted, would not be
costly and difficult to administer or to maintain.

A closer scrutiny of the numerical growth of a
few "prestigious" professions supports the contention that a rapid expansion was, in fact, taking
place and suggests such an expansion provided
opportunities for the Jewish population as well.[13]

The doubling of the size of the three professional categories (medicine, dentistry and law)
since 1950 has without any doubt, provided employment opportunities for the Jewish population. Even
if we would assume that the share of Jewish employment in those categories remained unchanged, rather
than increased, it would permit a numerical growth
that would have affected the employment structure
of the Jewish population. That assumption (minimally the preservation of the proportion of Jewish
professionals in those categories) appears to be
reasonable for the following reasons. First, the
Jews' level of education made them eligible to
study those subjects in the various professinal
schools. Second, given the preexisting relatively
high share of Jews in those professions and the
slight advantage that children of professionals
have to enter their parents' professions, Jewish
children might be more favorably inclined to follow
suit.

The participation of Jews in the educational
professions is significant but is not easily interpreted. In the past, the penetration of Jews into
the area of education was made primarily by women
at the level of elementary and secondary school
teaching. The last two decades witnessed a very
substantial increase of employment in teaching at
institutions of higher learning, in which Jewish
males participated. Therefore, we could base our
assumption about the relative stability or even
growth, in the number of Jews in the teaching profession, not only upon the overall increase in
educational employment, but also upon the rapid
growth of employment in higher education, which in
the case of the Jews, more than compensated for
their possible relative decline in employment at
the elementary or secondary levels.

There is, in addition, the area of Jewish
education in institutions supported by local Jewish
communities. Beginning with the 1950s, an expansion of both educational facilities and employment
took place here. Although this line of employment
is growing slowly (given the low rate of Jewish
population growth in the United States), it nevertheless provided some additional employment opportunities in education which in all likelihood, were
not accounted for by the official data upon which

Table 2
SELECTED INDICATORS OF GROWTH OF
PROFESSIONAL AND TECHNICAL EMPLOYMENT
(IN THOUSANDS)

	1950	1955	1960	1965	1970	1975
Total professional and technical	5000	--	7090	--	11561	--
Miscellaneous business services	384	528	728	1107	1581	1957
Miscellaneous professional services	270	328	466	566	798	1016
Educational services	502	552	699	902	1046	1164
Legal services	234	248	297	330	385	460
Accountants and auditors	385	--	496	--	712	--
Editors and reporters	73	--	106	--	151	--
Social and welfare workers	94	--	124	--	274	--
Personnel and labor relations	53	--	103	--	296	--
Natural scientists	43	--	62	--	95	--
Social scientists	36	--	42	--	110	--

Sources: U.S. Bureau of the Census, Historical
Statistics of the United States, Colonial
Times to 1970 (Washington, D.C., 1975),
pp. 140-141; U.S. Bureau of the Census,
Statistical Abstract of the United
States, 1977 (Washington,D.C., 1977).

not accounted for by the official data upon which
our previous discussion is based.

Since these groups of "prestigious" professional-technical employment (to which also the
categories labelled natural scientists and social
scientists belong) all have in common a relatively
high education prerequisite, it is incumbent upon
us to discuss the problem of education as one of
the most important vehicles of upward social mobility and as one of the factors explaining the change
in the employment structure of the Jewish population.

EDUCATION

The historical dimensions of the educational
achievements of the Jewish population in the United
States, when viewed against all denominational
groups, can be seen from the table presented by
A.M. Greeley[14] on the proportion of denominational
groups attending college by cohorts. (Table 3).

Although an analysis of the accuracy and consistency of the National Opinion Research Center
samples and Greeley's results is beyond the purview
of this essay, the main results can be accepted as
a rough approximation. Not only did the Jews in
his sample lead all other groups in the level of
many years of education - 14 years, a national average of 11.5 years during 1973 and 1974[15] - but
they also clearly overcame the disadvantage of having less educated parents than Episcopalians or
Presbyterians.[16] For somewhat more detailed data
of the last two decades, which illustrate the
change in the distribution of the Jewish population
by years of achieved formal education for 1957 and
1970 consider Table 4.

While this table does not illustrate the
relative change that was also taking place among
the general population in the United States,[17a-b]
it represents the cumulative results of an ongoing
process, which appears somewhat slower because of
the increased longevity of the earlier age cohorts. There is no doubt that, historically
speaking, the Jewish community in the United States
is the best educated large community in the history
of the Jews. The stock of human capital that
became embodied in the labor force of the Jewish
population provided the basis for seeking opportunities in the areas of employment in which the
highest return could be obtained for this type of
capital and specific skills.

Thus we find a very high degree of correlation between the levels of education and particular

Table 3

PROPORTION DENOMINATIONAL GROUPS ATTENDING COLLEGE BY COHORTS (IN PERCENT)

Cohorts	Jews	All
1900-1909	17	17
1910-1919	29	18
1920-1929	42	18
1930-1939	47	23
1940-1949	69	29
1950-1959	64	32
1960-1969	88	43

Source: A.M. Greeley, Ethnicity, Denomination and Inequality (Beverly Hills, California: Sage Publications, 1976), p.32.

Table 4

PERCENT DISTRIBUTION OF YEARS OF SCHOOLING COMPLETED OF JEWISH POPULATION 25 YEARS AND OVER

	Males		Females		Both sexes	
	1957	1970	1957	1970	1957	1970
Less than 12 years	37.5	15.2	39.9	16.0	38.7	15.6
12 years	21.5	22.5	35.8	35.3	29.0	29.2
College 1-3 years	12.6	17.3	12.8	21.0	12.7	19.2
College 4 years or more	25.6	41.4	9.7	24.2	17.3	32.4
Unknown	2.8	3.5	1.8	3.5	2.3	3.5

Sources: U.S. Bureau of the Census "Tabulations of Data on the Social and Economic Character- istics of Major Religious Groups: March 1957" (unpublished). Fred Massarik and Alvin Chenkin "United States National Population Study: A First Report," American Jewish Year Book, vol. 74 (1973), p. 280.

types or categories of employment. Table 5, which presents a comparison between the employment distribution of all college graduates and Jewish college graduates for 1957, and which indicates the similarity of both distributions, illustrates this pattern of strong correlation between levels of education and employment status. For the labor force of the Jewish population with its relatively high educational endowment, a general distribution heavily weighted toward professional and managerial employment would be the one suggested by both economic theory and evidence.

The fact that the acquisition of formal education on a large scale started early in this century provided the Jews with an advantage over other immigrant groups as far as occupational mobility is concerned, and during the recent periods permitted them to overtake such "educationally minded" denominations as the Episcopalians and

Table 5

PERCENT DISTRIBUTION OF EMPLOYED COLLEGE GRADUATES
IN URBAN AREAS BY MAJOR OCCUPATION GROUP
TOTAL U.S. AND JEWISH POPULATION, 1957

Major Occupation Group	Total	Jewish
Professional	63.2	58.2
Managers and proprietors	15.7	22.1
Clerical	8.2	8.9
Sales workers	5.8	7.8
Skilled laborers	3.2	.9
Semi-skilled laborers	1.5	1.3
Other occupations	2.4	.9

Source: U.S. Bureau of the Census, 1957 sample survey from unpublished data. Courtesy of Dr. Herbert Bienstock.

Presbyterians. A high level of educational achievement, which enabled Jewish members of the labor force to enter into the professional and managerial categories, has provided its bearers with a degree of social esteem. When measured, by the National Opinion Research Center occupational prestige scale, the Jews have a mean of 48.8 points

(on a scale of zero to 99), or 8.5 points above the
national average of 40.3 points.

THE INCOME PROFILES

While the educational data certainly support
and partly explain the relationship between educational achievement, occupational mobility and
structure of populations, it is also important to
examine their implications for income levels.
Economic logic would suggest, on the basis of the
previous discussion of educational levels and occupational structure, that the incomes of the Jewish
members of the labor force should be high relative
to other groups of the United States, labor force
in the absence of discrimination. A few exogeneous
factors contributed to this development. One factor was the urban character of the Jewish population with its wider opportunities and higher
incomes than those of the rural population. Another factor that contributed to the economic
success of the Jews in the United States was the
change in demographic patter beginning with the
immigrant generations. Most significant was the
reduction in family size. Not only did child mortality decline and the birth rate adjust itself to
the diminished death rate, but birth control practices were adopted that reduced the numbers of
births even further. The decline in the size of
the family led to a decrease in expenditures for
goods and services and permitted either an increase
in the share of savings or a greater investment in
the education and training of children relative to
that of the previous generations. The results were
higher quality children. While family incomes increased, per capita income increased even more
owing to the subsequent reductions in family size.
Recent data for the New York boroughs provide
some insight in the sizes of Jewish families or
households. In the boroughs of Queens, Westchester, and Nassau-Suffolk, where the percentage
of the Jewish population in the age groups between
20 and 59 were 57.8, 54, and 53.9 respectively, the
average household sizes were 2.85, 3.28, and 3.64
persons. Needless to say that in Brooklyn, the
Bronx and Manhattan, with high percentages in the
age groups of 60 years and above (25.4 percent in
Brooklyn, 34.6 percent in Manhattan, and 43 percent
in the Bronx), the average size of Jewish households were considerably smaller (as low as 1.84
persons in Manhattan). Although it is clear that

the two-person household is primarily an age-
related phenomenon, nevertheless the fact that
households have a size of fewer than four persons
has a number of implications for population growth
rates and for transfers of resources to younger
generations. It is conceivable that under certain
conditions the average size of the Jewish family
could decrease somewhat further, but such a decline
will have a relatively small effect upon the income
position or occupational structure of the Jewish
communities.[18]

Still another demographic factor, namely the
age distribution of the Jewish population, has an
effect upon the level of family incomes. The age
distribution of the Jewish labor force contains a
higher percentage of individuals above 30 years of
age than does the total labor force.[19] To the extent that this age category contains more income
earners at the peak of their earning capacity, it
may raise the level of the family income. Therefore, given an age distribution which, in addition
to the occupational structure, was favorable to
increasing family incomes, the process of upward
economic mobility continued. Although we do not
know exactly when the median family income of the
Jewish population reached the average for the total
population, a 1956 study indicated that the median
income of the Jewish urban labor force, both male
and female, was higher than the median for the total United States population. The median income
for Jewish males reported $4773 compared to $4472
for the total population and Jewish females earned
$2352 as opposed to $2255 for the total female population.[20] During the subsequent period the differential tended to increase, and A.M. Greeley in
his survey sample of 1974 finds the family income
for his Jewish respondents to be $13,340 and
$13,512 for men only compared to a national average
of $9953. Greely estimates Jewish incomes outside
the South to be $12,918 whereas they were $10,623
for the total population, and $11,204 for Jews in
metropolitan regions of over two million inhabit-
ants, all in 1974 dollars.[21] The data of the sample survey conducted by A.M. Greeley enabled him to
indicate the rank order of a number of denominational groups in average family income in which the
relative position of the Jewish group is indicated.[22]

Apart from the income position of the Jewish
participants in the labor force relative to other
denominational groups, it is important to place
them in the distribution of family incomes of the

general population. In view of the absence of
direct recent data - the latest being collected for
1956[23] - one has to find in the distribution of
family incomes of the general population the
particular groups whose occupational distribution
and educational endowment approximate the characteristics of the Jewish population described
above. Such categories were found in the range
between the highest fifth of the families income
distribution and between the top 5 percent of the
distribution, both for occupations and education.[24a-b] Although the results are not exact,
they appear to approximate the actual range.

Both economic logic and empirical observations, furthermore, suggest that for high income
groups earnings from work do not constitute the
only source of income, but that property incomes
constitute an important component of the total
income.[25] Such property incomes might consist of
dividends, interest, or rents. The holding of such
assets is related both to the previous level of
income or past savings, and changes over the life
cycle of individuals. While for younger age
cohorts current earnings from work might predomi-
nate, such earnings might peak at a certain point
in the life cycle, while real estate and corporate
stock holdings (both providing a growing capital
appreciation) would tend to increase with age as a
part of the asset portfolio. Circumstantial evidence for the incomes of the Jewish population
indicates the growth of real estate in total asset
holdings, as a protection against inflation and an
anticipation of urban growth. Accompanying the
relative shift to real estate from other means to
holding wealth was the active involvement of Jewish
entrepreneurs in both real estate, housing, and
commercial and industrial construction. Data from
smaller and middle size Jewish communities indicate
the rise in these above described forms of economic
activity.

The occupational and age structure of the Jews
help to explain income disparity within the Jewish
community. As the average life span has extended,
there has been a high degree of concentration of
Jews with limited means in advanced age groups.
This concentration of low income people is a combination of demographic factors (in spite of the fact
that Jews were employed more than other groups
beyond the statutory retirement age) and the socioeconomic or occupational structure of earlier
decades. This bipolarity of the income distribution might diminish in the future, but during the

present period of protracted inflationary pres-
sures, which tend to erode accumulated savings and
affect people who depend upon fixed incomes, both
the problem and the sufferings are real.

Perhaps some of this bipolarity of incomes
might also be owing to the nature of income or
asset transfers from generation to generation.
Some of our data indicate that the costs of educa-
ting children was higher among Jews than among
other groups. There is a possibility that in some
cases the investment in their children's education
went beyond the point of maximizing returns and
might better be considered consumption expenses.
There is also reason to believe that transfers of
assets to their children took place not at the time
of death and inheritance but earlier, during the
life of the parents, in the expectation of subsequent support from the children, which might have
turned out to be below expectations.

GAZING INTO THE FUTURE

Granted that the present Jewish generation in
the United States has found itself within the upper
stratum of the socioeconomic pyramid, one might in-
quire or speculate about their changes of remaining
there within the foreseeable future. The history
of minority groups within larger populations provides a number of examples which question the ability of minorities to maintain their socioeconomic
status vis-a-vis either discrimination or intensified competition on the part of the majority. The
problem of intensified competition deserves serious
consideration; some knowledgeable scholars of the
contemporary Jewish scene in the United States have
begun addressing themselves to it.[26]

It has been argued on the basis of observable
trends that the differences in income, status, education, between the Jews and other denominational
groups (such as the Catholics) are diminishing and
that competition in areas which were previously
considered as open for entry of Jews is becoming
fierce. I, for one, would not dispute such
findings nor the possibility that in the longer run
future generations of Jews would find it necessary
to return to some of the occupations which were
given up by their parents for what once appeared to
be more lucrative or prestigious. Earnings in different occupations might change in the longer run,
and adjustments will probably be necessary and will
doubtless take place. However, for the shorter

run, given no major shifts in society's preferences
and assuming a general continuity of employment
trends, one might still argue for the likelihood
that the Jews will maintain their present
position. It is necessary to emphasize that while
we are dealing with particular categories of
employment (whether defined by the census or
otherwise) we are not differentiating sufficiently
the composition or the scope of such categories.
In other words, while concentrating upon the differences between or among the categories, we are
not allowing for the quality differences within the
categories.
    Perhaps a simple example might suffice to
illustrate our contention. If we are to measure
the effects of the participation of Jews (or any
other group) in the category of educational services, one general number will be insufficient because we could not differentiate between teachers
in elementary schools, in secondary and in higher
education. A net decrease in the category of educational services could yield a positive result if
a moderate decrease in elementary school teachers
were compensated for by a small increase in teaching at the college level. Thus, the gist of my argument is the trade-off between quantity and quality. A graduate from Harvard Law School will,
other things being equal, earn more than a graduate
from Alabama Law School. Thus, given the high educational endowment, experience in the professions,
in management and business proprietorships, it is
still possible for the foreseeable future, to compete in the marketplace for high quality (and high
income) positions in a number of occupations. Our
competitive model also includes an increase in the
employment of Jewish women, which should help to
strengthen the relative economic position by aug-
menting the size of family earnings. Thus while my
argument does not negate my argument that there
will be an increase in competition for the long
run, it postpones more painful and disruptive adjustments to a later period.
    While this review of some selected economic
aspects of the Jewish communities in the United
States is by necessity brief and incomplete, it
does point to the need for a more extensive collection of data and a more rigorous analysis of
phenomena which are perhaps mundane but, nevertheless, significantly touch everyone's life.

NOTES

* The author owes a special debt of gratitude to Dr. Herbert Bienstock, Regional Commissioner of the Bureau of Labor Statistics in New York, who generously provided the results of his penetrating analysis of the trends in the employment structure of the Jewish population. A discussion with Mr. Joel Shinsky of the Jewish Federation of Chicago was very fruitful. My colleagues Professors Alexander Erlich, Joseph B. Gittler, Ralph Lerner and Roger Weiss read an earlier version of this essay and offered constructive criticism. Responsibility of possible errors of judgment rests solely with the author.

1. See the chapter by Professor Sidney Goldstein in this volume.

2. On the degree of congruence of the employment structure of Jewish immigrants in the country of origin and in the U.S., see, Simon Kuznets, "Immigration of Russian Jews to the United States: Background and Structure," Perspectives in American History, vol. 9 (1975), pp. 35-126, and Arcadius Kahan, "Economic Opportunities and Some Pilgrims' Progress: Jewish Immigrants from Eastern Europe in the U.S., 1890-1914," The Journal of Economic History vol. 1 (1978), pp. 235-251.

3. It is also possible, that many of the immigrant wage workers, were aided by the relatively high level of unionization in their trades in localities, which provided them with a somewhat higher starting point for individual advancement and socialization in American society relative to other immigrant groups.

4. The number of World War II veterans who returned to civilian life can be estimated approximately at 11.6 million. The direct cost to the United States government of the educational and training programs for war veterans constituted $14,182 million between 1946 and 1952. (U.S. Bureau of the Census, Historical Statistics of the United States, Colonial Times to 1970 (Washington, D.C., 1975), vol. I, p. 340; vol. II, p. 1145).

5. U.S. Bureau of the Census, Statistical Abstract of the United States, 1977 (Washington, D.C., 1977), pp. 406-411, and U.S. Bureau of the Census, Ibid; vol. I, pp. 140-145.. For the general trends in the occupational structure of the American labor force and

economically active population, see these
sources. For comparison of the Jewish
occupational pattern and the general one, see
Tables A1 and A2 of the Appendix to this
chapter.

6. The professional technical group increased
during 1950-1970 from 5.0 millions to 11.6
millions, while the total rose from 59.2 to
79.8 millions. See U.S. Bureau of the Census,
Historical Statistics of the United States,
Colonial Times to 1970 (Washington, D.C.,
1975).

7. The decline in the proportion of the blue-
collar workers in the total employed white
population (inclusive of farm workers and
service workers) was from 53.4 percent in 1960
to 48.2 percent in 1976. The slower pace
among the general population can in part be
explained by the shift of some blue-collar
workers into the service workers category and
by their having a lower level of education
than do the Jews. See U.S. Bureau of the
Census, Statistical Abstract of the United
States, 1977 (Washington, D.C. 1977), p. 407.

(Footnote 8, on page 256).

8. For the area of retail trade the following table should be of interest.

Volume of Retail Trade Sales (in billion dollars)

	1950	1955	1960	1965	1970	1975
All retail	147.2	183.9	219.5	284.1	375.5	584.0
Durable goods	54.3	67.0	70.6	94.2	114.3	180.7
Automotive	27.4	36.3	37.0	56.9	65.0	102.1
Furniture	8.3	10.1	10.6	13.4	17.8	26.1
Building materials, hardware	9.7	11.0	11.3	17.1	20.5	43.2
Non-durable goods	92.9	116.9	149.0	189.9	261.2	403.7
Men's apparel	2.3	2.3	2.6	na	4.6	6.1
Women's apparel	3.7	4.2	5.3	na	7.6	10.4
Liquor	2.7	3.5	4.9	5.7	8.0	11.0
Food	31.9	42.0	54.0	64.0	86.1	131.7
General merchandise	17.3	20.1	24.1	42.3	61.3	95.4
Employment (in thousands)	8,185	8,801	9,262	9,706	10,906	11,961

Sources: U.S. Bureau of the Census, Historical Statistics of the United States, Colonial Times to 1970 (Washington, D.C., 1975), pp. 848-849. U.S. Bureau of the Census, Statistical Abstract of the United States, 1977 (Washington, D.C. 1977), p. 831.

9. This assumption rests not only upon economic logic, but upon scattered data on declining and increasing participation of groups of retail merchants from various branches in the affairs of some major Jewish communities especially fund raising.

10. The total value of sales of the United States wholesale trade is given in the following table.

VOLUME IF WHOLESALE TRADE SALES
(in billion dollars)

Years	Durables	Non-Durables	Total
1950	37.7	54.6	92.3
1955	51.4	67.3	118.7
1960	58.6	81.3	139.9
1965	82.9	104.5	187.3
1970	112.0	135.0	247.0
1975	185.9	253.1	439.0

The data in the table and the more detailed breakdown of wholesale trade branches provide the information about the growth trends. For details for the years between 1948 and 1972, see U.S. Bureau of the Census, Historical Statistics of the United States, Colonial Times to 1970 (Washington, D.C., 1975), pp. 850-853 and U.S. Bureau of Census, Statistical Abstract of the United States, 1977 (Washington, D.C. 1977), p. 829.

11. The circumstantial evidence is provided by the patterns of shifts in the charitable contributions of Jewish wholesale merchants in a number of large Jewish communities, and in the changing relationship between the numbers of retail and wholesale merchants.

12. See U.S. Bureau of the Census, Historical Statistics of the United States, Colonial Times to 1970 (Washington, D.C. 1975), pp. 140-41 and U.S. Bureau of the Census, Statistical Abstract of the United States, 1977 (Washington, D.C. 1977).

13. The assumption of existing opportunities for Jewish employment in the selected categories of service professions is based upon our knowledge of the educational endowment of Jews in the labor force, a topic which is discussed later in this essay. See U.S. Bureau of the Census, Statistical Abstract of the United States, 1977 (Washington, D.C. 1977), pp. 99, 154, 181.

258

14. A.M. Greeley, <u>Ethnicity, Denomination and Inequality</u>, Beverly Hills, California, Sage Publications, 1976.

(Footnote 15, on page 259).

15. The rank order of American denominational groups on mean educational achievement (Non-Spanish-speaking Whites Only) for 1973 and 1974 is given in the following table.

DENOMINATIONAL GROUPS	ALL RESPONDENTS		MEN	
	Mean Years of Education	Standard Deviation	Mean Yars of Education	Standard Deviation
Jews (357)	14.0	(7.1)	14.0	(3.4)
Episcopalians (320)	13.5	(5.6)	13.9	(7.6)
Presbyterians (649)	12.7	(4.6)	12.4	(3.6)
Methodists (1535)	11.9	(4.9)	11.8	(4.6)
Catholics (5733)	11.5	(4.7)	11.4	(5.6)
Lutherans (1105)	11.2	(4.0)	11.3	(5.1)
Baptists (1825)	10.7	(5.2)	10.6	(6.3)

SOURCE: A. M. Greeley, Ethnicity, Denomination and Inequality (Beverly Hills, Calif.: Sage Publications, 1976, p. 19).

16. The parental education of American denomination groups (non-Spanish speaking whites only) is given in the following table.

Denominational Groups	Father's Education	Mother's Education
Jews	10.2	9.9
Episcopalians	12.2	12.2
Presbyterians	10.7	10.7
Methodists	9.4	10.0
Catholics	8.5	8.7
Lutherans	8.8	9.1
Baptists	8.2	8.9

SOURCE: A. M. Greeley, Ethnicity, Denomination and Inequality (Beverly Hills, Calif.: Sage Publications, 1976, p. 20).

17a. The percent distribution of years of school completed by persons 25 years old and over, Jewish and total population (by sex in the United States in 1957), is given in the following table.

Years of School Completed	Males		Females		Total	
	Total Population	Jewish	Total Population	Jewish	Total Population	Jewish
Elementary 0-7	23.2	14.7	20.3	16.6	21.7	15.6
8	18.5	13.1	17.4	13.1	17.9	13.1
High School 1-3	17.3	9.7	18.1	10.2	17.7	10.0
4	22.1	21.5	29.5	35.8	26.0	29.0
College 1-3	7.3	12.6	7.4	12.8	7.3	12.7
4 or More	9.4	25.6	5.7	9.7	7.5	17.3
Not reported	2.2	2.8	1.6	1.8	1.9	2.3
Total percent	100.0	100.0	100.0	100.0	100.0	100.0
Median school Years completed	10.3	12.5	10.9	12.3	10.6	12.3

Source: U.S. Bureau of the Census, "Tabulations of Data on the Social and Economic Characteristics of Major Religious Groups," March, 1957 (unpublished).

17b. The percent distribution of years of school completed by persons aged 25 and over, Jewish and total white population (by sex in the United States in 1970) is given in the following table.

Years of School Completed	Males		Females		Both Sexes	
	Jewish	Total White	Jewish	Total White	Jewish	Total White
Less than 12 years	15.2	46.1	16.0	44.9	15.6	45.5
12 Years	22.5	28.5	35.3	35.5	29.2	32.1
College:						
1-3 years	17.3	11.1	21.0	11.1	19.2	11.1
4 years	14.9	7.2	13.6	5.7	14.2	6.4
5 or more years	26.5	7.1	10.6	2.8	18.2	4.9
Unknown	3.5	-	3.5	-	3.5	-
Total percent	100.0	100.0	100.0	100.0	100.0	100.0

Sources: For the Jewish population see Fred Massarik and Alvin Chenkin, "United States National Jewish Population Study: A First Report," American Jewish Year Book, vol. 74 (1973), p. 280; for the United States white population: U.S. Bureau of the Census, 1970 U.S. Census of Population: General Social and Economic Characteristics, PC(1)-C1 (Washington: Government Printing Office, 1972), p. 386.

18. Fred Massarik, "Basic Characteristics of the Greater New York Jewish Population," <u>American Jewish Year Book 1976</u> (1975), pp. 239-48.
19. <u>The Gallup Opinion Index</u>, Report 130, "Religion in America" (Princeton, N.J., 1976), pp. 39, 49.
20. See U.S. Bureau of the Census, <u>1957 Sample Survey</u>, unpublished data.
21. See A.M. Greeley, op. cit., p. 27.

(Footnote 22, on page 264).

22. The rank order of American denominational groups in average family income (1974 Dollars) for non-Spanish-speaking whites only is given in the following table.

Denominational Group	All Respondents	Standard Deviation	Men	Deviation
Jews	$13,340	(11,382)	$13,512	(11,896)
Catholics	11,374	(8,064)	11,811	(8,082)
Episcopalians	11,032	(10,447)	12,975	(10,911)
Presbyterians	10,796	(10,265)	11,723	(10,291)
Methodists	10,103	(8,987)	10,419	(9,087)
Lutherans	9,702	(9,037)	9,725	(7,871)
Baptists	8,693	(7,985)	9,128	(8,176)

SOURCE: Greeley, op. cit., table 14, p. 27.

23. The percent distribution of persons 14 years old and over by income in 1956 (total and Jewish urban population by sex) standardized by occupation groups is given in the following table.

Income	MALES		FEMALES	
	Total Population	Jewish	Total Population	Jewish
Under $1000	5.6	4.1	23.2	22.5
$ 1,000 to 1999	6.1	6.4	20.6	18.8
2,000 to 2999	10.8	7.6	24.3	24.7
3,000 to 3999	17.4	13.9	19.6	19.1
4,000 to 4999	21.4	23.3	7.8	9.7
5,000 to 5999	16.0	17.0	2.7	2.8
6,000 to 9999	17.6	18.9	1.4	1.7
10,000 and over	5.0	8.7	.3	.7
Median Income	$4472	$4773	$2255	$2352

Source: U.S. Bureau of the Census, 1957 sample survey, unpublished data. Courtesy of Dr. Herbert Bienstock.

24a. The occupational distribution of Jewishmales in 1970 and the occupational distribution of highest fifth and top 5 percent of the American heads of families by size of total money income in 1974 in percentages is given in the following table.

	Highest Fifth	Top 5%	Jewish Males
Professional, technical	27.5	33.1	29.3
Self-employed	4.5	10.6	--
Salaried	22.5	22.5	--
Managers and administrators	29.9	39.7	40.7
Self-employed	4.1	4.7	--
Salaried	25.8	35.0	--
Clerical workers	5.4	3.0	3.2
Sales workers	8.4	7.6	14.2
Skilled workers	14.4	7.0	5.6
Semi-skilled workers	7.4	4.1	3.9
Service workers	3.2	.8	1.2
Laborers	1.5	1.0	.3
Unknown	--	--	1.7

Sources: For the occupational distribution of Jewish males in 1970 see Table A2. For the occupational distribution of American heads of families by size of total money Income, see, U.S. Bureau of the Census, Current Population Reports. Series P. 60, #101, "Monetary Income in 1974 of Families and Persons in the United States" (Washington, D.C.: U.S. Government Printing Office, 1976), p. 29.

24b. Percent distribution of families ranked by
size of total money income in 1974 and the
percent distribution of years of schooling
completed by the Jewish populatin, 25 years
and over in 1970, see the following table.

American Families		Jews		
	Highest Fifth	Top 5 Percent	Both Sexes	Males Only
Less than 12 years	16.6	11.8	15.6	15.2
12 years	30.8	24.7	29.2	22.5
College 1-3	17.0	16.6	19.2	17.3
4 years or more	35.6	46.8	32.4	41.4
Unknown	--	--	3.5	3.5

Sources: U.S. Bureau of the Census, Current
Population Reports, Series P-60, #101,
"Monetary Income in 1974 of Families and
Persons in the United States" (Washington,
D.C.: U.S. Government Printing Office,
1976), p. 29.

25. Out of the vast economic literature on this
subject, one would like to single out the
volume by Lee Soltow, ed., Six Papers on the
Size Distribution of Wealth and Income (New
York: National Bureau of Economic Research,
1969). The papers by Melvyn W. Reder, John B.
Lansing, John Sonquist, Dorothy S. Projector,
Gertrude S. Weiss, and Erling T. Thoresen are
pertinent to some of the aspects of our
discussion.

26. The most interesting treatments of this issue
was provided by Dr. Herbert Bienstock.

APPENDIX
Table A1
PERCENT DISTRIBUTION OF EMPLOYED PERSONS 18 YEARS OLD AND OVER
BY MAJOR OCCUPATION GROUP, JEWISH AND TOTAL POPULATION
IN URBAN UNITED STATES, 1957[a]

Major Occupation Group	Males		Females	
	Total Population	Jewish	Total Population	Jewish
Professional	9.9	20.3	12.2	15.5
Farmers and farm managers	7.3	0.1	0.7	0.2
Managers and proprietors	13.3	35.1	5.5	8.9
Clerical workers	6.9	8.0	30.3	43.9
Sales workers	5.4	14.1	6.9	14.4
Skilled laborers	20.0	8.9	1.0	0.7
Semiskilled laborers	20.9	10.1	17.1	11.2
Service workers	6.1	2.3	22.7	5.1
Farm laborers	2.5	0.1	3.0	–
Unskilled laborers	7.7	0.8	0.6	–
Total percent	100.0	100.0	100.0	100.0
Total white-collar	35.5	77.6	54.9	82.7
Total blue-collar	57.2	22.2	44.4	17.0

[a]Standardized by years of school completed.
Source: U.S. Bureau of the Census, "Tabulations of Data on the Social and Economic Characteristics of Major Religious Groups, March 1957" (Unpublished).

Table A2
OCCUPATIONAL DISTRIBUTION OF THE JEWISH AND TOTAL UNITED STATES WHITE POPULATION, BY SEX, 1970[a]

Occupation	Males		Females		Both Sexes	
	Jewish	Total White	Jewish	Total White	Jewish	Total White
Professional and technical	29.3	15.0	23.8	16.3	27.4	15.5
Managers, administrators	40.7	12.0	15.5	3.9	32.2	9.0
Clerical	3.2	7.6	41.7	8.1	16.2	18.4
Sales	14.2	7.4	8.3	36.8	12.2	7.7
Crafts	5.6	21.8	1.5	1.9	4.2	14.4
Operatives	3.9	18.7	2.3	14.0	3.4	17.0
Service	1.2	7.3	3.6	17.4	2.0	11.0
Laborers	0.3	5.7	0.2	0.9	0.3	3.9
Agriculture[b]	-	4.5	-	0.7	-	3.1
Unknown	1.7	-	3.1	-	2.2	-
Total percent	100.0	100.0	100.0	100.0	100.0	100.0

[a] The Jewish population includes persons aged 25 and over; the total white population includes persons aged 16 and over.

[b] No separate category for agriculture was included in the National Jewish Population Study data.

Source: For the Jewish population see Fred Massarik and Alvin Chenkin, "United States National Jewish Population Study: A First Report," American Jewish Year Book, vol. 74 (1973), pp. 284-285. For the United States white population see U.S. Bureau of the Census, 1970 U.S. Census of Population: General Social and Economic Characteristics, PC(1)-C1 (Washington, D.C.: Government Printing Office, 1972), p. 392.

Chapter VII

JEWISH LIFE IN THE UNITED STATES:
PERSPECTIVES FROM HISTORY

HENRY L. FEINGOLD

George Santayana once observed that "American
life is a powerful solvent" and so it was for the
millions of immigrants who have been reshaped in
America's image for over three centuries.[1] For the
most part it was a benevolent slow process achieved
more by seduction than coercion. Once having left
the "old home" America substituted its own culture
which was plastic enough to allow for the retention
of some of the sentimental facets of the old. Much
ethnicity today reflects that sentimentalism.
    The underlying theme of this discussion is
that the Americanizing solvent did not work the
same way for Jews and it is that fact which continues to differentiate them in the American culture. To be sure the Jewish immigrant became Americanized, even an "exaggerated American," but he
did so on different terms than other immigrants who
having abandoned the territory of the "old home"
became malleable human clay ready for remolding.
Jews too have an "old home" but it is not the country from which they emigrated. It was the fact
that the original society despised them which compelled them to set out on their perilous journey.
They possess a cultural identity not rooted in territorial space, and mere physical removal cannot
separate them from it. It is that residual feeling
of belonging to the Jewish people that gives American Jewry a strange and persistent duality which is
reflected in virtually every facet of its

experience in America. They are in America but
never completely of it. Something is held back.
American Jewry seems always to be trying to achieve
a delicate balance between two cultural pulls, the
tangible America with which they have cast their
temporal lot and the preexisting Jewish which
continues to lay claim to much of their spirit.

I have elsewhere called that phenomenon
"American Jewish exceptionalism" by which I mean
not its superior achievement but the unique duality
it possesses.[2] It bedevils those social scientists
who naively seek a classification, ethnic group,
religious denomination, hyphenate, to make their
task easier. I leave these problems to them in the
certain knowledge that none of their categories
will precisely fit American Jewry. Instead let us
examine how this internal tension between the American and the Jewish plays itself out first in the
writing of American Jewish history and then in the
actual Jewish experience in America.

*   *   *

Confronted by two independent historical
streams, the historian of American Jewry faces
unique problems of perspective. To whose history
does American Jewry belong? Is it part of American
migration, or ethnic or urban history, or a brief
and as yet unheralded chapter in the millenial
stream of Jewish history, another Diaspora in a
history full of Diasporas? One can, for example,
compare the American Jewish historical experience
to that of other Jewries in the Western Hemi-
sphers.[3] Not too long ago the comparison of the
position of American Jewry with German Jewry especially during the Weimar period was popular.[4] At
the same time one can read the American Jewish
experience as being solely part of the American
historical canvas. Two of the most prodigious
workers in the field, Bertram Korn and Rudolf
Glanz, have used such an approach with fruitful
results. But most find it impossible to separate
one from the other neatly. They find that some
amalgamation or at least some reference to the
other stream is necessary if a full historical
picture is to emerge.

Problems of historical perspective in viewing
the history of the host culture can be especially
vexing for the Jewishly conscious historian. As
part of the process of self identification, all

cultures produce heroes and myths which define the
values it holds dear. Historians must take them
into account because, as members of the community,
they are themselves subject to their impact and
because they do tell us something about the society
under study. But the Jewish historical perspective, which is richly furnished with its own heroes
and myths, can find itself in conflict with what
the host culture deems as heroic or important.
Salo Baron uses the illustration of the Roman emperor Titus who was well considered by Roman historians but is rarely mentioned in rabbinic sources
without the epithet ha-rasha (The Wicked) since he
is held responsible for the destruction of the
temple.[5]

Such a lack of confluence abounds in a Jewish
view of American history. What, for example, shall
we do with Henry Ford who American historians consider an ingenious, if somewhat eccentric mechani-
cal whiz who successfully produced an automobile
within the purchasing power of the average American
and thereby changed the face of America? But from
the Jewish perspective he is also the man who
fueled the anti Semitic imagination in the xeno-
phobic twenties by publishing The Protocols of the
Elders of Zion in his Dearborn Independent.[6] For
most Americans Charles Lindbergh may be a folk
hero. His flight symbolized the values small town
America held dear, coolness in the face of danger,
love of nature, self reliance, even inarticu-
lateness. But Jews also note an easy ability to
fall into Nazi-type racial attitudes which held
their group in low esteem.[7] General Ulysses Grant
has gone down in American history as a rather medi-
ocre president but nevertheless the military leader
who saved the union by developing the strategy
which finally brought the Confederacy to its
knees. For Jewish historians, however, he is also
the leader who issued Federal Order Number 11, the
only instance of government sponsored collective
punishment of Jews in American history.[8]

Sometimes an incident barely mentioned in
American history books, such as the lynching of Leo
Frank or the harassment of Jewish merchants in the
Confederacy, warrants special attention from the
Jewish perspective.[9] Every student knows the dramatic story of how William Jennings Bryan stampeded
the Democratic convention in Chicago with his famous "Cross of Gold" speech. But the innocent use
of that Christian metaphor, "You shall not crucify
mankind upon a cross of gold," may strike the Jewish historian who is aware of the deicide polemic

and the link many Populists sought between the currency problem and Jewish money lenders "in the temple," as far from innocent. Much depends on how one looks at things and from what vantage. In the actual writing of history the result may be merely a difference in emphasis but it can go much further than that. Thus the outspoken editor of the Jewish Spectator maintained in a recently published essay that much of what consists of American Jewish culture should not be sought in its contribution to American belles lettres or its impact on popular culture, that is to say the culture actually generated by American Jews, but the humanistic values such as the love of learning which originate in the Jewish religious tradition.[10]

An entire episode may look different from a Jewish perspective. American historians, for example, have given little attention to the role played by organized anti-Semitism in the isolationist trend of the thirties. An ethnic component, to be sure, has been found in the Midwest, but disillusionment with America's entry into World War I and other factors have been stressed.[11] Only recently has a new work emphasised the link between isolationism and anti-Semitism. Spokesmen like Smith, Palley, Coughlin, and Kuhn cloaked their cause in legitimacy and amplified their voice by successfully linking themselves to the isolationist nexus.[12] Then Lindbergh, in Des Moines in September 1941, warned that Jews and anglophiles were puching the nation into a war against the best national interest. Jewish historians long ago noted a linkage between isolationism, the anti-refugee policy and anti-Semitism.[13]

In the area of European history the classic example of how a Jewish historical perspective differs from that held by non-Jewish historians can be gleaned from the recent prize winning work by Lucy Dawidowicz.[14] She gives the holocaust a centrality in World War II which is shared by few specialists in this area. It is not possible to dismiss such views as distortion caused by ethnocentrism or parochialism, as failure by the Jewish historian to muster sufficient detachment to write value-free history. When one dwells on it there are many areas in American history, the abolitionist movement, the Populists, the Progressive period, the Red Scare and even the New Deal which simply look different when viewed through Jewish eyes. That vision stems from a separate Jewish historical experience and identity which many Jewish historians, by no means all, carry with them. It is an example of how the duality of the Jewish presence penetrates even to the writing of history.

History is not a seamless garment. Historians break-up the stream of events into periods, and how they do so gives us a clue about what they think is important and what ephemeral. Nowhere is the interaction between two separate historical streams, the American and the Jewish, more evident than in the different periodizations employed. The major periods in antebellum American historiography are the colonial period (which can be subdivided further) the revolutionary period, the national or federal period, the Era of Good Feeling, sectionalism, Jacksonian democracy, the Civil War and so on. Of course things are really not so neat, since historians at the same time may employ topical ways of breaking up or organizing the time stream (labor history, women's history, urban history, slavery, and the history of reform movements, among others). Now, while American Jewish history also deals with such sequences, its major periodization originates in the stream of Jewish history. As outlined by Jacob Marcus, the dean of American Jewish history, the first period of Sephardic hegemony (1654 to 1840) is linked to the Iberian expulsion and the subsequent growth and influence of Jews and Maranos in the viceroyalties of Spanish America. The second period (1840-1920) is one of German-Jewish dominance and is again linked to the mass emigration of Jews triggered partly by the new wave of anti-Semitism during the restoration period. The period of Eastern Jewish predominance (1881-1920) is again related in part to the strident official anti-Somitism of the governments of that region. Only the last period which starts in 1921, called by Marcus simple the "American period," has no visible links to the Jewish experience elsewhere.[15]

The existence of a periodization scheme whose reference points relate to Jewish rather than American history reflects the natural tension in American Jewish historiography created by two separate and independent pulls. That tension does not exist in a vaccuum. It is merely a reflection of the tension or duality which is present in the actual Jewish experience in America. Like all history, American Jewish history relates closely to the people whose story it seeks to tell. How could it be otherwise?

*   *   *

We turn next to four developments in that
story, Jewish mobility, the Jewish labor movement,
Jewish organizational life, and Jewish interest in
foreign affairs, to demonstrate how a link to
Jewish peoplehood, the memory of corporateness
called K'lal Yisrael, has come virtually to define
what remains Jewish about American Jewry.

Under ordinary circumstances the amazing success story of American Jewry would best be left to
sociologists or Cliometricians who gleefully toll
the numbers to prove or disprove their case. But
the story of Jewish mobility is so quintessentially
American and at the same time so apparent in many
Jewish communities the world over that it serves as
an almost irresistable illustration of our theme of
duality.

Jewish mobility in America remains problematic. Few have been able to state with any precision how much more mobile Jews were than other
subgroups in America. We know today that other
immigrant groups have now also "made it," that is
they have gone beyond the founding Protestant denominations in income and job status.[16] Moreover
the Jewish climb "from rags to riches" has not been
nearly as uniform as was imagined. That much the
recent discovery of the Jewish poor attests. Yet a
concensus is developing that Jews were somehow
faster in their climb; they leaped over the generational increments in income and job status to which
most other immigrants were heir.[17] It seemed as if
this society had released energy and talent stored
up for millenia. What the lovers of statistics,
paradigms, and trends could not see, because they
focused primarily on the contemporary picture, was
that over three centuries American Jewry had actually repeated the success story three times and
produced three separate commercial elites. It did
not matter if it was an agricultural preindustrial
economy, as in the colonial period, or a post industrial one, as today, Jews were successful on the
terms laid down by the society. More interesting
is the fact that, to some extent, their success was
contingent on connection with a Jewish nexus.

The Sephardic Jews of colonial America produced a commercial elite by doing many things
including the manufacture of spermaceti candles and
merchandizing. But their greatest wealth came from
their participation in ocean commerce which touched
Africa and the West Indies and found its American
anchor in Newport which for a time boasted the
largest Jewish community in colonial America. The
success of merchant princes like Aron Lopez was, in

some measure, the result of a strategic and profit-
able connection with the equally successful Jewish
merchants of the original Jewish communities in the
Caribbean. The second elite, recently called "Our
Crowd" by a popularizer, attached themselves to the
westward movement where they filled a merchandizing
vacuum by peddling and by establishing stores.[18]
By the final decades of the nineteenth century a
small group of the most successful merchants, the
tip of the iceberg, made their way into investment
banking where they were joined by an equally successful group of Jews stemming from the banking
houses established by Jews in Germany.[19]   Again it
was a conduit furnished by the connection with German and European Jewish banking houses that contributed to their success. These houses were important because they could supply the risk capital
required by intense industrial development which
occurred in America after the Civil War.

The third wave of eastern Jews repeated the
success story at a somewhat slower pace and on different terms. First they dominated the rapidly
expanding ready-to-wear garment industry which was
previously the scene of German-Jewish commercial
activity. At the same time they entered and developed many marginal industries such as the second-
hand business. Eastern Jewish input into commerce
was for various reasons destined to be less sustained. A good number of the second and third
generation chose to enter the professions rather
than small business, so that today medicine, law,
dentistry and the professorial ranks are disproportionately practiced by Jews.[20]   In all three cases
we may take note of a phenomenon called "courageous
enterprizing," the peculiar ability of American
Jews to strike out as pioneers into relatively new
fields such as fur trading in the colonial period,
or plastics today, or to take old components and
combine them in a new way.[21]   (Many of the so-
called "egg-head millionaires," new Jewish millionaires of the post-World War II period, combined a
professional skill such as chemistry or engineering
with traditional business acumen to make a fortune
in plastics or transistors).[22]

Most important for our story, however, is not
that a disproportionate number of Jews were successful in America but that such success stories
were not confined to America. To some extent Jewish success was a phenomenon which could be observed in all developing Western economies during the
post-emancipation period. The rapid mobility of
Soviet Jewry in the twenties, although it came

about in "socialist" terms, indicates that we need
not confine our story to the West. That is noteworthy because it raises the question of the
sources of Jewish success. Does it stem from the
relative openess of the American economy or does
its driving force come from within the Jewish
culture and condition in the Diaspora? Or was it
caused by the linkage of the two at a particularly
fortunate historical juncture? We have seen how
the success of the Sephardic and German Jews was
based, at least partly, on a strategic position
vis-a-vis other established Jewish communities. To
some extent even the dominance by eastern Jews of
the garment industry, which served as their principle economic base, was contingent on the prior role
of German-Jewish entrepreneurs.

When the full story of American Jewish mobility finally comes to light it will be difficult to
overlook the dual cultural generating force which
was at its heart and which the historical focus
reveals. Like so many facets of the American Jewish experience, Jewish success in America appears
to rest partly on the preexisting Jewish culture,
which gives it behavioral cues, a unique entrepreneurial vision as well as connections and capital,
and American culture which gives it a success
ethos, economic opportunity and an open society.

                    *   *   *

A parallel interconnectedness of the Jewish
and American cultural stream can be noted in the
remarkable development of the Jewish labor movement. The Jewish contribution to business is
matched by its contribution to organized labor.
The eastern Jews were one of two American subgroups
who organized their own labor movement. (The other
was the German-American). The existence of organized Jewish workers is a rather strange phenomenon
related to the rapid proletarianization of Jews in
the Russian Pale in the final quarter of the nineteenth century.[23] The process was intensified by
the immigration and transplantation experience
which converted many Jews from artisans, craftsmen,
and petit merchants to mere "hands" in shops. The
skills they possessed in the Pale were frequently
not usable in the more advanced industrial economy
of America. They were unaccustomed to thinking of
themselves as factory workers nor did they readily
abandon aspiration levels, often reinforced in the

new environment, which might more readily be associated with the middle class. We know that it was
extremely difficult to organize them and keep them
organized.[24] Indeed their sojourn in the working
class, which so won their loyalty, was temporary.
It lasted but one generation. But during that eye
blink in American history the Jewish labor movement
had a profound impact.

For the historian the movement represents
something of a paradox, for while the ideology it
advocated and the methods it employed had a distinctly foreign, if not precisely Jewish flavor, it
also served as a prime Americanizing agency, especially through the press. It also was the Jewish
institution in America which came into possession
of real power which could directly effect the lives
of thousands of people. How that power was used,
rather than the radical rhetoric it projected,
tells the historian a great deal about its real
character.[25]

For men like Samuel Gompers, the English born
Jewish cigar maker who came to lead the American
Federation of Labor, the very idea of a separate
labor movement based on the Jewishness of its rank
and file smacked of parochialism and dual
loyalty. Undoubtedly patrician "uptowners" shared
that view since it resonated what they felt about
all manifestations of Jewish separatism. But for
the Jewish immigrant, who actually perceived that
he was different, separate Jewish locals seemed the
most natural thing in the world. It did not mean
that he did not want to be American. That was in
fact very dear to him. But he wanted to do so on
his own terms, and his conception of how much of
his original culture could be maintained in the new
world was simply more generous. The Jewish labor
movement therefore not only espoused a philosophy
at odds with that of the mainline unions, its
methods of organization from top down also departed
markedly from the normal local craft unions which
were the most enduring components of the American
labor movement. The priority given by Terence
Powderly's Knights of Labor to fraternalism and the
cooperative movement seemed to the radical intellectuals who organized the Jewish Labor Movement as
merely ameliorative.[26] The idea of business
unionism based on "bread and butter" objectives
lacked ideological depth. More crucial was the
restrictionist position taken by the mainline
organization which flew in the face of the Jewish
interest. But it was the socialist approach of
Jewish labor leaders which was the primary source

of contention. Leaders like Samuel Gompers were convinced, and so testified before congressional investigation committees, that the "pie in the sky," instrumentalist approach to unionism advocated by Jewish labor leaders was cynical and based on a fundamental misunderstanding of the American economy and culture. Yet while it was true that organizing workers was, for men like Cahan, Miller, De Leon, and others, not an end in itself but merely a step towards the day when a new order of society would give the worker the fruits of his labor and the social priority he deserved, they also realized that steps to improve conditions of the workers in the "here and now" were necessary. They fought against the sweating system and to attain some security for the worker. But ultimately it would have to be the "new day" that socialism would bring that would solve the basic problems of the working class. In the heavy moral responsibility they bore they were quintessentially part of Jewish political culture.

It was primarily that socialist instrumentalism coupled with moral righteousness and the separatism they insisted upon which alienated them from the mainline unions. One of the largest units of the Jewish Labor Movement, the Amalgamated Clothing Workers, did not join the American Federation of Labor until 1933, and those unions who were affiliated, like the powerful International Ladies Garment Workers, had almost no influence in the inner councils of the federation. One historian concludes that "until the period of the 1930's the Jewish unions were largely in, but not of, the mainstream of the American labor movement."[27] That condition, we have seen, is not unlike that of American Jewry in general.

Yet such apartness did not mean that the movement could avoid the effects of the pull of Americanization. Indeed one way to view the internal tensions within the movement is to see them as generated by the conflict between European secular-Jewish and American modalities. The Forverts, like other Yiddish dailies, prominently featured columns on citizenship education and did present news of the American environment even if it was viewed through socialist eyes. Moreover the socialist ideology and other factors which kept it separate were not destined to endure when the American solvent became fully operative. The socialist rhetoric could fly high when it was not tested in the real world. It was linked to powerlessness. But once power came, once the triad which served as its

base, the United Hebrew Trades, the Forverts and
the Workmen's Circle, were firmly established that
rhetoric had to be muted. In the real world there
were "bosses" with countervailing power whose
truths derived from the ledger sheet not from Socialism. And there was a perpetual threat from the
extreme left which wanted to coopt the movement.
To be sure the influence of socialist ideology did
not disappear entirely but its preeminence gradually gave way to a pragmatic operationalism which
was recognizably American in its problem solving
approach. The "clerics" who founded the movement
remained dedicated and incorruptible, but much of
their creative energy was now devoted to conceiving
of the ameliorative steps which some had previously
opposed because they would dull the edges of the
class struggle. Initially the struggle to organize
the garment industry was especially bitter. Both
the shop owners and the workers were Jewish and
conflict between brothers sometimes takes on a more
passionate quality. But ways were ultimately found
to bring peace to the industry. When Hart,
Schaffner and Marx contemplated liquidation in the
early days of the Depression threatening the jobs
of 4000 members of the Amalgamated, Sidney Hillman
gave the firm an extraordinary "loan" in the form
of a voluntary wage cut for one year.[28] During
contract negotiations the management team was sometimes astonished by the expertize brought to bear
by the "professionals" of the union team. The
union "experts" often had a better knowledge of
what ailed the industry than management.
     It was in one sense the ameliorative measures
first recommended by Jewish unions which found
their way into Roosevelt's welfare state program,
especially its program for labor. It was Sidney
Hillman who urged upon Roosevelt the idea of minimum wages and maximum hours. The provision guar-
enteeing the right to organize and bargain collec-
tively which found its way into the path-breaking
clause 7a of the National Industrial Recovery Act
had its prototype in contracts negotiated by Jewish
unions during the three decades of the century.
Roosevelt's appointment of Sidney Hillman and Dr.
Leo Wollman to the Labor Advisory Board was a recognition of what garment unions had contributed.
Other facets of the welfare state program such as
unemployment insurance, codes of fair competition,
and old-age pensions stemmed directly from contracts negotiated by Jewish unions.[30] The Amalgamated and Cloakmakers pioneering unemployment com-
pensation plan of the twenties was precedent for

the Federal Social Security Act of 1935.   In addition the Jewish unions pioneered in other areas.
The International Ladies Garment Workers Union was
first to operate a Health Center, a prototype for
other unions.   The Workmen's Circle "cradle to the
grave" total approach to social services, including
old-age medical care, is suggestive of the direction government policy is taking today.[31]   Cooperative housing, credit associations, supermarkets,
paid vacations, and scholarships for the children
of members, now a normal part of the program of
established labor unions, were pioneered by the
Jewish Labor Movement.

     One might note that except for the fact that
these programs were conceived by secular Jewish
unionists from eastern Europe there is nothing in
them that makes them substantively Jewish.   In
fact, addicted to universalism as a solution to the
Jewish problem, one might argue that they advocated
an end to Jewish particularism.   Yet the Jewish Labor Movement somehow remained bound to Jewish peoplehood despite its ideology.   Within their socialist ideology one could often find a "folk religious
ethic", sometimes buttressed by scriptural references.[32]   Eventually the connection to Jewish peoplehood was reestablished through a secular labor-
Zionist conduit.   While the Jewish Labor Movement
refused to support the American Federation of
Labor's pressure on behalf of the Balfour
Declaration and other Zionist causes in 1917, that
policy soon changed.[33]   By 1924 the United Hebrew
Trades, led by Max Pine, joined with Labor Zionists
in forming the Geverkshaftn campaign on behalf of
Histadrut.   By the mid thirties one could note an
increasingly generous outpouring of funds and
support from Jewish unions.   After the holocaust
the support of the now much changed United Hebrew
Trades was unstinting.   It played an important role
in the struggle to recognize the state of Israel in
1948 and has been active in financing programs in
Israel since that time.   It had found its way back.

     While much of what was once alien in the Jew-
ish Labor Movement had been melded into an acceptable American pattern by the thirties, its approach
to politics and political action continued to be
differentiated.   It favored more direct political
action by the labor movement.   When John L. Lewis
organized the Congress of Industrial Organization
in 1935 some movement in that direction could be
noted in the establishment of the Political Action
Committee.   Under David Dubinsky the International
Ladies Garment Workers Union and other elements of

the liberal coalition went one step further by
organizing the American Labor Party in New York
state. What was desired was not so much a party
that could enact a labor program. Under the
governship of Roosevelt and Lehman a good part of
their objectives had been made into law. It was an
important part of the "Little New Deal."[34] What
was needed was a party ticket whereby socialist-
oriented Jewish voters could cast their ballots for
Roosevelt, a high born patrician Episcopalian,
without compromising their socialist principles.

Like other facets of the American Jewish
experience, the Jewish Labor Movement had become
part of America and yet it kept something apart.
"The Jewish labor movement," notes one historian
"had become 'Americanized' and the American labor
movement had assimilated many of the 'foreign'
ideas and practices of the immigrant Jewish labor
movement."[35] That is the transaction we can observe in many other areas of the Jewish relation
with America.

*   *   *

We come next to a discussion of one of the
major differentiating characteristics of American
Jewry, its rich organizational structure. The
elaboration of Jewish organizational life at the
turn of the century had two basic objectives. The
first was to evolve a strategy for survival which
called for the reestablishment of some kind of
Jewish corporateness on a voluntary basis. The
second was to build some kind of bridge between
themselves and the Jewish world overseas. That is,
of course, an observation made possible only by the
vantage point of time. At the turn of the century
there was a myriad of immediate causes which led to
the establishment of a rich organizational
network.[36]

Several studies during the sixties indicated
that American Jews living in suburbia continue to
find most of their primary associations among themselves even while religious ties among them are
weaker than among Catholics and Protestants.[37]
What holds Jews together when the thrust of moder-
nity is towards atomization, individuation, and
fragmentation is something of a mystery. If the
answer were known, a good portion of the mystery of
Jewish survival through the ages would be revealed. The historian Bernard Lewis rather than

targeting organization or religion as a primary
factor in Jewish cohesiveness signals out a factor
called "corporate historical memory."[38]   It is
ostensibly from that memory, a thing of the spirit
to be sure, that the concrete manifestations of
Jewish peoplehood, congregations, secular
organizations, and thousands of simple social
circles come to be.

It should come as no surprise that Jewish
organizations have something to do with Jewishness
but that it should be based on a memory of once
having been one people and a longing to build again
a bridge to the remnant of that people is difficult
to substantiate. Yet there are some suggestions
that such may be the case. The landsmannschaften
which dotted the Jewish social landscape at the
turn of the century fit into such a classification
as do fraternal orders like B'nai B'rith and B'rith
Abraham. On the national level the establishment
of the American Jewish Congress in 1916 and the New
York Kehillah in 1908 are, from one point of view,
attempts at some kind of reincorporation or perhaps
simply communalization.

To be sure the Kehillah was a local organization, but its implications were clearly national
since it sought to bring some order to the heart of
American Jewry. The name Kehillah was chosen to
conjure up the image of former corporateness.[39]
That had its dual roots in the organization of
society into separate but inter-dependent corporations during the Middle Ages and in the Jewish
religious culture which emphasized collectivity and
group response. The memory of such corporateness
was reinforced by the manner of Jewish organization
in eastern Europe. There communal organization
permitted Jews to exercise a high degree of autonomy and self-government between the sixteenth and
seventeenth century when it reached its zenith.[40]
A residuum of that cohesiveness remained in the
shtetlach they had left. In their concentration in
the Pale they formed in effect, a separate nation
with its own culture, language, religion, and even
territory. The only thing that was missing was
power.
Ostensibly the American Jewish Congress was
organized to bring "democracy" to Jewish life which
ostensibly was dominated and mismanaged by the "up-
town" patricians who knew little of Yiddishkeit and
simply saw their Jewishness in denominational
terms. The idea that more democracy can cure the
ills of a community is a progressive notion which
led to such new instruments as the initiative, the

referendum and recall, as well as party prima-
ries. But we should note that the idea of applying
it to Jews presupposed that there was a living
Jewish community that required a better form of
governance. Members of the "illustrious obscure"
like Bernard Richards and Gedaliah Bublick, editor
of the Tageblatt, in their fetish for community
wide elections, seemed never to have heard of the
"melting pot" idea. Elections to determine who
would govern the community, even when there was no
longer any sanction to make Jews obey, seemed
natural.

In a similar way the idea behind the founding
of the Kehillah was based on a nostalgia for the
order which ostensibly once ruled Jewish life. It
was the chaos and lack of governance which made the
Jewish enterprise vulnerable to charges of
criminality like those of Police Commissioner
Bingham. The Jewish community would take care of
its own without the help of outsiders. Behind the
arguments for the establishment of both organizations was the assumption that such a thing as a
Jewish community existed and required protection if
Judaism was to survive in America. If the idea of
community was abandoned, as had been done by the
Reform movement, if peoplehood was to be replaced
by denominationalism in order to fit into the American scheme, the Jewish presence was bound to disappear. A separate Jewish people required organization. Indeed, "organization was in the air" and
never far beneath it was the notion of Jewish
peoplehood.[41]

If the establishment of the Kehillah and the
American Jewish Congress were secular reflections
of corporate peoplehood then the revitalization of
the Conservative movement by Solomon Shechter with
its support of cultural Zionism and the notion of
"Catholic Israel" was its spiritual reflection.
But something more was required, something to dress
the ideological nakedness of Jewish separateness so
that it could be rationalized for Americans and for
Jews.

That ideological rationale which pointed to a
separate tradition with its own claims was articu-
lated in its clearest form by Mordecai Kaplan who
taught at the Jewish Theological Seminary of America for 50 years and founded the Reconstructionist
movement in 1924. Perhaps the only theologian to
be produced by American Jewry, Kaplan was unique
because his theology, if one could call it that,
addressed itself not to mediating between God and
his people, the normal task of a Jewish theology,

but rather mediating between the Jewish people and
the secular society. Kaplan maintained that
Judaism was a separate evolving religious civilization "whose common denominator is neither belief,
nor tenet, nor practice, but rather the continuous
life of the Jewish people."[42] Here was an open
acknowledgement of Jewish exceptionalism. To be a
Jew was not merely to adhere to a certain faith,
although that could be part of it, nor did it mean
belonging to a certain ethnic or hyphenate group.
It meant belonging to a separate religious
civilization, receiving separate cultural cues and
possessing a separate identity which could never
fit entirely into another culture. For Kaplan it
seemed as if American Jews had instinctively been
Reconstructionists all along without knowing it.

   Such an avowal of separateness and unmeltabil-
ity was not without risks in turn-of-the-century
America and positively foolhardy in the America of
the twenties. Doubts about the assimilation potential of the "new" immigrants had become common currency. The Progressives, largely of native stock,
were particularly disturbed by developments in the
American city. They agreed with Lord Bryce that it
was the worst governed unit in Christendom.
"Bosses" managed corrupt political machines. Their
power was based on being able to lead immigrants to
the polls like so many head of cattle. Loyalty was
the least that could be expected, but with a Jewish
avowal of separateness even that was doubtful.[43]
The Progressives were tolerant about the need to
Americanize. It would be achieved gradually
through the school curriculum, the church, and the
settlement house. But after World War I an intense
mood of nativism and xenophobia demanded something
more, a cultural gleichhaltung in which Jewish separatism and radicalism would find little social
space.[44]

   It fell to Horace Kallen to propound a philosophy that would create such space. Cultural pluralism, he maintained, was the natural and desirable state of a democratic society which should
permit and even encourage dual and multiple loyalties. He saw American society as an "orchestration
of cultures" which permitted a minimum of "injus-
tice," "suppression," and "frustration" of one culture by another.[45] Kallen was not addressing himself directly to the Jewish condition in America
but few could fail to note that the concept of cultural pluralism, if accepted, would make allowances
for the peculiar way American Jews sought to

accommodate to American society without forgetting
their own.

The idea of a Jewish lump in the melting pot
gained only gradual acceptance and in some quarters
it remained anathema. But ultimately a relationship which in an earlier time would have been rejected on the grounds that it demanded dual loyalty
was accepted by the host culture. It is precisely
the relationship which American Jewry has with America today.[46] Yet strangely enough during the
twenties the idea of physically recreating some
form of Jewish corporateness, the Kehillah and the
American Jewish Congress, withered on the vine. It
would be the weak and fledgling Zionist movement
which would carry the idea of Jewish peoplehood
forward and eventually anchor it in a living symbol
of separateness, a national Jewish homeland.

Yet what has won such seemingly easy acceptance from the American culture today was once the
source of great apprehension in the Zionist
movement as well. The contribution of Louis
Brandeis to American Zionism comes precisely in the
way he handled the vexing question of dual loyalties. He did so by muting the nationalist separatist component in a favor of philanthropic operationalism without abandoning the idea that such an
entity as a separate Jewish people and culture did
in fact exist. He legitimized it by insisting that
to be a good American one had to be a good Jew and
to be a good Jew one had to be a good Zionist.[47]
Once that idea became acceptable a new Americanized
Zionism, devoid of the strong separatist component
which characterized it in eastern Europe, but retaining a strong implication of the feeling of
peoplehood was able to play a mediating role between Jews and their Judaism as well as Jews and
Americanism. Zionism became a crucial element in a
new kind of civil religion for American Jews when
the purely religious modality could no longer be
fully accepted. By the late thirties it would be
the peoplehood element in Zionism that was most
reminiscent of the Jewish corporateness of long
ago. It would be that spiritual sense of belonging
rather than the physical efforts represented by the
Kehillah and the American Jewish Congress which
came to hold sway. Today, whether it is called
Israelism or Zionism, it is the cement which holds
Jews to its corporate memory.

*   *   *

There remains one area which deserves brief
mention beause the duality of the American Jewish
posture is so clearly reflected in it. It is the
overriding concern American Jews display for their
brethren in other lands which is manifested in
their interest in American foreign policy. That
interest became apparent early in the century when
we note that, four major Jewish organizational
efforts were triggered by problems Jews faced in
foreign lands.[48] The American Jewish Committee was
organized as a result of the Russian depredations
especially the Kishineff pogrom; the American Jewish Congress was concerned primarily with an American Jewish input to the forthcoming peace conference; the American Jewish Joint Distribution
Committee was concerned primarily with the physical
nurture of Jewish communities abroad; and the Federation of American Zionists (including Hadassah
and Mizrachi) concerned itself with the development
of the Yishuv in Palestine. (Its name was changed
to Zionist Organization of America in 1918.) Today
that interest is part of all Jewish organizations,
fraternal, religious, professional, and philanthropic. It is reflected in their budgets, their
travel and educational programs and the cultural
activities that they sponsor. It is natural that
it should be so since the tie to Israel is what defines them as Jewish.

Historians of American foreign relations long
ago discovered the externalization phenomenon in
American Jewish political culture.[49] Jews are more
interested in American foreign policy than other
subgroups and that interest is more sustained and
more apt to result in efforts at projecting pressure on decision makers.

Students of other disciplines will undoubtedly
be able to point out many reasons for such an
interest which do not impinge on a Jewish nexus.
People with a high level of formal education such
as American Jews possess are typically less parochial and more concerned with world events.
Moreover Jewish interest in domestic affairs is
also higher than that of many other groups.[50] Jews
as a highly urbanized cosmopolitan group, simply
are more universally minded, more aware that their
own interest impinges on what happens abroad.
While all these factors bear on Jewish interest in
American foreign affairs, the fact that there seems
always to be beleaguered Jews somewhere in the
world which has claim to their attention figures
prominently in their interest. It has compelled
them to learn the arts of projecting pressure on

the American government whose benevolent interces-
sion is required to insure the well-being of such
communities. That fact is most apparent in American Jewish interest in Middle East policy, but it
is not confined to it. It was true of immigration
policy in the early decades of the century and
policy towards Nazi Germany during the thirties.
It is natural that it should be so, since it reflects the continual attempt by American Jewry to
find an accommodation between the pulls and seduc-
tions of a benevolent American culture and the
demands of an age old Jewish civilization from
which it continues to draw spiritual nourishment.
The turning of at least one eye outward to see what
is happening in that Jewish world is necessary and
predictable. All of which is to say that the overriding interest Jews exhibit in the foreign affairs
of the nation is like their mobility, the founding
of a separate labor movement, and their unique
organizational life, yet another manifestation of
the duality which appears to be at the center of
American Jewish life and defines what is Jewish
about it.

                *   *   *

        Ultimately the historian viewing the American
Jewish experience realizes that at its most crucial
interstices is the connection with k'lal yisrael
which in its most pristine form is the love of
Zion. It can take many different forms, -- the receiving of messengers during the colonial period,
the connection of American Jewish bankers with
Jewish banking houses in Europe or perhaps merely a
socialist Jewish labor leader citing scripture to
wring better treatment for Jewish workers from Jewish employers. It is at the heart of American
Jewish exceptionalism, what has made them come to
different terms with the American culture.
        Finally it may be instructive to risk projec-
ting our theme of the persistance of Jewish corporateness to note its implications for Jewish con-
tinuance in America. I say risk because the
historian is on dangerous ground when he adds to
the problematics of explaining the past, the role
of prophet. Yet the vision presented by other
disciplines in the social sciences is one of such
unreleaved gloom that it might be argued that one
ought to do so if only to give the general prognosis some balance. The sociologists and social

psychologists studying Jewish identification in
America have concluded that it is weakening. A
recent prediction of a demographer informs us with
utter certainty that given present trends American
Jewry will have virtually vanished in a century.
Others who nervously take the pulse of American
Jewry repeatedly note failing life signs, -- the
Jewish population is aging rapidly; the birthrate
is ominously low; attrition by intermarriage and
other factors is high; the ramshakle Jewish education system is a dismal failure. These are realities ignored only at great peril. Yet the historian might well wonder if that picture is complete
and balanced. He recalls that throughout Jewish
history at any given juncture the prospect of
survival was open to question. The Jewish enterprise always appeared fragile; disappearance seemed
imminent. Indeed concern over survival is perhaps
as old as Jewish history itself. One might note
that had the projections of demographers really
been applicable to the Jewish condition, Jewish
civilization should have vanished a long time
ago. That it did not and does not may also be part
of Jewish exceptionalism. It may well be that
Judaism is governed by different rules. And as for
American Jewry the signs of an attachment to k'lal
yisrael which has come to define what is Jewish
about it, an overriding commitment to Israel's survival, a watchful eye on Soviet Jewry, a growing
interest in the holocaust is perhaps stronger today
than ever before. At the same time the Americanization and secularization process goes on relent-
lessly. What appears to be happening is that the
American Jewish life equation itself has grown
larger on both sides of the equal sign. Jews are
more American and less distinguishable from other
subgroups in this plastic society but they are also
more Jewish as measured by the concern for Jewish
peoplehood the world over. The American solvent
remakes them but somehow they remain a definable
separate presence in American society. That America permits them to be so is a measure of its
greatness and that Jews continue to cherish that
unique duality which marks them as different is a
measure of their vitality.

NOTES

1. Quoted in D.J. Boorstin, The Americans: The Democratic Experience (New York: Vintage Books, 1974), title page.

2. H.L. Feingold, Zion in America: The Jewish Experience From Colonial Times To the Present (New York: Hippocrene Books, Inc., 1974), preface.

3. M. Davis, "Centers of Jewry in the Western Hemisphere: A Comparative Approach," Jewish Journal of Sociology, vol. V (1963), pp. 4ff.

4. For a discussion of the pitfalls of the Weimar analogy see H.L. Feingold, "German Jewry and the American Jewish Condition: A View From Weimer," Judaism, vol. XX (Winter 1971), pp. 108-119.

5. S.W. Baron, History and Jewish Historians: Essays and Addresses, (Philadelphia: Jewish Publication Society of America, 1964), p. 39.

6. See M. Rosenstock, Louis Marshall, Defender of Jewish Rights, (Detroit: Wayne State University Press, 1965), pp. 128-200.

7. C.A. Lindbergh, The Wartime Journals of Charles A. Lindbergh, 1937-1945, (New York: Harcourt, Brace Jovanovish Co., Inc., 1970); Wayne Cole, Charles A. Lindbergh And The Battle Against Intervention in World War II (New York: The Library of Social Science, 1974).

8. B.W. Korn, American Jewry and the Civil War (New York: Atheneum, 1970), pp. 121-155.

9. L. Dinnerstein, The Leo Frank Case (New York: Columbia University (New York: Dell Publishing Co., 1956).

10. T. Weiss-Rosmarin, "The Cultural Tradition of the American Jew," in Stanley M. Wagner, ed., Traditions of the American Jew (New York: Ktav Publishing House, Inc., 1977), pp. 1-19.

11. S. Lubell, The Future of American Politics (New York: Anchor Book, Inc., 1956).

12. G. Smith, To Save A Nation: American Countersubversives, The New Deal and the Coming of World War II (New York: Basic Books, Inc., 1973).

13. H.L. Feingold, The Politics of Rescue: The Roosevelt Administration and the Holocaust, 1938-1945 (New Brunswick: Rutgers University Press, 1970); Saul Friedman, No Haven For the Oppressed: United States Policy Toward Jewish Refugees, 1938-1945 (Detroit: Wayne State University Press, 1973).

14. L. Dawidowicz, The War Against The Jews, 1933-1945 (New York: Holt Rinehart, Winston, 1975).

15. J.R. Marcus, "The Periodization of American Jewish History," in J.R. Marcus, Studies in American Jewish History (Cincinnati: American Jewish Archives, 1969).

16. A.M. Greeley, "American Catholics, Making It Or Loosing It?" The Public Interest (Summer 1972), pp. 26-37.

17. S. Thernstrom, The Other Bostonians: Poverty and Progress in the American Metropolis, 1800-1915 (Cambridge: Harvard University Press, 1973), p. 143; T. Kessner, The Golden Door: Italian and Jewish Immigrant Mobility in New York City, 1880-1915 (New York: Oxford University Press, 1977), pp. 161-177. S. Hertzberg, "Unsettled Jews: Geographic Mobility in a Nineteenth Century City," American Jewish Historical Quarterly, vol. LXVII, (December 1977), pp. 125-139. N. Glazer, "The American Jew and the Attainment of Middle Class Rank: Some Trends and Explanations," in Marshall Sklare, ed., The Jews: Social Patterns of an American Group (New York: The Free Press, 1958), pp. 138-146.

18. Stephen Birmingham, Our Crowd, The Great Jewish Families of New York (New York: Harper & Row, 1967).

19. B.E. Supple, "A Business Elite: German-Jewish Financiers in Nineteenth Century New York," Business History Review, vol. XXXI (Summer 1957), pp. 143-178; V.P. Carosso, "A Financial Elite: New York's German-Jewish Investment Bankers," American Jewish Historical Quarterly, vol. LXVI (September 1976), pp. 67-88.; L.R. Rachman, "Julius Rosenwald," ibid., pp. 89-104.; K. Grunwald, "Three Chapters of German Jewish Banking History," Leo Baeck Yearbook, vol. XXII (1977), pp. 191-208.

20. J.S. Auerbach, "From Rags to Robes: The Legal Profession, Social Mobility and the American Jewish Experience," American Jewish Historical Quarterly, vol. LXVI (December 1976), pp. 249-284.; S.M. Lipset and E. Ladd Jr., "Jewish Academics in the United States: Their Achievement, Culture and Politics," American Jewish Yearbook, vol. 72 (1971).; R.S. Willis, The College of the City of New York, A History 1847-1947, (New York: The City College Press, 1949); S. Steinberg, The Academic Melting Pot,

Catholics and Jews in American Higher
Education (New York: Carnegie Foundation,
1974). For a personal account see N.
Podhoretz, Making It (New York: Random House,
1967); "Professional Tendencies Among Jewish
Students in Colleges, Universities and Professional Schools," American Jewish Yearbook,
1920-1921, pp. 383-393.
21. J.R. Marcus, Early American Jewry,
     (Philadelphia: Jewish Publication Society of
     America, 1953), vol. III, p. 53.
22. N. Glazer and D. Moynihan, Beyond The Melting
     Pot (Cambridge: Harvard University Press,
     1969), p. 155. See also "The Egghead
     Millionaires," Fortune (September, 1960),
     p. 172ff.
23. E. Mendelsohn, "The Russian Roots of the
     American Jewish Labor Movement," in E.
     Mendelsohn, ed., Essays on the American Jewish
     Labor Movement, YIVO Annual of Jewish Social
     Science, vol. XVI (1976), pp. 150-176; M.
     Rischin, The Promised City: New York's Jews,
     1870-1914 (New York: Harper and Row, 1970),
     pp. 25-31, 125-194.
24. M. Hillquit, Loose Leaves From A Busy Life,
     (New York: Macmillan Co., 1934), pp. 15-40.
     See also R. Sanders, The Downtown Jews:
     Portrait of an Immigrant Generation (New
     York: Harper and Row, 1969) chpts. 4 and 5;
     H.L. Feingold, Zion In America, op. cit. ch.
     11.
25. Joseph Brandes, "From Sweatshop to Stability,
     Jewish Labor Between Two World Wars," in E.
     Mendelsohn, op. cit.
26. Ibid., p. 7.
27. R. Asher, "Jewish Unions and the American
     Federation of Labor Power Structure, 1903-
     1905," American Jewish Historical Quarterly,
     vol. LXV, (March 1976), p. 226.
28. Brandes, op. cit., p. 62.
29. Ibid; pp. 68-69.
30. Ibid., pp. 76-77. See also M. Rischin, "The
     Jewish Labor Movement in America, A Social
     Interpretation," Labor History, vol. IV (Fall
     1963), p. 231ff.
31. Brandes, op. cit., p. 77.
32. Rischin, op. cit., p. 234. See also J.B.S.
     Hardman, "The Jewish Labor Movement in the
     United States: Jewish and Non-Jewish
     Influences," American Jewish Historical
     Quarterly, vol. XLI, (December 1952).

33. S. Polishook, "The American Federation of
     Labor, Zionism and the First World War,"
     American Jewish Historical Quarterly, vol. LXV
     (March 1976), pp. 228-244.
34. R.P. Ingalls, Herbert H. Lehman and New York's
     Little New Deal, (New York: New York
     University Press, 1975), pp. 131-142.
35. Asher, op. cit., p. 227.
36. For a description and analysis of Jewish
     organizational life see D. Elazar, Community
     and Polity, The Organizational Dynamics of
     American Jewry (Philadelphia: Jewish Publi-
     cation Society of America, 1976); C.S.
     Liebman, "American Jewry: Identity and Affil-
     iation," in D. Sidorsky, ed., The Future of
     the Jewish Community in America
     (Philadelphia: Jewish Publication Society of
     America, 1973), pp. 127-152; H.L. Feingold,
     Zion in America, pp. 208-227.
37. G. Lenski, The Religious Factor, (New York:
     Anchor Books, 1963), p. 37; M. Sklare and J.
     Greenblum, Jewish Identity on the Suburban
     Frontier (New York: Basic Books, 1967),
     pp. 280-281.
38. B. Lewis, "The Meaning of Jewish History," in
     Land of Immigrants, Proceedings, B'nai B'rith
     Commission on Adult Education (March 1976),
     p. 10.
39. A.A. Goren, New York Jews and the Quest For
     Community: The Kehillah Experiment, 1908-
     1922, (New York: Columbia University Press,
     1970), p. 3.
40. Ibid., pp. 7-12.
41. N.W. Cohen, Not Free To Desist, A History of
     the American Jewish Committee, 1906-1966,
     (Philadelphia: Jewish Publication Society of
     America, 1972), ch. 1.
42. Quoted in C.S. Liebman, "Reconstructionism in
     American Life," American Jewish Yearbook, vol.
     71 (1970), pp. 3-100. For additional
     information see M.M. Kaplan, Judaism As A
     Civilization; Toward A. Reconstruction of
     American Jewish Life, (New York: Schocken
     Books, 1967), Parts II, IV and V; M. Scult,
     "Mordecai M. Kaplan, Challenges and Conflicts
     in the Twenties," American Jewish Historical
     Quarterly, vol. LXVI (March 1977), pp. 401-
     416; S.M. Cahn, "Religion Without Super
     Naturalism." in R.A. Brauner ed., Shiv'im:
     Essays and Studies in Honor of Ira Eisenstein
     (New York: Ktav Publishing Co., 1977), pp.
     225-229.

43. M. Curti, The Roots of American Loyalty (New York: Atheneum, 1968), p. 184ff.

44. J. Higham, Strangers in the Land: Patterns of American Nativism, 1860-1925 (New York: Atheneum, 1968), pp. 236-239.

45. H.M. Kallen, Cultural Pluralism and the American Idea (Philadelphia: University of Pennsylvania Press, 1956), p. 100. See also "American Jews. What Now?" Jewish Social Service Quarterly, (Fall 1955), p. 22.

46. That is an observation made by A. Hertzberg, "Some Reflections on Zionism Today," Congress Monthly vol. 44 (March/April 1977), pp. 5-6.

47. M.I. Urofsky, American Zionism, From Herzl to Holocaust (New York: Doubleday, 1975), pp. 123-124, 128-130; "Zionism, An American Experience," American Jewish Historical Quarterly, vol. LXIII, (March 1974), pp. 215-230; N.W. Cohen, American Jews and the Zionist Idea (New York: Ktav Pub., 1975), pp. 16-17.

48. See Elazar, op. cit.; Cohen, op. cit.; Urofsky, op. cit.; Yehuda Bauer, My Brother's Keeper: A History of the American Jewish Joint Distribution Committee (Philadelphia: Jewish Publication Society of America, 1974), pp. 1-18.

49. T.A. Bailey, The Man In the Street: The Impact of American Public Opinion on Foreign Policy (New York: Macmillan, 1948), pp. 187-190; G. Almond, The American People and Foreign Policy (New York: Praeger, 1960), p. 185; A.O. Hero, American Religious Groups View Foreign Policy (Durham: Duke University Press, 1973), pp. 201-204; Louis L. Gerson, The Hyphenate in Recent American Politics and Diplomacy (Lawrence: University of Kansas Press, 1964), pp. 86-87.

50. According to Rabbi Hertzberg it is far higher and more intense for foreign concerns. Herzberg, op. cit.

51. Elihu Bergman, "The American Jewish Population Erosion," Midstream, vol. XXIII (October 1977), pp. 9-19.

Chapter VIII

Jewish Life in the United States:
Perspectives from Anthropology

SOL TAX

My task is to develop an anthropological perspective on Jewish life in America. In the anthropological tradition this paper should rather be the
culmination of intensive study and fieldwork of a
colleague produced by one of the cultures of, say
India, or Japan, or Brazil, or Nigeria. One needs
the fresh look from outside. But in recent years
we have understood that it is equally important for
anthropology to include what we call in-culture
studies, done not only by members of the subject
society itself but even by members who are naive.
Thus for example Navajo Indians have been taught by
anthropologists minimum motion-picture camera and
film editing techniques and encouraged to film
Navajo subjects in their own way. Although all had
doubtless seen finished films and quickly learned
to handle the equipment, they now provided views
quite different from those of their teachers; presumably their own films better reflect Navajo
thought. This is no new practice in anthropology,
of course, since our major learning has always come
from listening to the words and observing the behavior of the people we study, as well as from
their arts and their folklore which reflect their
culture. The newer structuralist and cognitive
anthropological theory only requires greater sys-
tematization and refinement of these traditional
fieldwork methods.
So if I find myself in the position of writing
on the life of American Jews, I am inclined to
treat as a virtue my identity as one of the six

million members of the subject society. Although a
student of other cultures, as I write this paper I
also find that I am surely as naive about my own as
are the Navajos aiming the camera, or the people in
Guatemalan villages who have helped me to understand their cultures; indeed, much more naive than
any of them, relative to the size, heterogeneity,
and mobility of the society whose culture I pretend
to represent. Unlike others who are not only participants in the culture but are students of it,
who read the literature on Judaism, professionally,
in the languages in which it comes, I am the igno-
rant layman; and I would quickly send to them any
visiting anthropologist who tried to interview
me. But the naive native serves, too, as the
expert at least on his own life experience, for
what that may be worth. Perhaps as a student of
other cultures, impressions of my own have added
value. Moreover, as an anthropologist, I know
something about other peoples in America who are
like and unlike Jews in different ways, and whose
lives and cultures have been opposed to or
interwoven with ours. Perhaps this knowledge can
illuminate some of the changing problems that concern leaders of the American Jewish community.

So, I imagine here that the visiting anthropologist has selected me to interview, and asks me
to address two questions. First, I am to look back
over the last 50 years and give my impression--as a
naive participant--of how the perception of being
Jewish in America, and the concerns of the Jewish
Community, have changed; and second, whether as
participant or as anthropologist, I am to compare
the place of Jews in America with that of other
groups. The visitor also suggests that I might
draw on these perceptions to look backward and
forward for any general observations.

CHANGING CONCERNS

The major concern today of the professional
leadership--as I read and hear and sense it in the
Jewish community--can be labelled demographic attrition. After the destruction of Jews in Europe,
the United States contained the world's largest
Jewish community with a complex feeling of responsibility. On the one hand, the holocaust itself
gave us a feeling of renewed defiance. Our enemies
had wanted us dead, and our answer is to more than
compensate for the numbers who were murdered. Survival thus is an important value. The danger to it

is said to be threefold. First, there is the falling birthrate itself; we are not reproducing
ourselves. Second, there is a continuing or growing loss of practicing Jews, who thus disappear
into the general American population. Although
intermarriage does not necessarily reduce--and
presently in fact increases--the number of Jews,
our leadership fears it greatly. Third, we are
geographically so mobile that Jewish institutions
find it hard to catch and keep us, and some fear
that dispersion into more and more smaller communities from the fewer larger ones will increase the
rate of acculturation and attrition. Although
these fears are greatly exaggerated, certainly the
age structure of Jews, like that of other Americans, is radically changing so that the proportion
of children to be served by schools is becoming
smaller and the proportion of the aging larger, and
this requires readjustment of our institutions.
Perhaps the change is also socially discomfiting;
who likes to give up eager young children for us
ailing old folks? So whether or not survival itself is the issue, there appears to be at least a
temporary demographic problem about which I say no
more.

The problem of survival may well be the deep-
est and most important Jewish concern, and perhaps
cannot be understood without knowing Jewish history. I do not know how many Jews in America are
aware of Jewish history, but every year most of us
in greater or less seriousness, celebrate festivals
which keep alive some moments of triumph. The
Passover seders celebrate our exodus from slavery
in Egypt and the beginning of a Jewish nation in
Palestine. Purim records a triumph -- again during
a colonial period -- against the genocidal plot of
a prime minister. Chanukah celebrates a military
victory -- again when we were politically dependent -- in a guerrilla war to preserve our
religion.

We also commemorate with prayer and fasting
several contrary events, most noteworthy among them
the destruction of the Temple in Jerusalem on the
9th of Av, first by the Babylonians in 586 Before
The Common Era and again by the Romans 656 years
later, to the day. In both cases the loss of the
Temple meant also the loss of the nation and exile
for our people. From the 17th of Tamuz--the date
of an earlier breaching of the wall--to the 9th of
Av are three weeks of mourning, the last nine days
of which are severe, and ending with the most serious fast of the yearly calendar. Yet in my part of

Jewish America, except among the few most pious,
Tishe'ah Be'av is no more than the name of a vaguely known holy day.

For whatever it may be worth I point up a
contrast between the way we commemorate the happy
and the sad events of our history, in the one case
public celebrations by almost everybody emphasizing
their public character, in the other case private
observance by only a few. Must it be said that
American Jews prefer to hide and thus to forget the
more painful episodes of our past? That we shall
soon forget also the Nazi holocaust is suggested by
our ignorance of the centuries of similar episodes
in Europe which led right up to what was to be in
the 1940s the "final" solution.

However one deals with these facts, I suspect
that the happy occasions serve to remind us of the
dangers through which we have successfully
passed. Celebrating occasions of our miraculous
survival suggests that others lie ahead. It has
been rare in our history to have had a period of
three centuries, as here in America, of relative
freedom, equality, and belonging. And if we are
fortunate enough for this to continue, might we not
join the 40 percent of Americans who are not otherwise identified? Will the very lack of a Great
Threat ease us into the oblivion of assimilation?
Are those Israelis right who argue that we cannot
survive as Jews in America?

The second and third concerns of American Jews
today, however, are for the security of the new
nation, Israel, and the safety and freedom of the
two and a half million Jews in the U.S.S.R.

These concerns seem to me all new, strikingly
different from those even 20 years ago. Let me
therefore start over again.

Fifty years ago, in the spring of 1928, I was
finishing my second year at the University of Wisconsin in Madison and had already turned to anthropology. I was also about to become president of
the Hillel Foundation, which was in its third or
fourth year, and only the second such in the country. The big issue was campus anti-Semitism. I
had written an editorial on the subject in the
Hillel Review, of which I was editor, and this
seemed important enough to be reprinted at once in
the Daily Cardinal, the student newspaper, and then
in the Capital Times, a Madison newspaper. (Anti-
Semitism then was the sort of thing that became the
issue in the novel Gentlemen's Agreement). Two
years later I was to pass through Munich and see
brownshirts marching in the street and to come home

to the depression and to the American fascist
movement blaring anti-semitism of another kind over
national radio. One had to ask with Sinclair Lewis
if indeed "it couldn't happen here,"--but that was
later. Back in 1928, at least for Jews on campus,
it was the gentlemanly anti-Semitism that was the
leading concern. Zionism was a lesser issue. I
had grown up in Milwaukee of socialist, Zionist,
and Orthodix Jewish parents who had come from
different parts of Russia in their teens and spoke
Yiddish when we four children were not supposed to
understand something.

From earlier years I remembered the name of
Goldie Meyerson, as well as of an election of delegates to a World Zionist Congress, one evening
inside the Yiddische Folk Schule while we played
outside and heard in loud unforgettable cadences
the counting of the votes for what must have been
the two winners: "E.E. Levitzky, Nathan Sand."
But I at least soon became much more interested in
the politics of Milwaukee, of Wisconsin, and of the
United States, than in Zionism, which then for me
became one of my new discoveries at the university. I was a member of our Avukah debating team,
famous for its symphony of the names of its four
members, Max Wax, Sol Tax, Moe Max, and Maurie Zox,
which debated a visiting British team from Oxford
on the proposition that the founding of a Jewish
homeland in Palestine would end anti-Semitism in
the world. Unlike gentlemanly anti-Semitism, which
was real to us, Zionism for us was more a theoretical, intellectual game. It became a little more
real when we brought Ralph Linton, my anthropology
teacher, to speak at Hillel on the subject. He
concluded that the oldest crossroads in the world
was an unlikely place for a lasting, peaceful
settlement.

In addition to defense against anti-Semitism,
and interest in Zionism, a third concern was the
general lack of interest in Jewish matters and especially in religion. Those were years of struggle
among various leftist political sects, as well as
between competing fraternity and sorority groups on
one side and independents on the other. We also
had a hard time filling our hall even for speakers
like Maurice Samuels, Ludwig Lewisohn, and Rabbi
Abba Hillel Silver. For individual students, and
hence indirectly for the community, problems of
personal identity and affiliation were probably
also important. Most of the Jewish students I knew
were children of immigrants, the first American
born generation, and the first in our respective

family circles to be in an American University.
Although liberal Wisconsin attracted an unusual
number of students from New York and other Eastern
cities, the half of my friends I knew through
Hillel were mainly Midwesterners, with scant Jewish
education and little or no interest in getting
more. The Jews among the other half ranged in
their Jewish feeling from indifferent to hostile.
Even we at Hillel were probably there less from
positive Jewish interest than one would suppose.
Hillel was an easy place to organize and take
charge of, which gave us satisfaction much harder
to get in the wider campus community. So much for
Jewish life in mid-America in the late twenties.

Let us move now to December of 1945, to a conference in New York on Jewish Adjustment in America
and sponsored by the American Jewish Committee.
The participants were Jewish academics and leaders
working mainly in the Northeast but including four
of us from the University of Chicago. We were
probably more representative of America's Jewish
Intellectuals in 1945 than were my fellow students
in Madison of the American Jewish College population in 1928. From the summary of the proceedings
I offer two of the most interesting assertions
about the situation of our people at that time.
The first (page 3) hints that in 1945 anti-Semitism
still appeared to be a problem:

> The conferees noted that there was little
> relationship between the degree of minority
> adaptation and the security of that minor-
> ity. While the Jews have acclimated them-
> selves to a far greater extent than other
> white minorities of comparable length of
> residence in the United States, they were,
> perhaps, the most insecure of all minority
> peoples. It was observed that despite war
> with Italy, the insecurity of the Italian
> group was not to any noticeable extent en-
> hanced. Yet, in this same period, although
> American Jewry was identified with the anti-
> fascist cause, its insecurity increased.

The second quote (page 4) shows that survival was
also a concern:

> ...In the future, America might be increas-
> ingly less receptive to deviants from what
> might approximate, if the present tendency
> toward standardization continued, a cultural
> norm. However, it was felt that with regard
> to the Jewish group, the impact of the Euro-
> pean catastrophe, the movement for a Palestine
> homeland, anti-Semitism, the religious content

of Jewish culture, were factors making for
Jewish preservation over and above those involved in the survival of non-Jewish ethnic
groups. The opinion was expressed that in the
United States ethnic cultures have survived to
the extent that they are religiously oriented,
and that Jews will endure as a religious group
long after their ethnic characteristics and
those of other ethnic groups have vanished.

The concerns which appear to be new in 1978
are those which respond to more recent political
events: concern for the safety of the new nation
of Israel and concern for the Jews in an increasingly anti-Jewish U.S.S.R. There is also a growing
secondary fear that our pressure for help for
Israel and Russian Jews might weaken the security
we in the United States have recently come to feel.

I shall postpone observations on these concerns until I have dealt with the second question,
on how Jews in America fit into the patchwork quilt
of ethnicity in America which includes hundreds of
groups, large and small.

OTHER GROUPS

Since we are dealing with a perceived danger
that Jews may be assimilating into some generality
or non-group American society, I shall begin with
what is said to be our largest minority, which
consists of people with no special identity. Is it
true that these may constitute 45 percent of the
population of the United States? To get a figure
would require first some statistics on all groups
which do identify as special groups. I do not mean
races, like Black and white; or religions, like
Protestant, Catholic and Jewish; or nationalities
or countries of origin; or, derived from these, the
convenient class called Wasps--White, Anglo-Saxon,
Protestants--to contrast with Blacks, Latinos,
Catholics, and Jews. None of these refer to
functioning social groups. To Blacks as to
Catholics, as examples, the differences are what
matter.

It is an endless task, of course, to begin at
the other end, with the small groups who identify
themselves by some name. For example, among Blacks
in Chicago there is an important network of families who originated in Holmes County, Mississippi;
among Latinos are specific groups of Puerto Ricans
or of people from parts of Texas or California;
among American Indians the Winnebago or the Ojibwa

function as two separate groups among the 100-odd
different tribes represented. Among Chinese,
Japanese, Filipinos, Arabs, Greeks, Italians,
Ukranians, Poles, Bohemians, Croatians,
Lithuanians, Swedes, and all the other "nationalities" there are subdivisions which are of great
significance to their members. It is, I repeat,
laborious to start with the functioning groups to
develop the patchwork quilt which would show us
also which and how many Americans are left over.
Are there indeed so many who float free as individuals attached at most to close kin and accidental
neighbors? I hope any new studies will be able to
collect sample data on groups--not individuals--to
determine this.

A new study would also find useful a major
distinction between groups in our population who
came here to seek a new life, as did many or most
who migrated from Europe, and those who did not.
Large numbers of our present population never asked
to become part of our American population. The
native peoples of all the Americas were of course
here from time immemorial; they were moved in on
first by the Spanish and Portuguese. The Spanish
in Central Mexico mixed with the native population,
and it was a Spanish-speaking mixed population
which spread north into what is now our South-
western states and California, where they found
North American Indian towns, bands, tribes or
nations near whom they settled. When the United
States moved west and took this territory they
engulfed both the Spanish-speakers whom we continued to call Mexicans and also the Indian communities.

Meanwhile, Europeans also were bringing slaves
from Africa, resulting in populations of English-
speaking Africans mainly in our Southeastern states
and of mainly Spanish-speaking Africans in the
Caribbean. When we annexed Puerto Rico we added to
the United States a second population of Spanish-
speakers. So the rural population came to include
not only a large number of people who had come from
Europe to be farmers in America, but also Blacks,
Indians, Mexican-Americans, and Puerto Ricans. The
Europeans who settled first in our Atlantic colo-
nies were the heart of the original westward movement into West Virginia, Tennessee, Kentuckky, and
beyond. These settled in, though later many also
moved west to be joined by newer rural immigrants
from northern Europe who came directly to the
Midwest.

All eventually settled peacefully into their
new rural homelands: Europeans, Africans, Latinos,
Indians. Then at least those in poor marginal
areas were again uprooted and forced to go to cities, all victims alike of the new industrial and
money economy. Meanwhile, agricultural technology
increasingly made manual labor unnecessary on
farms, and growing numbers of rural people on the
richer lands were attracted to city and eventually
suburban life, where they joined and were joined by
large numbers of European immigrants who had come
there directly. These more voluntary urbanites,
virtually all of European origin, constituted the
dominant metropolitan populations when the in-
voluntary urbanites came in poverty to live and to
make a living. Note that most of them were precisely those who had not even asked to come to the
United States. They had their own languages or
dialects, their own respective social values and
customs, their own family systems. Above all, they
had and valued their traditional religious beliefs
and practices which had remained central to their
communities. Indeed, they generally have a folklike and sacred world view with the specific
character--as contrasted with the "Middle Americans" who had preceded them in the city--of being
economically relaxed; the willingness to cooperate
and share is dominant over the competitive and
acquisitive. They especially value persons and
personal dignity, and equality, over hierarchy.
Not worldly, but good people of whom others can
take advantage, they do not see why they should
change from what they think are good ways.

My native American friends are one example.
The term "Indian" we introduced. They are rather
Hopi and Hupa and Choctaw and Chippewa and Tlingit
and Tuscarora and all the other nations too many to
name. But they share a value and concept of harmo-
ny among people and with the earth.

Survival is no problem for them; they have
always been here, through many troubles. If they
behave properly, they will survive. They worry
rather about the rest of the world; the Great
Spirit may be staying his hand only because the end
of the world would be the end too of the Indian
people. So they wait for others to behave properly
again. Indians feel strongly their obligations as
a chosen people, and, of course also feel frustrated. You will get some notion of this from Stan
Steiner's book The Vanishing White Man[1] in which he
quotes "testaments" of a number of North American
Indians, and from Alicja Iwanska's book The Truths

of Others: An Essay on Nativistic Intellectuals in
Mexico².
         The major point made by American Indians is
that they and this continent are one, having grown
up together from the time we first became Homo
sapiens.   The Cherokee Indian anthropologist,
Robert K. Thomas, who teaches at Wayne State
University in Detroit, told me that:

> Italians in London can be called an ethnic
> group.   Basques in Spain can best be consid-
> ered a minority nationality or, better put
> perhaps, a submerged national group.   An old,
> in-situ people with a land base and a politi-
> cal consciousness of themselves does not react
> the same to acculturation pressures or to po-
> litical submergence as does a relatively
> recently removed community of foreigners in a
> strange land far from their fellows and their
> roots.   The dynamics of group relations be-
> tween the French speakers and the English ma-
> jority in Windsor are not the same as between
> Quebec and the rest of Canada.   American
> Indians in the city can be thought of as a
> forming ethnic group, but rural American
> Indian societies more closely resemble the
> Basques of Spain than they do the Poles of
> Detroit.   And, of course, this means that city
> Indians will never resemble a European ethnic
> group in the city.   Even the Jews and the
> Gypsies do not fit the ethnic model well.
> Further, race complicates the ethnic model in
> America.   The ethnic model can be used as an
> "ideal type" to explore similarities and dif-
> ference between groups rather than as a blan-
> ket category.   I think we are yet much in the
> dark as to the dynamics of the American
> system.³

         It seems to me that Thomas might accept that
Blacks, having naturalized themselves in the cotton
fields, could say something like this.   He hints
this by distinguishing the French-speakers in
Quebec from those in Windsor.   Jews certainly will
find these ideas familiar with respect to the land
of Israel; but I wonder if the case might not be
made also for Diaspora Jewry in relation now not to
the symbolic homeland but to our interrelated God,
Torah, and social idealism, with food preferences,
the Sabbath and festivals, family traditions, and
humor as helpful handmaidens.   The case might begin
with the fact of our survival and argue that without a land the challenge was even greater; continue
by recalling that even when the second Temple was

standing in Jerusalem many more Jews lived in the
Diaspora than in the homeland; and it might interpret anti-Semitism as a response to our function
universally as teachers of monotheism and its corresponding ethic, with resulting hostility from the
omnipresent wicked sons.

In any case, it seems to me worthwhile to
think positively of the miracle of Jewish survival
and to study other cases, including the innumerable
societies of a few dozen or hundreds of North American Indians surviving against impossible odds with
their basic religion and world view intact. Since
the North American Indians that I have met, are
without any exception deeply and genuinely religious -- more so than any other people I have known
-- I suggest that survival depends on passing on to
very young children a religious world view with its
underlying unexpressed premises for thought and
action. I imagine that this world view is so deep
that nobody knows its content. Once transmitted it
is virtually unchangeable and emotionally important, so that ideas that conflict with it are
rejected without trial if indeed they are even
received.

OBSERVATIONS

And now I shall try to provide the general
observations for which our imaginary visiting
anthropologist has asked. My first would be to
express pleasure that a major study is finally
underway. The 1945 Conference noted that "Negroes
had done far more than Jews in investigating their
history and status in the United States; that no
study...had been made comparable to Myrdal's defin-
itive treatment of the American Negro." That study
combined direction by Gunnar Myrdal, an outsider,
with assistance from a variety of American social
scientists who developed monographs for him on
special topics. One would indeed welcome now a
similar effort on the nature of our democracy to
explain not only what has recently happened to
Blacks but what is happening to all of us. Myrdal
showed that there had never been "a negro problem"
but rather a white problem of a conflict of values
in the dominant society. Likewise clearly there
never has been an Indian problem, or a Latino problem, or a woman problem. These have been protests
which call attention to problems somewhere in the
whole system and therefore call for new and of
course interdisciplinary study. It would be

excellent indeed for this to be an out-culture
study using in-culture talent (like Myrdal's) with
a significant component relating to Jews in
America. I could only add "Better late than never,
and Godspeed!"

In turning now to more personal observations,
I should make explicit a relevant part of my basic
point of view in anthropology, and since it may be
influenced by my Jewish background, I will begin
with an incident that occurred in 1930 when I accompanied an archeological expedition from Beloit
College to the Constantine area of Algeria, to
excavate mounds mainly of snail shells left by
people who had lived some 25,000 years ago. We
camped separately and hired Arabic-speaking Berber
workmen to help us. I was interested in their culture and visited their camps. But I also noticed
that there were Jews living in the town of Aïn
Beïda where the camp director, Alonzo Pond, bought
supplies. At my request he told a Jewish merchant,
Solomon Melloul that he had on his expedition a
Jewish young man. His family begged to let me be
their guest for the eight days of Passover, and
Pond promised to bring me for the first and last
days.

My first professional publication describes
this experience.[4] I found that two kinds of Jews
lived in rural Algeria in what happened to be its
hundredth year as a French colony. "The mayor's
family had come from Algiers....Sephardic Jews more
Western than the other Jews of Aïn Beïda [who] had
come to the Constantine area a hundred years before
from Bône and Tunis. Before that they had been in
Alexandria. Beyond that they could not trace their
origin. These were truly Eastern Jews and had had
practically no contact with European-Jewish ancestors for almost 2000 years. Separated from American Jews thus by 20 centuries and six thousand
miles, I was not surprised to find them very different."[5] Most of the article describes the interesting differences; but there is this paragraph
which gives the point I want to make:

"As the days passed, and I grew to know them
better, more and more their likeness to the
Jews back home impressed me. The same ritual,
of course, with slightly different pronunci-
ation of the Hebrew, but the same nevertheless; the same mannerisms, the same quickness
of thought and of speech; and above all, and
this became apparent in our discussions, the
same premise of and passion for social justice
that I knew distinguished our people in

America. And my feeling of kin grew upon me
with the hours, and, before I finally left, I
actually felt closer to these Jews, far off in
Algeria, living in an Eastern culture, than I
did to those Gentile friends of mine in our
archeological camp brought up with me in my
own country as they were. What deep traditions to bind us so!"[6]
This may have been an emotional reaction without significance, though written in Wisconsin eight
months after the experience. But I realize now
that in my subsequent professional theories I have
generally seen cultural continuities as stronger
than fluctuations from environmental changes. In
Guatemala in the 1930s and early 1940s I continu-
ally cautioned against taking seriously the views
of the older generation that their way of life was
falling apart. I recall returning to Panajachel in
1956 after a 15-year absence to find that indeed
what I had called the men's "old-fashioned" cos-
tume, so-named because we all supposed it was on
the way out, was being worn as always by the elders. We sat together in the Cofradia where the
patron saint is housed. I had the eerie feeling
that this was where I had come in as these elders
complained about the younger generation in just the
terms their parents had. Beginning in the 1960s
Robert Hinshaw has been publishing precise data of
the changes which have occurred in this very village. It happens that Panajachel has undergone a
population explosion. By now twice the number of
children and grandchildren of my friends of the
1930s are living on the same limited land base.
The area has a perfect climate and is scenic and
picturesque. Aldous Huxley once called its com-
manding view of Lake Atitlan the most beautiful in
the world. Two hours on a paved road from
Guatemala City, a few hours by air from Los
Angeles, New Orleans, or Miami, it is not surprising that Panajachel has become attractive to city
people and to tourists. The Panajachel Indians
added to their earlier single occupation of
agriculture many construction and management
skills. Hinshaw estimates that in addition to the
people who have moved into chalets and condomin-
iums, there are at least 120,000 tourists a year,
half of them from abroad. The Indians were already
market oriented and entreprenurial and needed no
change in orientation to take advantage of new
opportunities.[7] But one would expect that their
folklike beliefs would be greatly affected by an
excellent new clinic and improved schools and by

the tremendously increased contacts with thousands
of sophisticated people, not to mention the permanent settlement among them of about 200 Americans
called by them Hippies. But the fact is that the
world view of the parents and grandparents has
stayed remarkably intact in the children and
grandchildren.

Long before I had seen this evidence in Guatemala, however, I was confirmed in my conviction by
experience with North American Indian groups. From
1948 onward my students and I struggled to understand The Indians' relations with their neighbors
and with our larger society. And by 1952 I had
become convinced that our concepts of acccultur-
ation--and certainly the notion we had of the
inevitability of assimilation--were simply invalid,
possibly the mistaken product of our experiences as
immigrants. So here again, historical cultural
continuities were for me confirmed and emphasized.

It is therefore no surprise that I doubt that
Jews in America will disappear into the general
society. Like the Basques, the Gypsies, the Arme-
nians, the Iroquois, the Navajos, and the hundreds
of other peoples who have been here from the beginning of recorded time, the Jews too will be here
because they want to be here. If they are threatened, more of them will want to carry on. If they
are not threatened at all, more of those who want
less to carry on will find it easier to go their
individual ways, leaving to carry on -- and to grow
in number -- a harder core of those who care
more. Probably it has always been so with all the
hundreds of groups. The lesson is not that those
who worry about attrition should stop worrying;
their voiced concern is their show of caring, which
is an essential element in the process by which we
shall survive. But we also need equally to avoid
the fear that leads to panic and to warfare among
groups of Jews each believing that the ways of life
of other groups endanger the survival of all.

I now return to my earlier observations concerning the place of religion in all of this. I
implied that first I distinguish between particular
beliefs and practices on one side and a basic world
view on the other. Both among Maya Indian villag-
ers in Central America and among smaller and larger
bands and nations of North American Indians, it has
become clear to me that a unique world view maintains its integrity precisely because it is resil-
ient and permissive of a large variety of particular beliefs and practices which can change in
response to external changes or be passed from one

to another or from a wholly different culture.
Just as the English language remains even when new
and alternative expressions are coined or borrowed,
so one has the same world view while those who hold
it add to and change their repertory of beliefs and
practices. Presumably those beliefs and practices
will be rejected which seriously clash with the
structure, which in turn can be known only by knowing which beliefs and patterns at any time are
there; so there is much which is tautological in
the proposition. But it is useful to make the general point that probably the unique larger world
view patterns of different people in contact do not
themselves easily "mix." What may be at the heart
of cultural continuity and continuing group identity is the intuitive recognition of a common world
view too abstract to be defined by counting up any
number of pieces. In a crisis a single sign, like
the word Jew, may be worth a thousand mixed up
criteria.

      With that understanding, the question is what
difference does it make if some Jews are orthodox,
others reformed, and still others conservative--or
any of the changing varieties of these. Or what
difference does it makes whether they live individually or as parts of congregations; or if they are
observant or not, or what in particular they
observe.

      I recall a letter in Commentary some 20 years
ago by a gentile anthropologist who argued that we
should recognize as Jews people like himself who
were not ethnically Jewish but who shared our ways
of looking at things. This raises the further
question of what difference it makes if a Jew is
native or naturalized, so to speak. Or what is the
difference between two people who both "feel Jewish" and recognize one another as sharing the
Jewish way of thinking, one of whom traces ancestry
through generations of known Jews, while the other
descends from an old American high church family
but grew up happily in a Jewish neighborhood?

      Whether or not the Jewish world view which I
am positing as integral, unique, and recognizable
to others who share it--whether or not it can "mix"
with another world view--it can evidently be adopted successfully by one whose biological ancestors
had some other world view, and just as evidently it
can be absent in a person whose ancestors identified as Jewish. However rare these cases may be, I
suggest that they are critical for understanding
the more important usual cases. The non-Jew who
has come into a Jewish identity is likely to

gravitate to like-minded, preponderantly Jewish people to adopt specific beliefs and practices, and thus reinforce his or her Jewish identity. The Jew in whom the Jewish outlook is absent, in contrast, is likely to gravitate to like-minded non-Jews; unless rejected because of anti-Semitism, he or she will drop more and more Jewish practices and beliefs and evidences of Jewish identity.

With this understanding of marginal cases, let me now return finally to the community of Jews who share the basic Jewish world view. By my definitions the whole range of them from orthodox to reformed are more alike in their world view than they are in beliefs and practices. This does not say that they will be equally compatible. Imagine a row of a hundred persons spaced equally from one end to the other along this supposed single axis called orthodox to reformed. Two persons within 10 positions of one another will be more compatible than two who are 50 positions apart. That is because of their more-different beliefs and practices. But their world views are much less different, and they are presumed to identify one another as Jews. Unlike the Irish in Northern Ireland our people have not drawn even temporarily a hard line at any point of the continuum. Thus, increasing contact is possible at all distances, and tendencies toward integration go relatively unimpeded even though least likely between the extremes.

Now suppose that it is argued that Jews with more orthodox practices are more likely to pass on the Jewish world view to their children than are Jews with more reformed practices, perhaps because of their greater separateness from the non-Jewish world. One would then say that for survival in America orthodoxy is safer and should be preferred. Or suppose that the contrary is posited, on the ground that orthodoxy in America encourages rejection by children of their parents, so that realistic compromises give a better statistical chance for survival. If either of these cases could be established, it would follow that greater or less adherence to traditional beliefs and practices is significant for Jewish survival; and we would have something to fight about. But of course that statistical difference would be indeterminable as its very suggestion roused suspicions that discrimination by religious practice was imminent. Therefore, wisdom counsels a continuing pluralism among us, and the strengthening of the religious basis of Judaism at all points on the scale. This

accords happily with the general view in America
that religion is good and everybody should have one
-- no matter which.

NOTES

1. (New York: Harper and Row, 1976).
2. (Cambridge: Schenkman, 1977).
3. Personal communication.
4. "An Algerian Passover," The American Hebrew,
    April 3, 1931, p. 548ff.
5. Ibid.
6. Ibid.
7. I called my study of the Indians Penny
    Capitalism.

INDEX

Abelson, R., 27-28
Abrahams, Gerald, 24
Age composition
    of Jews in the United States, 76-80
Aggregate, definition of, 17
Ajdukiewicz, Kasimir, 26
Allen, G. N., 119
Allinsmith, Wesley, 145
Allport, Gordon W., 118
Almond, G., 295
American Council for Judaism, 22, 25
American Jewish Congress, 284-85, 287
Anthropological perspectives
    of Jews in the United States, chapter 8
Anti-semitism, chapters 1, 3, 6, 7, 8
Antonovsky, Aaron, 100
Ash, Roberta, 22-23
Ashby, W. R., 16
Asher, R., 293-94
Assimilation
    of Jews in the United States, 50-59, 226,
        chapter 7
Auerbach, J. S. 292
Axelrod, Morris, 98-101
Ayer, A. J., 27

Bachi, Roberto, 98
Bahn, A., 121
Bailey, T. A., 295
Bales, Robert F., 28
Bauer, Yehuda, 295
Baron, Salo, 96, 219, 291
Bergman, Elihu, 96, 295
Berman, Michael D., 134, 146, 149
Berrien, Kenneth F., 28
Berry, Brewton, 24
Bertalanffy, Ludwig von, 16, 28
Bettelheim, B., 120
Bienstock, Herbert, 248, 254, 265, 267
Birmingham, Stephen, 292
Birthrates, comparative, 39-50
Blumer, Herbert, 26
Bonham, Gordon Scott, 97
Boorstin, D. J., 243
Boroff, D. J., 121
Boulding, Kenneth, 16

Brandes, Joseph, 293
Bryan, William Jennings, 273
Bublick, Gedaliah, 285
Buckley, Walter, 28
Bury, R. G., 26

Cahn, S. M., 294-95
Campbell, Arthur A., 95
Cantril, Hadley, 295
Carosso, V. P., 292
Cassel, J., 120-21
Category, definition of, 17
Chein, Isidore, 24
Chenkin, Alvin, 94-100, 262-69
Cohen, Morris Raphael, 21, 26-27, 29
Cohen, N. W., 294-95
Cohen, Steven, 97
Concepts, 173-76
Copi, I. M., 27
Correlation analysis, limitations of, 212-15
Curti, M., 295

Definition
    by per genus et differentiam, 6-7
        critique, 14-17
    by traditional Aristotelian logic, 6
Definition, guidelines, 16
Definition
    of a collectivity, 6-7
    of an ethnic group, 7-9
    of an ethnic minority group, 13
    of general systems, 17-20
    of a human social group, 7-8
    of a Jew, 1-15
    of an organized human social group, 7-8
    of a social collectivity, 6-7
    of a system, 17-18
    of an unorganized human social group, 7-8
Definitions, criteria and types, 4-14
Demography
    of Jews in the United States, chapter 2
        future trends, 90-94
Deutscher, Isaac, 23, 27
Dewey, John, 17, 20-21, 26
Diamond, Jack, 99
Dinnerstein, L., 291
Dotterer, Ray H., 29
Dramatological approach
    to life in an Orthodox synagogue, 176-90

Dubinsky, David, 282-83
Dubnow, Simon, 25

Eagle, Morris N., vii, chapter 3
Eaton, R. W., 28
Erickson, Judith B., 99
Economic perspectives
    of Jews in the United States, chapter 6
Education
    of Jews in the United States, 80-85, 246-49
Einstein, Albert, 11, 22
Erickson, Erik, H., 23, 104-06, 120
Ethnic group, 7-12
    definition, 7-9
    psychological supports, 109
Ethnic groups
    and mental illness, 109, 120-21
Ethnicity and religion, 216

Family size
    of Jews in the United States, 39-50
Feigl, Herbert, 21, 26-27
Feingold, Henry L., chapter 7, 291-94
Ferguson, Leonard W., 22
Fertility
    among Jews in the United States, 39-50
Field, G. C., 26
Fisher, Allan M., 146
Fishman, Joshua A., 118-19
Fitzgerald, R., 120
Ford, Kathleen, 97
Foreign affairs interest
    among Jews in the United States, 276, 288-89
Fowler, Floyd J., 98-101
Freud, Sigmund, 11, 116, 121
Friedlander, Paul, 26
Fuchs, Lawrence H., 145

General systems, 16-20
Generation status
    of Jews in the United States, 74-76
Gerson, Louis L., 295
Gerth, Hans H., 25
Gittler, Joseph B., vii-viii, chapter 1, 254
Glanz, Rudolf, 272
Glazer, Nathan, 29, 101, 175-76, 216-30, 292-93
Goldscheider, Calvin, 49, 96-100
Goldstein, Sidney, viii, chapter 2, 96-101, 254
Gompers, Samuel, 276, 280

Goodman, Leo A., 25
Goodman, Saul L., 23, 25
Goren, B. B., 294
Gorwitz, K., 119, 121
Grant, Ulysses S., 273
Gray, William, 28
Greenberg, Meyer, 24
Greeley, A. M., 246, 259-64, 292
Greenblatt, Robert, 23
Greenblum, Joseph, 174-75, 199-215, 230, 294
Greenwald, K., 292
Gurin, Arnold, 98-99, 101
Gurion, David Ben, 23

Harlow, H. G., 119
Harris, Louis, 146-47
Hart, Jeffrey, 136-37, 149
Hasidic Community of Williamsburg,
    analysis and critique, 190-99
Heilman, Samuel, 174-190, 230-33
Hempel, Carl G., 21
Hero, A. O., 295
Hertzberg, A., 295
Hillman, Sidney, 281
Hillquit, Morris, 293
Himmelfarb, Milton, 149
Hinshaw, Robert, 309
Historical perspectives
    of Jews in the United States, chapter 7

Income
    of Jews in the United States, 249-52
Ingalls, R. P., 294
Intermarriage
    of Jews in the United States, 50-57
Isaacs, Stephen D., 145
Iwanska, Alicja, 305

Jackson, G., 120
Jew, definitions, chapter 1
Jewish Identity on the Suburban Frontier,
    analysis and critique, 199-215
Jewish traditions
    and social change, 110-115
Jews in the United States
    age composition, 76-80
    anthropological perspectives, chapter 8
    assimilation, 57-59
    birth rates, 39-50

education, 73-85, 246-49
family size, 39-50
foreign born, 74-76
future demographic trends, 90-94
generation status, 74-76
historical perspectives, chapter 7
in small towns, 65-67
income profiles, 249-52
interest in foreign affairs, 288-89, 311-12
intermarriage, 50-57
labor movement, 276-83
migration and population distribution, 59-73,
    276-78
mortality rates, 37-39
native born, 73-89
occupational composition, 85-89, 240-48
organizational life, 276, 283-87
political liberalism, 124, 134-36, 153
political values, chapter 4
psychological perspectives, 103-21
population growth, 33-37
size of family, 20-48
suburbanization, 64-65
socio-demographic composition, 73-89
sociological perspectives, chapter 5
Joergensen, Joergen, 19
Judaism
    Neo-orthodoxy, 12
    Orthodox, 12, 176-90
    Reform, 12
    Samson Raphael Hirsch School, 12
Judaism in America
    analysis and critique, 216-28

Kahler, Erich, 22
Kahan, Arcadius, viii, chapter 6, 254
Kahn, Benjamin M., 90
Kallen, Horace M., 286-87, 295
Kant, Immanuel, 20, 115
Kaplan, Mordecai, 285-86, 294
Kessner, T., 292
Kiser, Clyde V., 96
Klausner, Joseph, 219
Klausner, Samuel Z., viii, chapter 5
Klir, George J., 28
Korn, Bertram, 272, 291
Kramer, Michael S., 149
Kuhn, Alfred, 29
Kuznets, Simon, 87, 96, 101

Labor movement
    among Jews in the United States, 276-83
Ladd, Everett Carll, ix, chapter 4, 292
Langner, T., 119
Lansing, John B., 267
Laszlo, Ervin, 28
Lazarus, Mitchel J., 99
Leighton, A., 120
Lenski, Gerhard, 100, 294
Leo Frank Case, 291
Lerner, Ralph, 254
Lestchinsky, Jacob, 96
Levine, Gene N., 98
Levinson, Boris M., 119
Levy, L., 120
Levy, Mark R., 149
Lewin, Kurt, 103, 118
Lewis, Bernard, 283-84, 294
Liberalism index, 132, 147-52, 170-71
Lieberman, Samuel S., 96
Liebman, C. S., 294
Lindbergh, Charles A., 273-74, 291
Lipset, Seymour M., 137-38, 149, 292
Loewe, Raphael, 24
Lopez, Aron, 276
Lotka, A., 16
Lubell, S., 291

MacIver, Robert M., 27
Malcolm X, 120
Marcus, Jacob, 275
Marshall, Louis, 29
Massarik, Fred, 24, 57, 94, 98-100, 262-63, 269
Mayer, Albert J., 99
Mayer, Egon, 55, 98
Maynard, Betty J., 99
Mead, George H., 177
Mendelsohn, E., 293
Mesarovic, M. D., 28
Mesthene, Emmanuel G., 29
Migration of Jews in the United States, 59-73
Miller, J. G., 16
Mills, C. Wright, 25
Minority group, 7, 13
Miran, Maynard, 95-96
Mishler, Eliot, 95, 97
Montagu, M. F. A., 27
Moynihan, Daniel P., 137, 293
Murphy, H. B. M., 120
Myrdal, Gunnar, 307

Nagel, Ernest, 26, 28
Nam, Charles B., 100
Neurath, Otto, 21
Newman, William M., 99
Niger, Schmuel, 23

Occupational composition
    of Jews in the United States, 85-90, 240-48
Organizational life
    of Jews in the United States, 276, 283-87

Parsons, Talcott, 28, 232
Pascal, Blaise, 23
Patterson, John E., 95
Pearl, Raymond, 96
Pergola, Sergio Della, 45, 97
Piaget, Jean, 28
Pine, Max, 282
Plato, 3, 26
Podhoretz, M., 293
Polishook, S., 294
Political values
    of Catholics, 136-40
    of college professors, 164-71
    of Jews, chapter 4
Poll, Solomon, 174-75, 190-99, 233
Populatin growth
    of Jews. See demography.
Potter, Robert, 95, 97
Powderly, Terence, 279
Projector, Dorothy S., 267
Protestant Ethic, 118
Protocols of the Elders of Zion, 273
Psychological perspectives
    of Jewish life in the United States, Chapter 3
Psathas, George, 22

Rabkin, J. G., 120-21
Race, 9
Rachman, L. R., 292
Rachovsky, B., 121
Ramsperger, A. C., 27
Reconstructionism, 285-86
Reder, Melvyn W., 267
Reform Judaism, 12
Religion and ethnicity, 216
Rhodes, A. Lewis, 100
Richards, Bernard, 285
Richards, I. A., 28

Rischin, M., 293
Rizzo, Nicholas D., 28
Rootman, I., 120
Rosenstock, M., 291
Rosenthal, Erich, 24, 52, 54, 97
Rosenwaite, Ira, 99
Rothman, Jack, 22
Rotenstreich, Nathan, 25
Rowitz, L., 120
Russell, Bertrand, 20-21, 27
Ryder, Norman B., 95, 97

Sagi, Philip, 95, 97
Samson Raphael Hirsch School
    of Neo-orthodoxy, 12
Sandberg, Neil C., 98
Sanders, R., 293
Santayana, George, 271
Sanua, Victor, 119
Savitz, Leonard D., 25
Schechter, Soloman, 285
Schindler, Alexander, 98
Schneider, William, 134, 146, 149
Schoen, Douglas E., 146, 149
Schoenfeld, Eugen, 99
Schultz, Mark, 134, 146, 149
Schutz, Alfred, 177
Seligman, Ben, 100
Sellars, Wilfrid, 26
Selzer, Michael, 25-26
Sidorsky, S., 294
Simmel, Georg, 25
Singer, C., 22
Sklare, Marshall, 22, 174-75, 199-215, 230, 292-94
Smith, G., 29
Social Classes in the United States, 9, 125-34
Social collectivity, 6-7
Social group. See human social group,
    organized human social group,
    unorganized human social group
Sociological concepts, 173-76
Sociology, applied, 173
Soltow, Lee, 267
Sombart, Werner, 228
Sonquist, John, 267
Spiro, E., 121
Srole, Leo, 119
Stix, R. K., 96
Steinberg, S., 292
Steiner, Stan, 305
Stonequist, Everett V., 25

Stouffer, Samuel A., 150
Struening, E. L., 120-21
Sumner, Graham, 233
Supple, B. E., 292
Sydiaha, D., 120
Synagogue Life,
    analysis and critique, 176-90
System, definition of, 17-18

Tax, Sol, ix, chapter 8
Thernstrom, S., 292
Thomas, Robert K., 306
Thoresen, Erling T., 267
Tomasson, Richard F., 25
Toynbee, Arnold J., 22, 235

Uhlenberg, Peter R., 49
Unorganized human social group, 7-8
Urofsky, M. I., 295

Veblen, Thorstein, 24
Verbit, Mervin F., 101
Vosk, Mark, 22

Wagner, Stanley M., 291
Weinfeld, Morton, 96
Westoff, Charles F., 95-99
Whelpton, Pascal K., 95-97
Whitehead, Alfred North, 20, 27
Weber, Max, 118, 121, 197, 216, 231, 234
Weiss, Gertrude, 267
Weiss, Roger, 254
Weiss-Rosmarin, T., 291
Willis, R. S., 292
Winnicott, D. W., 106, 119
Wirth, Louis, 27
Wittgenstein, Ludwig, 3
Wolfe, Ann G., 79, 100
Wollman, Leo, 281
Woodger, Joseph, 21

YIVO Institute of Jewish Research, v

Zeitlin, Solomon, 22, 25
Zimmer, Basil, 100
Zimmerman, R. R., 119
Zionism, American, 287-88